LANDSCAPING

A Five-Year Plan

◆

LANDSCAPING

A Five-Year Plan

◆

Theodore James, Jr.

Photography by Harry Haralambou

Burford Books

Printed in the United States of America

10 9 8 7 6 5 4 3 2 1

Library of Congress Cataloging in Publication Data
James, Theodore.
    Landscaping : a five-year plan / Theodore James, Jr. ;
photography by Harry Haralambou.
        p.   cm.
    Originally published: New York : Macmillan, c1988.
    Includes index.
    ISBN 1-58080-026-2 (pbk.)
    1. Landscape gardening. 2. Landscape plants. I. Title.
SB473.J26   1999
635.9—DC21
                                                    98-46036
                                                        CIP

To the Contessa Elaine and T.P.

Contents

◆

Contents

Preface

♦

Twelve years ago, I decided to buy a house in the country. My city apartment was filled to the gills with greenery—houseplants by the hundreds—but looking around one day, it occurred to me I really wanted a house of my own and a plot of ground on which I could grow more than just houseplants. I had grown up in the country and thus had some experience with growing things, but at that point I was by no means an experienced gardener. Nevertheless, I eagerly looked forward to being able to pursue my horticultural interests. Well, I bought the house in the country and found, much to my surprise, that I enjoyed country living so much that within three years I had relinquished my apartment and taken up full-time residence on the North Fork of Long Island, out in the "mid-Atlantic," according to some waggish friends.

I enthusiastically embraced my gardening interest and set out to land-scape my property. Although I was blessed with the best soil this side of Kansas—four feet of topsoil—with the exception of one monumental, 100-year-old yew and a magnificent 150-year-old copper beech, there was nothing else on the property but countless "junk" trees and overgrown bushes. I'm not complaining; the two fine old specimens are indeed rare, and had the previous owner known of their value, he could probably have asked for and received twice the price I paid for the property. I cherish these trees and will be grateful until the day I die to the fine, old gentleman who planted them more than a century ago. (I took the time to find out who he was from elderly neighbors, who knew his children and grandchildren.)

When I first took title, armies of friends and family began arriving with station wagons filled with furniture, odds and ends, and planting ma-terial. I soon found I had container after container of unidentified cultivars, which I proceeded to plant here and there, if only to ensure their survival. I had read scores of books on landscaping, but none seemed to answer the questions I had. How do I start to landscape my property? Where should I plant trees? Should I cut down any trees? What do I do with overgrown bushes? If you have recently bought a house, I'm sure you understand by now exactly what I'm talking about, as you are going through exactly the same experience yourself.

At any rate, I plunged right into my landscaping project, learning what I could from books, friends, family, and neighbors. All the time I kept thinking, "If only there was a book for me." Landscaping books abounded, filled with beautiful pictures of swimming pools with elaborate bathhouses, decks, plantings, fountains, and flowering plants. But the magnificent photographs of extensive perennial borders, perfectly maintained vegetable gardens, and elegant patios were more appropriate to Beverly Hills or Hampton bunkers than to my modest, 250-year-old, half-cape house set amid the potato fields and vineyards of the area. The authors, many of whom were landscape architects or designers, didn't seem to understand that I couldn't afford to spend $5,000 to install a Japanese garden complete with lily pond and fountains. I had to have some cellar work done, and I had to replace the water heater and insulate the place. That took care of the $5,000. Further, they seemed to assume that I was acquainted with the thousands of varieties of cultivars they were recommending and that I knew exactly how to maintain all of them.

After spending about five years making one mistake after another and learning the hard way, I thought it would be a good idea to write a book about how to landscape a piece of property based on my own experiences, which are doubtless quite similar to those of most new home owners. So, here it is. From the start, I want to emphasize that I am not a landscape architect or a landscape designer. I do not hold a degree in horticulture but in fact, one in art and archaeology. I am an avid gardener, have read volumes on the subject, and have written three other books on specialized areas of gardening and hundreds of articles about gardening for the *New York Times, Family Circle, Horticulture, Ladies' Home Journal,* and other publications. I acquired my gardening expertise by reading, consulting with experts, and, most important, *doing* it.

The goal of this book is to give you a *framework* within which you can bring beauty to your new world. It is not intended to be definitive. Should a particular aspect of landscaping and gardening be of interest to you, bear in mind that this book is intended to serve merely as an introduction. Definitive books exist on each area covered here, and within each area, even more specialized books are available.

I have made many mistakes in landscaping my property, and you will too, but I hope that you can learn from my experiences and avoid wasting time, effort, and money unnecessarily.

I sincerely hope that this book will help you create beauty in your surroundings. And while I hope that beauty is your aim, keep in mind that statistics reveal a beautiful landscape can add from 20 to 30 percent to the value of your property. Should you ever decide to sell, you will be rewarded for your landscaping efforts in dollars and cents.

I have divided this five-year-plan book into chapters corresponding to each year of the project. You may find, depending on your priorities and the nature of your property, that you do not follow this sequence exactly, but for most new home owners, this division should prove to be workable. Because novice gardeners are always full of questions—I know I certainly was—the text is presented in a question-and-answer format. I've included selective encyclopedias throughout the book. Again, they are not intended to be definitive, but include cultivars most readily available at nurseries and garden centers and those that are easily grown.

Good luck with your project. If the time spent working at it and the end results give you only a fraction of the gratification I have received, then my work is completed.

Acknowledgments

♦

The author and photographer wish to thank the following for their interest, cooperation, suggestions and/or encouragement.

Rosemary Verey; Valerie Finnis and the late Sir David Scott; Robert Dash; Ida Vail; Pamela Lord; Roz Cole; Alexia Dorszynski; Alfred and Delfina Smith; Duncan and Barbara Hoxworth; Dr. George Broniek; Steadwell Gnehm; L. Herndon Werth; Leila Combs Leathers; Edith and the late F. R. (Ady) Schreiber; Betsy Baker; Sue Blair; Bill and Barbara Wilhelm; Martin and Janet Garrell; John and Brenda Scranton; Douglas Campbell; Sherry Schreiber; David Palladini; Mr. and Mrs. Theodore James, Sr.; Mr. and Mrs. Philip Haralambou; Pierre Bennerup; Bob LaRue; W. Atlee Burpee Seed Company, Inc., Warminster, Pennsylvania; Park Seed Company, Inc., Greenwood, South Carolina; Bluestone Perennials, Inc., Madison, Ohio; K. Van Bourgondien and Sons, Inc., Babylon, New York; C. J. Van Bourgondien, Inc., Peconic, New York; Commercial Nursery Company, Decherd, Tennessee; Richard Belanger and the Netherlands Flower Bulb Institute; Thompson and Morgan, Inc., Jackson, New Jersey; Johnny's Selected Seeds, Albion, Maine; Kelly Brothers Nursery, Dansville, New York; Shaw Nurseries, Manorville, New York; Stoves and Stone, Southampton, New York; Homeside Florist and Greenhouses, Inc., Riverhead, New York; Jackson and Perkins, Inc., Medford, Oregon; Victor Hasselblad, Inc.

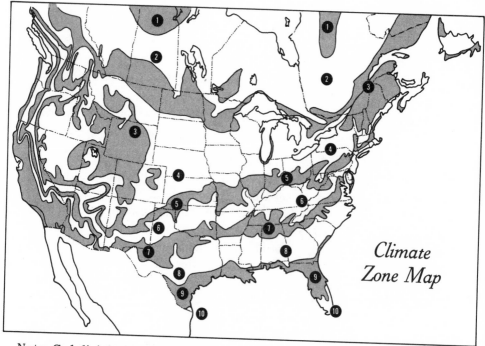

Climate
Zone Map

Note: Subdivisions to the climate zones have recently been adopted, but for simplicity and congruity with the text references, this map identifies the main zones only.

Chapter One

♦

THE FIRST YEAR

Assessing Your Property and
Getting Your Feet Wet

The Colors that Tide You Over in Summer
and Fall: Annuals

The Annual Encyclopedia

Attracting Birds to Your Property

Assessing Your Property and Getting Your Feet Wet

The first year of your landscape project should be spent assessing your property—that is, learning what you already have in terms of established plantings; deciding what your needs are and what use you wish to make of the property; deciding which existing structures, such as patios, paths, or steps, are properly located for your needs—in short, getting to know your land. Landscaping is quite similar to redesigning or installing a new kitchen. Before you spent money on new cabinets and appliances, you would seek the advice of kitchen design experts, read books and magazine articles about design, and use your present kitchen to ascertain traffic patterns and personal needs. You should approach a landscape project in the same way.

How do I begin to assess my property? Start by walking around day in and day out, at different times of the year, to familiarize yourself with your property. If you have a detached garage, for example, learn the best path to the garage in spring, summer, fall, and winter. You might find that a particular area of your property is subject to flooding in late winter or spring. If you install a path before learning of this situation it would mean that in order to get to the garage, you might have to walk through six inches of water. Decide upon a convenient area for garbage. Stake out your vegetable garden to see if it is conveniently located to the kitchen. Decide where you wish to locate your outdoor living area. Gaze out your windows and envision plantings of bulbs in spring, flowers in summer and fall. Start to think about shrub borders, perennial borders, bulb plantings, annual flower plantings, possible garden structures, privacy screens, and fences—all the aspects of your future landscape.

3

Should I take notes on my thoughts and existing plantings? Absolutely. A gardener's best friend is a notebook. The best way to do this is to purchase a yearly diary. Then, each year you can take notes on the appropriate date, jotting down what is in bloom, what should be removed or changed, your success with various cultivars, the heights of cultivars, and so on. Every time you walk around your property, jot down your thoughts on landscaping in the notebook on the appropriate date. Take extensive notes on existing plantings. If, for example, you move into your house in the fall, you will have absolutely no idea whether or not there are any spring bulbs, such as daffodils or tulips, planted on the property. Perennial plantings will be scruffy, usually going into dormancy, and you will not know what cultivars are already planted.

Spring-blooming shrubs will be cloaked in autumn foliage, with no flowers. In the spring, when things begin to grow and flowers and flowering shrubs and trees bloom, take more notes. All of this will help you decide what you wish to maintain, what you wish to remove, and what you wish to plant.

Learn what plants you have during the first year and jot this information down in your notebook. Write down date of bloom, color, height, and width of each cultivar—anything that might help you later on in designing or redesigning your landscape.

Aside from my own notes, is there anyone or anything else that I can refer to for advice and more information? Yes. The following are good sources of information:

- Knowledgeable friends, family, and neighbors can provide you with a great deal of information about your particular property, existing plantings, and future plans. Avail yourself of their knowledge; they are usually more than willing to share it with you.
- Personnel at local garden centers and nurseries are also a great source of information about local growing conditions and cultivars suitable for your area, as well as planting and maintenance advice. If nobody in a particular nursery or garden center has any knowledgeable advice to offer, seek a different source, not only for information but for purchasing plants.
- All over the country, almost every county of every state has a County Cooperative Extension Service, set up to provide you with information about many things, including horticulture. They are usually listed in the telephone book under "County Offices." These offices are staffed by personnel with credentials in horticulture, whose job it is to provide infor-

mation about pests and diseases that might affect your area, local growing conditions, recommended varieties of plants to install—in short, just about anything you might need to know in the area of gardening and landscaping.

● Local libraries usually have extensive collections of books on gardening. Read books about trees, shrubs, perennials, annuals, vegetables, bulbs—indeed, any aspect of landscaping you decide to undertake. Learn as much as you can about each area *before* you begin a project.

● Bookstores and most garden centers also carry numerous books on gardening. I have found that the Ortho books, a series of about fifty reasonably priced titles on many aspects of gardening and landscaping, are among the best.

● Catalogues from mail-order nurseries are an excellent source of all kinds of information about plants and landscaping (see pp. 247–49). I recommend that you send postcards to all of the mail-order sources listed there, requesting their catalogues. Once you do so, you will be put on their mailing lists and will receive their catalogues every January, in time for spring planting, and often in the late summer, in time for fall planting.

How do I start to design my personal landscape? After several months of walking around your property and taking notes, you will begin to have some idea of what you need and want in terms of your landscape. Now is the time to sit down with a pencil and a pad of graph paper to begin your design. Keep in mind, however, that this is only a beginning. Using a scale of one inch to five feet, mark out your property on the graph paper. If one piece of paper is not sufficient, tape several together before you start. Measure your house and any other existing buildings and structures and sketch them onto the graph paper in the appropriate place(s). Measure the driveway if it exists, and mark that on the graph paper. Sketch shrub borders, foundation plantings, and trees, if they exist. In other words, sketch everything you have on your property onto the graph paper.

Now, after you have read the information in this chapter, begin to sketch in an outdoor living area, service area, children's play area, dog run, compost heap, "nursery" area, vegetable garden, annual flower garden, new foundation plantings, new tree and shrub plantings, and so forth. After you have done your preliminary sketch, put it aside for a week or so. Then, go back to it and make any changes you deem fit. You might want to show your plan to a few knowledgeable people, such as those recommended above as sources of information, for their comments. Continue to rework this plan during the first year of your project. You will undoubtedly find yourself making many changes as you start to "live" with your paper design. In fact, even after the first year, or the first five years, you will still be making changes. This is part of landscaping, so be prepared for it.

Sketching on graph paper should become a permanent aspect of your entire landscape project, not just something you do in the initial stages. Later on, when you begin to think about installing perennial borders, a rock garden, a rose garden, shrub borders, and trees, you should once again start your project by designing on graph paper.

What is a "nursery" area? A nursery area is a plot located in an out-of-the-way part of your property, usually out of sight. It is a place where you can install unidentified plants given to you by friends so that you can see how tall they ultimately grow, what color their flowers are, and whether or not they thrive on your property. You can also use it to install very young shrubs, trees, or perennials, which you can purchase very reasonably, until they are large enough for permanent installation in a border, foundation planting, or bed. You can use this area to experiment with various plants before installing them permanently, thus ascertaining whether or not they are right for a particular location without letting other people see your mistakes.

What is a compost heap? A compost heap is a pile of organic waste material from your garden, such as grass clippings, leaves, and weeds. Organic waste material from the kitchen, such as citrus rinds, melon rinds, potato peelings, egg shells, or any vegetable waste, can also be included. This is combined with fertilizer and kept reasonably moist. After several months, the organic material decomposes. It is full of all kinds of nutrients and is probably the best fertilizer you can add to your soil, either by working it into the soil as a nutrient or using it as mulch.

What is mulch? Mulch is probably the gardener's best friend, and for that reason, I include this explanation in the first chapter of this book. Mulch serves as a protective covering for plants and might consist of rotted compost, pine or cedar bark chips (available at garden centers or nurseries), grass clippings, and, depending on availability in your locale, ground-up corn cobs or cocoa bean hulls (though their chocolate odor, in my opinion, is inappropriate in a garden). The material is spread on the surface of the soil between shrubs, vegetables, flowers, or anywhere that bare soil is exposed. Mulch serves several purposes: it helps retain moisture, cutting down on watering time; it helps retard weed growth, cutting down on weeding time; it dresses up a garden; and, as it decomposes, it adds nutrients to the soil. If you are smart, you will use a great deal of mulch throughout your gardening career.

How do I make a compost pile so that I have homemade fertilizer and lots of mulch? If possible, locate your compost pile out of sight of your house, close to a source of water, and in a shady area so that moisture will be retained. Once located, it is easy to make a compost pile.

First, dig a shallow pit six to eight inches deep, and lay the soil aside. You will need some kind of retaining fence or wire mesh to keep the pile in a manageable area and to ensure that the material is properly compacted. You can use old doors, chicken wire, railroad ties, or cement blocks for this purpose. I have found that cement blocks are best. However, the microbes that decompose the composting material need air, so if you use cement blocks, leave spaces in between them so that air can get into the pile.

Gather all of the organic material from your kitchen garbage, lawn clippings, flower beds, and garden trimmings. Do *not* include stones, tin cans or boxes, plastic or paper cartons, metal, or wood. Spread the refuse evenly over the pit area to a depth of eight to ten inches. As you add layers of organic material, try to form the pile so that the sides slant toward the middle. When it is finished—and it shouldn't be more than five feet high—fashion a shallow depression in the top layer so that rain can soak into the pile.

Moisture is essential to make compost. If you do not maintain moisture, some of the material may become dried out and then scorched by the sun, destroying the nutrients and rendering the compost useless as a soil amendment. You should water your compost heap after each layer of refuse has been added on the top. Using a fine spray from the garden hose, moisten the pile thoroughly. In dry climates, cover the pile with plastic to keep moisture in.

Nitrogen will help rot the organic matter as you build the pile. Apply a thin layer of sheep, horse, chicken, or cow manure, enough to cover the pile, after you add a layer of material. If fresh manure is not available, dried cow or sheep manure is available at garden centers and nurseries. You can use a layer of chemical 5-10-10 fertilizer if you cannot get manure. The numbers 5-10-10 indicate five pounds of actual nitrogen, ten pounds of actual phosphorus, and ten pounds of actual potassium per one hundred pounds of fertilizer, or 5 percent, 10 percent, and 10 percent of any other quantity. Nitrogen is necessary for good vegetative growth; phosphorus is essential for photosynthesis, fruiting, and root growth; and potassium strengthens stems and improves fruiting or blossoming. Other materials, such as dried blood, soybean or cottonseed meal, and fish scraps, also provide nitrogen and can be added to speed decomposition. An average-size compost heap—five feet square by four feet high—should have about twenty-five pounds of 5-10-10 fertilizer distributed in five applications of five pounds each. One or two pounds of lime should be mixed thoroughly into the pile as well to keep it from becoming too acidic.

Cover the pile with a two-inch layer of soil. The soil will introduce microbes, keep loose materials from blowing away, and help retain heat and odors. However, if you have constructed your compost pile properly, there should be no disagreeable odor.

A compost pile must breathe. To ensure this, you must turn the pile over every three to four weeks. Try to turn from the inside out, exchanging material that is more decomposed with the raw outside material.

Here is a list of organic materials you can add to a compost heap:

- Leaves from maple, oak, birch, willow, and other trees
- Pine needles
- Weeds, preferably before they set seeds
- Lawn clippings
- Small clippings from bushes or hedges
- Spoiled vegetables or fruits from the garden or kitchen
- Sawdust
- Horse, cow, chicken, or sheep manure
- Manure from dogs, but not cats
- Cornstalks, if well chopped up
- Hay
- Garbage from the kitchen
- Small wood chips

Your compost should be well rotted and ready to use in about three months.

What is a service area? This is the place where you install your clothesline, where you keep your garbage cans, and where you can pile bags of peat moss and other things necessary to maintaining your property as well as necessities for day-to-day living—in short, things that are ugly and thus best kept out of sight.

Where should I place my service area for garbage and what problems can I expect? When you locate your service area, keep in mind that you will probably have to take the garbage out several times a day, in both the heat of summer and the cold of winter. It should therefore be situated near the kitchen or rear entrance of the house. And, each week or biweekly, depending on your garbage service, the cans will have to be carted out to the pick-up point, usually in the front of the house at curbside. So, if possible, your service area should also be located as close to the curb as possible.

I have found that containers made of rubberized material hold up better than those made of galvanized metal. The galvanized versions rust out within a few years. Heavy-duty rubber containers are also preferable to stiff, heavy, plastic containers, for plastic tends to crack when exposed to cold temperatures.

If raccoons or stray dogs run around your neighborhood, it won't take them long to discover your garbage. Once they do, they will knock over the cans in search of food, spreading garbage all over the place. Beyond the nuisance factor, the strewn garbage can also attract rats. If this becomes a problem, the best solution is to build a small wooden compartment, with a covering, into which you place your garbage cans. If night marauders figure out how to open the top, simply place some sort of latch on the lid.

If you do not have the option of placing your service area out of sight, the wooden box can be painted, and flowers or shrubs can be planted in front of it to dress it up.

What about a place for my dog? First, find out whether or not there is a leash law in your area. If so, for the sake of good neighborly relations, it is best to abide by it, as a rambunctious dog can wreak havoc with a neighbor's garden. What is more, if a dog is permitted to roam loose, you may find it the victim of an accident, seriously maimed, or even dead. A motorist, in trying to avoid hitting your dog on the street, could have an accident, causing serious injury or even death. So for the safety of your dog and others, observe the leash law. If you do not do so, and your dog is snared by the local dog catcher and taken off to the pound, in most areas you will have to pay a fine to bail him out. In most areas, the fine becomes stiffer with each incarceration. If there is a leash law, and your dog has not been trained to remain on your property, you have several options. You can take him or her for walks at regular intervals, you can build a dog run, or you can install a chain somewhere on your property and tie your dog to it. If you have a large or very strong dog, make sure to get a heavy-duty chain, as the less sturdy chains can easily be broken if your dog sees another dog or is intent on roaming around.

What about a play area for the children? If you have children, and particularly young children, you will want to provide a play area for them. Here are a few things to keep in mind:

- Provide a green area for them, be it lawn or crab grass, as a hard surface can be dangerous if they fall.
- Locate the play area within sight of windows, particularly kitchen windows, so that you can keep an eye on them.
- Allow enough space for a sandbox, swings, trapeze, and other play apparatus.

What about assessing the trees on my property? One of the most important things you will want to do during the first year while assessing your property is to look over the trees you already have and decide which are worth maintaining, which need tree surgery, and which should be removed. You will have to learn what kinds of trees you actually have before you take any further steps. The best way to do this is to ask knowledgeable friends or neighbors or go to the library and take out books about trees. One of the most comprehensive is the *Illustrated Encyclopedia of Trees*, written by Hugh Johnson. Once you have identified all of your trees, sort out those commonly referred to as "junk trees" from those worth maintaining.

Which trees are "junk" trees that should be removed, and why? In addition to trees that provide edible fruit and nuts, there are many that produce inedible fruit, nuts, seed pods, and brittle limbs. The sooner you get rid of them and plant less troublesome trees in their place, the better. Perhaps my most obvious mistake in planning my landscape was not to remove an *Albizia*, also called pink mimosa or silk tree, *immediately*. (This tree, incidentally, is no relation to the beautiful yellow-flowering mimosa tree that grows in the south of France.) *Albizia* has feathery foliage that folds up at night and fluffy, pink flowers. The ultimate nuisance tree, it doesn't leaf out until July, and sits there in May and June amid the glorious spring spectacle resembling a hangman's tree. Then the flowers appear, smell sickeningly sweet, stay the rest of the summer, and drop on everything, leaving black stains. After flowering, pods about eight inches long form, again dropping on everything, germinating, and necessitating constant weeding. My pink mimosa has been gone for three years now and I am *still* pulling hundreds of seedlings from over the entire property. The tiny leaves drop early in the fall, without providing a display of color, and stick to your shoes, littering the floor of your house. Recently, a fungus that is spreading throughout the Northeast has mercifully started to attack and kill these trees—all the more reason to chop them down as soon as possible.

I put off chopping this tree down for many years, secretly hoping that an act of God, such as a hurricane, would do the job for me. I finally got rid of it about nine years after I bought my house, and it was a good thing that I did, because shortly thereafter, Hurricane Gloria passed through our area. The hurricane certainly would have taken the mimosa down, quite probably onto my house.

Here is a list of trees about which it can be said, "He who plants one or insists on maintaining one will live to regret it."

- Common catalpa: In the fall, beanlike pods, measuring up to twenty inches long, litter the lawn. The leaves of this genuine nuisance tree have a very disagreeable odor when crushed.
- Horse chestnut: Although this tree is nice along the Champs Elysée, on your property it will create a serious maintenance problem. All those hard-shelled nuts must be removed before mowing the lawn.
- Black locust: Locust is a sturdy wood; indeed, locust fence-posts have been sunk in the ground for one hundred years and stand unaffected by the elements. However, the trees are extremely brittle. In high winds, and sometimes even gentle winds, branches break and trunks splinter, littering the ground below and creating a safety hazard. Though it has lovely fragrant flowers, the thorns can be a menace. Black locusts are also subject to a disease that causes the leaves to fall, coating everything they touch with a black gummy substance.
- Swamp maples: Sometimes called red maple, this tree drops seed pods that end up in gutters and drainpipes. They sprout and produce more of the same all over your property. Should you decide to cut one down, be prepared for a yearly swing with the ax, for the trees persist and send up new shoots, which often attain a remarkable height in one year.
- Mulberry: This is a fast-growing tree, but don't plant the female fruiting variety near a driveway, clothesline, or patio. The fruit drops and badly stains anything on which it falls. Mulberries trod underfoot on pathways will cling to your shoes and stain your rugs when you get back home.

- Sweet gum: This tree produces inconspicuous flowers in the spring, which in fall turn into bushels of spiny, prickly fruits that drop in late winter. These fruits must be raked up and carted away. They are tough and almost nonbiodegradable; few compost piles welcome them.
- Osage orange: The American Indians used to make canoes out of the wood of these trees, and the early immigrants trimmed them into hedges to contain livestock. The trees grow thick and are covered with thorns. At one time there were fifty of them growing on the lane where I live. In 1938, according to elderly neighbors, a hurricane toppled forty-nine. As luck would have it, the one remaining stands directly across the street from my house. Every fall it treats us to a bonanza of useless green wrinkled fruit, the size of a grapefruit. This fruit has a foul odor and must be picked off the lawn and street.
- Weeping willow: This is a beautiful and graceful tree . . . in parks and on large estates. But its constantly shedding branches must be tended all summer. The roots search for water and find their way into septic tanks and drainpipes. In a feisty gale, let alone a hurricane, willows are always the first to uproot, generally pulling up half of the lawn with them.
- *Albizia* or pink mimosa: See above.

What should I do about very large, ancient fruit trees? Old apple and pear trees flower magnificently in the spring. However, unless they have been lovingly maintained through the years, you will find the fruit totally inedible—buggy, and disease ridden. Old varieties of pears do not ripen on the tree but have to be placed in cold storage for a number of weeks before they even begin to ripen. For this reason, unless you are willing to try to restore the tree (with the advice of a tree surgeon), to spray regularly (and bear in mind that to spray a pear tree thirty feet high requires professional orchard equipment), and then to pick up fruit as it falls in autumn (a menace underfoot, for you can trip and fall if you step on one), my advice to you is to get rid of old fruit trees. If you do not, be prepared for a constant mess—buggy leaves and fruit and litter on the lawn. If you decide you do wish to maintain an old fruit tree, *don't* locate a patio or a hammock beneath it. Falling fruit is as hard as a stone, and if one falls on your head or a guest's head, serious injury can result.

I've identified the trees I wish to eliminate. Now what do I do? If the trees are small, you can probably handle the job yourself. An ax or saw will do the trick. If you have a willing friend or companion who will help, two-person saws require the least strenuous effort and take the least time. If not, sharpen your ax with a honing stone and get to work. You can rent or buy a chain saw, but be advised: they are extremely dangerous to use if you do not have experience with them. You would do best to leave such work to professionals.

If the trees you wish to eliminate are large, call a professional landscape service and have them do the job. Large trees must be removed in stages. You must climb the tree and saw off top growth first, then the side limbs, and finally the main trunk. This is no job for an amateur.

I've identified the trees I wish to maintain. Now what do I do? Very often, large trees need work: thinning, repairing, fertilizing, and medication if they are diseased. The best thing to do is to call in a tree surgeon and ask his or her advice. Tree surgery is a complicated business and is also best left to professionals. A tree surgeon can also tell you whether or not a tree is worth saving.

I've eliminated "junk" trees, decided which other trees I wish to maintain, and taken care of work necessary on large trees. Should I plant replacement trees or other trees now? No. You do not know your property well enough to make these important decisions. It is better to spend the first year assessing your property to learn what use you wish the trees to serve, where you should plant them in your landscape, and what kinds of trees will best suit your needs. Spend the year observing your property, and read the section on trees in the next chapter for guidelines. Take extensive notes on areas of your property where you think you might wish to plant new trees. Is there any shade in that location now? Is there too much sun in a particular location now and would a shade tree make the area more compatible with outdoor summer living? Do you need a windbreak? (That is, is your yard very windy on some days, making it unpleasant to sit in?) If so, do you need trees for a windbreak?

What if I don't have any trees on my property? Should I plant trees now? The advice above applies to treeless properties as well: you do not know your property well enough to make these important decisions. Spend the year observing. Ask yourself the same questions as above and take extensive notes on what you think your needs are. Consult the section on trees in the next chapter for further guidelines.

The shrub borders on my property are overgrown. What should I do? Shrubs differ from trees in that old, overgrown shrubs can almost always be pruned and brought back to life and beauty. Therefore, if you've decided after lengthy walks around your property at different times of the year that your shrub borders are, in fact, in the right place, pruning is the road to take, unless the shrubs in the border do not appeal to you. In that case, remove them. Shrub pruning is a project you can undertake yourself. As a rule, most flowering shrubs should be pruned *after* flowering, and in most cases when you prune, you remove branches at the base of the plant, not halfway up. After removing overgrowth, cut the shrub back to about one-half its original height. For further information on shrubs, consult books in the library, seek advice from knowledgeable friends, family, or neighbors, or consult your local County Cooperative Extension Service, listed in the "County" pages of your telephone directory. Also, consult the shrub section in chapter 2.

There are shrubs planted willy-nilly all over my property. What should I do? It is probably best to remove these shrubs because they will undoubtedly be in the way of your landscape scheme. What is more, they can influence your landscaping decisions. You will find yourself saying things like, "Let's plan the patio around the forsythia bush." Don't let this happen. You will have to live with your patio for years to come, and you can always plant a new forsythia bush if you decide that is really what you want. You need not destroy these shrubs, however. You can transplant them into your nursery area in spring or fall and hold them there until you have designed your shrub plantings. Then you can decide if you really want to use them, and if so, replant them in the location *you* decide upon.

There are no shrubs on my property. What should I do? Don't do anything this year, unless you wish to purchase some very young shrubs and install them in a nursery area for future use. You do not know your property well enough yet to make decisions about a shrub border or planting.

What are foundation plantings? Foundation plantings are those that are planted around the foundation of the house. They set the house off in the landscape and add beauty to the surroundings.

What should I do about my present foundation plantings? If your house is more than twenty-five years old and foundation plantings exist, they are probably very overgrown and more likely than not consist of old-fashioned standard or tall-growing varieties of evergreens or conifers or broad-leaved evergreens, such as rhododendrons. (More recently, dwarf conifers and dwarf broad-leaved evergreens have been installed in most foundation plantings.) If they are overgrown, the best thing to do is to remove them. The most common foundation plantings of that vintage are common juniper, which becomes overgrown and sports dead brown lower branches with age; standard spruce, which becomes gigantic with age; and standard rhododendron, which also becomes gigantic with age. If any of your foundation plantings block light into windows, you will probably wish to remove them, regardless of their height. If your foundation plantings are within bounds, all that may be required is a pruning, either severe or slight. You can learn about how to prune shrubs from books. Again, however, it is probably wisest to hire a tree surgeon for this task, for these professionals know exactly how to prune each cultivar and can advise you about which cultivars you should remove.

I've removed overgrown foundation shrubs. Should I plant a new foundation planting now? No. As with trees, you do not know your property well enough yet and have not had time to decide on the aesthetics of your landscape plan. You may be concerned that the front of your house and other places where foundation plantings were removed will look bare. To offset this problem, you can plant annual flowers in these areas for summer color. In addition to adding aesthetic appeal to your home, this project will enable you to get your feet wet in planning an annual garden or filling in voids with annuals, tasks that will be necessary later on in your landscape project.

I want to install a patio or terrace for outdoor relaxation, entertaining, and dining. Should I do this now? How do I decide where to locate it? Do not install a patio during the first year; you don't know the traffic patterns on your property yet. There are a number of things you must decide before installing a patio, and it will probably take you an entire year until you feel secure enough to make these decisions. Keep in mind that if you plan on dining out of doors, you will want to situate the patio reasonably close to the kitchen. Remember, you will have to carry glasses, china, silver, and trays of food back and forth from the patio to the kitchen. Although full sunshine is delightful in May and early June, it can be unbearable in July and August, so you must plan your patio around existing shade or plan your new plantings to provide for it. Wind is another factor that must be considered. In some areas the prevailing winds are just too strong for comfortable outdoor living and entertaining, so you will want to situate your patio in a sheltered area.

The best way to go about situating your outdoor living area is to move a table and chairs to different locations during the year. Try placing them in one location for two weeks, then move them to another location for two weeks, and so forth. By the end of the first year, you will have a very good idea about which area works best in terms of convenience and comfort.

Patios will be discussed in detail in chapter 3.

What about other garden features such as walks, fences, and walls, and garden structures such as gazebos, arbors, terraces, and stairs? Should I install them now? You do not know your property well enough yet to start making permanent installations. There are some exceptions to this rule, however. Walks made of stepping-stones can be installed, but *not* permanently. You may find at this point that installing temporary walks—that is, simply laying stepping-stones on the ground—will help you to define your property and learn about traffic patterns. During the course of the first year you can move them around, trying different walk patterns. But again, *never* install permanent walks during the first year of property ownership.

If you desire privacy, and if for some reason your neighbors, neighboring structures, or the road in the front of your house denies you this, you may want to install a fence during your first year. However, it is best to wait until the second or third year to do this. A fence can be expensive, there are many options in style and design, and if you do put one up and then decide it is in the wrong place, you will have to dismantle it and reinstall it elsewhere, a time-consuming and expensive task.

But I am anxious to get started and to see some results. Are there any projects I can do the first year to get started on my landscape scheme? Well of course you don't just want to walk around your newly purchased piece of earth and assess what you have, what you don't have, and what you want. There are two things you can do the very first year for "instant gratification." All during the years you were waiting to buy your own home, with your own piece of land, you've been dreaming of growing something—anything other than those philodendrons, African violets, and other house plants. What about vegetables? Yes, even during your first year, there is no reason why you can't grow luscious, flavor-filled tomatoes, fresh Boston or Bibb lettuce, scallions, radishes, and other treats. Since almost all vegetables are annuals—that is, they complete their growing and bearing cycle in one season and then die—you don't have to decide on a permanent place for a vegetable garden just yet. And beyond the pride you will feel when you pick the first tomato you've grown from the vine, ruby-red ripe, and the first tender baby lettuce, carrots, beets, string beans, or radishes, growing vegetables the first year will serve a landscape purpose as well: you will begin to learn where your vegetable garden will be best situated. At this point, you can place it anywhere on your property as long as the area is reasonably well-drained (that is, water does not remain after heavy rains), and it receives full sun all day long, since almost all vegetables require such a light condition for maximum growth.

There are a few things you should keep in mind when situating even this temporary, first-year vegetable garden. Place it within reasonable distance of the house. Nobody wants to take a long walk to pick some fresh lettuce for a salad, some chives for an omelet, or parsley for the stew. I have found that the closer the vegetable garden is to the house, and to the kitchen in particular, the better. When I first bought my property, I situated the vegetable garden seventy-five feet to the rear. I learned that I rarely would venture out to the "south forty" for four or five sprigs of parsley or chives to add to this or that. Furthermore, if your vegetable garden is close to the house, you can easily keep your eye on weed growth each day, before the weeds get out of hand and the garden becomes a total mess. And, should the garden need watering during the summer, as it most assuredly will, you won't have to drag your hose a long distance.

Some people are of the opinion that a vegetable garden is not particularly attractive to look at. I disagree. If well maintained, it can be the brand-new, shining star of your landscape project. If you mulch, provide temporary surfaces for paths, weed conscientiously, and stake tall-growing plants such as tomatoes, it can be a beautiful sight indeed.

How do I start to prepare a vegetable garden? The first thing you must do is to stake out the area with stakes and string. It is always a good idea to stake out any garden project this way, for although you may feel you can trust your eye when it comes to edging a straight line, you can't. Any line you try to dig will inevitably be crooked. For ease of maintenance it is probably best to install a rectangular plot, perhaps ten feet across, leaving two feet on either side for a path. Your garden will thus be no wider than six feet, and you will have access to both sides from adjacent paths. The length of your garden depends, of course, on how much produce you wish to grow. I strongly advise you to think small. The temptation for most novice gardeners is to plant too many varieties of too many vegetables. Remember, you are just getting your feet wet and will be occupied with many other tasks during your first summer as a property owner, so don't overdo it. A small, well-maintained vegetable garden will yield considerably more produce than a large, neglected one.

Now start digging! And dig deep, about eighteen inches deep. Turn over the soil, remove rocks and debris, and rake out small stones. Then you must fortify the soil to make it hospitable to growing vegetables. First determine if your soil is very heavy in clay. You do this by squeezing it in your hand. If soil oozes through your fingers, it is heavy in clay. If so, spread considerable amounts of sand on top of the area, about one part sand to two parts soil. Then, for every two hundred square feet, spread about one bale of sphagnum peat moss on top, along with about three bushels of organic matter such as rotted compost or dried cow or sheep manure, all of which are available at garden centers and nurseries, over the entire plot. To determine if your soil is heavy in sand, squeeze it in your hand. If the soil falls all apart, it is too sandy. If your soil is very sandy, don't add sand and double the amount of sphagnum peat moss and organic matter you spread on top. A soil that is loamy and rich will not ooze through your fingers or fall apart in your hand when squeezed. If your soil is loamy and rich, incorporate half the amount of sand, sphagnum peat moss, and rotted organic matter indicated above for clayey soil. Then, using a spade, dig the additives into the soil. You can do this anytime after the ground is workable in the spring. (By workable, I mean after the ground has thawed and the soil is loamy in texture rather than waterlogged.) It is a good idea to prepare the bed well in advance of planting seeds. This will allow the soil to settle and help you avoid overworking (and accompanying back pains and muscle aches).

How do I protect my vegetable garden from rabbits and other animals? Once you've prepared the bed, you will have to provide protection from rabbits and other animals. Rabbits not only like carrots but baby lettuce, baby beets, baby spinach, baby peas, and so forth. It is best to install an inexpensive, temporary fence around your vegetable patch. It must be at least eighteen inches high, as rabbits can jump over anything lower. Purchase some metal stakes, which are inexpensive and available at garden centers and nurseries, and metal fencing material. You can use chicken wire, since its holes are small enough to prevent rabbits and their baby offspring from passing through. Drive the stakes into the ground, about one every five feet, and attach the fencing to them. The stakes, incidentally, can serve as supports for tomatoes, should you want to plant them. Be sure that the chicken wire or other material is sunk at least one inch into the ground around the perimeter of the garden plot. Inquire locally at a nursery or from your neighbors about other pests in the area. If stray dogs are a problem, make your fence four feet high. If deer are a problem, make your fence eight feet high. If woodchucks are a local pest, sink the fence one foot beneath the surface of the soil.

Pests indeed! What about a garden's friends? Many species of insects, birds, and reptiles will help you to grow fine produce. If you feed the birds during the winter, and every good gardener does, continue to do so in the summer. They will repay you tenfold by eating hundreds of thousands of undesirable insects. Do not kill toads or garter snakes; they consume their weight in pests every week. Learn which insects are beneficial to your garden. These include the ladybugs, the praying mantis, the ground beetle, the iridescent blue-green European ground beetle (chafer), the tiger beetle, the robber fly, the assassin bug, the goldeneyed lacewing, the ant lion (also called the doodlebug), the damselfly, the syrphid (also called the flower fly), and the wasp. These insects attack and kill many pests that rob your garden.

What about fertilizer? What are my options? At this point you will have to decide what kind of fertilizer you wish to use in your garden. Both organic and inorganic fertilizers are available. Inorganic, or chemical, fertilizer is available at garden centers and nurseries. The most commonly used type is 5-10-5. This is because 5-10-5 offers sufficient amounts of nitrogen, phosphorus, and potassium for most soil and growing conditions, without offering too much, which could create an imbalance in soil nutrition. If you decide on an organic or nonchemical fertilizer, here is a formula you can use to make your own. In an eight-gallon container mix about 30 percent dried sheep or cow manure (horse manure is not recommended until it has been thoroughly composted for one year), 20 percent well-rotted compost or sphagnum peat moss, 10 percent blood meal, 10 percent bone meal, 15 percent superphosphate or natural rock phosphate, 10 percent ground limestone, and 5 percent horticultural vermiculite. All of these ingredients are generally available at garden centers and nurseries. When it comes time to fertilize your garden, either at planting time or during the season, use this instead of 5-10-5 fertilizer, roughly doubling the amount specified in the instructions below for each application.

You have prepared your vegetable bed, fenced it in, and either purchased a supply of 5-10-5 fertilizer or made your own organic fertilizer. Now you are ready to plant your first vegetable garden.

Which varieties of vegetables should I plant and when should I plant them? As is true of plants in general, some vegetables are less problematical than others. There are four times of the year to plant vegetables. First, as soon as the soil is workable in spring. In most parts of the country this is in the end of March or the beginning of April. Next, about one month later, around mid-April to early May. Then, after all danger of frost, usually around mid-May. And finally, around the end of August or beginning of September, for a fall crop of some vegetables.

Which vegetables do I plant as soon as the ground becomes workable? Some vegetables require cold temperatures in order for the seeds to germinate. These vegetables are generally quite hardy and will withstand late frosts and even a snowfall. Included in this group are peas, onions, shallots, garlic, leek, celery, celeriac, salsify, lettuce, radishes, spinach, most greens, such as cress and arugula, and members of the brassica, or cabbage, family: bok choy, broccoli, brussels sprouts, cabbage, cauliflower, chinese cabbage, and kohlrabi. These same varieties, if planted in June, will not usually grow satisfactorily because the temperature is too high for germination and healthy growth. A good index as to when it is time to plant is the soil. If it is waterlogged and very cold, it is probably too early to plant the above varieties. If, on the other hand, the soil is friable—that is, if you take a handful and squeeze it a bit and it remains reasonably granular—it is usually a good time to plant.

Which vegetables do I plant about one month later but before all danger of frost is past? Certain vegetables require slightly cold conditions but some- what warmer than the above vegetables. These include Swiss chard, beets, and carrots. Although some recommend planting these at the same time as the varieties above, I have found that spring rains often rot the seeds, and germination is better if I wait a month or so before planting.

Which vegetables do I plant after all danger of frost? You must wait to plant some vegetables until all danger of frost is over and the ground has warmed up considerably. These vegetables are tender; that is, they will die if ex- posed to cold temperatures. Included in this group are all members of the bean family, such as string beans, lima beans, and kidney beans, tomatoes, eggplant, squash (both winter and summer varieties), melons, peppers, cucumbers, pumpkins, and corn.

Which vegetables do I plant at the end of summer or early fall? Early spring leaf vegetables such as lettuce, radishes, members of the cabbage family, spinach, cress, and arugula can all be planted at this time of year for a fall crop. Members of the onion family will not mature in time for harvest, so they are inappropriate for late planting. However, you can plant garlic in the fall, for it will winter over, that is, live through the winter, and grace you with an early spring crop. Beets may be harvestable before killing frost if you plant now, but carrots will not be. Do not plant any members of the bean family, tomatoes, eggplant, peppers, or any of the vine crops —melons, squash, pumpkins, or cucumbers—at this time of year, for they require hot weather to mature to eating stage and will not survive early fall frosts.

Which varieties of vegetables can I plant from seed and which are best planted from head-start six-packs? Vegetables that are best grown from seed include all salad greens, such as lettuce, arugula, cress, and mustard, peas, all beans, all vine crops, such as winter and summer squash, pumpkins, melons, and cucumbers, and most members of the cabbage family. Here's a time-saving tip: Many of these vegetable seeds are available in biodegradable strips, evenly spaced out, so that when you plant all you have to do is place the strip in the soil and the seeds will be spaced properly. Since all vegetables have to be thinned out once they reach an inch or so in height, this saves a great deal of time in the thinning process. Although these strips cost a little more than packages of seeds, they are worth the investment because of this savings in time. Since some varieties of vegetables require an early start under lights and indoors, these are best purchased in six-packs (plastic trays containing six compartments with one plant in each) from garden centers or nurseries. These include tomatoes, peppers, and eggplant. If you wish to start these indoors under lights, see *How do I start seedlings under lights?* (p. 30) in the section on annuals for further information. Tomatoes, peppers, and eggplant should be started indoors about six weeks before outdoor planting time in your area. Because of its slow germination and consequent tendency to rot in the ground if the earth is too moist, parsley is also best purchased in six-packs. Although members of the cabbage family do grow well from seed, it is often much easier to purchase six-packs of these varieties as well.

Are there any varieties of vegetables that are problematic and require advanced gardening knowledge? Yes, there are a few. Cauliflower is one, because rubber bands must be placed around the forming heads to hold the leaves around them in order to blanch them, that is, to ensure that heads are white. Cauliflower is also quite prone to insect infestation. Celery is also tricky, if you want the pale green or white blanched product. If you do not, celery is easy to grow. You may find that the carrots you grow in your garden are quite good. However, the carrots available in supermarkets, which are grown in California, are usually better and sweeter than those you grow at home. Radishes are prone to worm infestation if planted too late, though most other early-planted crops are not. To protect plants against worms, simply scatter some wood ashes onto the soil surface and with a cultivator scratch it into the soil before planting your seeds. Birds and corn borers love corn, so if local farmers grow and sell corn, it is perhaps less trouble and cheaper in the long run to buy theirs rather than grow your own.

Can I grow asparagus and rhubarb? Yes, and once installed, an asparagus bed will provide food for decades because it is a perennial plant—that is, it is winter hardy and does not die with frost. However, the first year is not the time to install an asparagus bud. Do this later in your landscape project when you have decided on a permanent location for your vegetable garden. Asparagus will be covered in greater detail in chapter 2, as will rhubarb, another perennial.

How do I plant seeds for my vegetable garden? Space rows for all early vegetables about one foot apart. Place two sticks in the ground, one at either end of the row, and tie a string between them. With a hoe, make a trench from six to eight inches deep. If you are using 5-10-5 chemical fertilizer, scatter one handful per six-foot row in the bottom of the trench. If you are using a nonchemical mix, per the above formula, scatter two handfuls in the bottom of the trench. Then scratch the fertilizer into the soil as you fill the trench with the soil that you removed.

Next, consult your seed packages for the proper depth and spacing of planting for each vegetable. With the handle of the hoe, make a furrow in the soil along the string that is tied between the two sticks at either end of the row. Then get down on your hands and knees and plant the seeds carefully. If you use seed tapes, simply lay each tape in place and cover it with soil. If you plant seeds, remember to plant them thinly, for you will have to remove many of them when they reach one inch in height. Then cover the seeds with soil, pressing it down firmly. Place a label in the soil to identify the vegetable. Move two stakes and your string one foot away from the planted row and continue on down the plot until you have installed all the vegetables you wish.

Peas should not be planted in rows with other vegetables because they are vines and need support to grow. They are best planted along the fence you installed to prevent rabbits from pillaging your crop.

Onions and shallots should be planted from sets purchased at local garden centers or nurseries. These look like tiny versions of the mature vegetable. Prepare a row as above. However, when you dig the furrow for the row, dig two inches deep. Place the onion or shallot sets about three or four inches apart and cover them with soil. Any garlic you buy can be divided into individual cloves and planted like onions. These cloves will grow to full size during the season. If larger garlic is desired, plant in spring or fall and harvest the following fall.

Be sure to leave space for tomatoes, string beans, and any other vegetables that you will plant later in the season, after all danger of frost.

When you have finished, water the entire garden, using the fine-spray setting on your hose nozzle. Do not flood the garden or use a powerful spray setting, as this will disturb the planting.

After the seeds germinate, and when they have reached a height of about one inch, thin the seedlings to the spacing recommended on the seed package. Continue to irrigate regularly during dry spells. In most parts of the country, however, this is not a problem during the spring and early summer.

You can usually start to harvest some of the vegetables you have planted—such as lettuce, arugula, spinach, and beet greens—after about a month. Many varieties of radishes are ready to harvest in two to three weeks. Other vegetables—such as tomatoes, peppers, melons, and cucumbers—take longer to reach edible maturity.

When hot weather arrives my lettuce becomes bitter and my other vegetables have flowers on them and are going to seed. What have I done wrong? Nothing. This is nature's way. Lettuce is a cool-weather crop and will "bolt" in hot weather; that is, it will go to seed and become bitter in taste. Pull it out and dispose of it. Then, when the cool weather of late summer arrives, plant a new crop of those vegetables that prefer cool growing conditions.

How do I plant tomatoes, peppers, and other vegetables that I have bought in six-packs from garden centers and nurseries? After all danger of frost, usually from the beginning to the end of May in most parts of the country, it is time to plant the tender vegetables. It is best to purchase six-packs of peppers, tomatoes, and eggplants from local garden centers or nurseries. For a full season of tomatoes, select one each of early, midseason, and late-bearing varieties. Select only those varieties that are disease resistant; almost all varieties available at retail outlets are, but you should ask the proprietors just to make sure. If they don't know, go elsewhere. If they tell you they are not, go elsewhere. If they tell you they are, buy them. Peppers and eggplant are usually not sold as early, midseason, or late-bearing. They generally bear around midseason or August.

Once you've purchased your plants, select an overcast day to plant. Set tomatoes about eighteen inches apart, peppers and eggplants about twelve inches apart. Dig holes about one-foot deep and scratch a handful of 5-10-5 fertilizer or two handfuls of your own organic fertilizer into the bottom of the hole. Fill in the hole with the removed soil. When you look at your tomato plants you will notice that they have long stems growing from the planting medium. Do not plant the tomato at the level in the six-pack, but sink it several inches into the ground so that only one or two sets of leaves are above the soil line. Roots will grow from the stems, providing a very strong root system for your plants. Peppers and eggplants can be planted about one inch below soil level for the same reason. Water these vegetables thoroughly and regularly during dry periods. It is a good idea to provide a mulch for your vegetables. Place about one inch of grass clippings or well-rotted compost over the area around the plants. As mentioned before, this mulch will help to retain moisture, cut down on weeding, and eventually, when it decomposes into the soil, will provide nutrients for plants.

As your tomatoes grow, you will notice "suckers" growing from between the main stem and vertical leaves. These are small green stems that sport small leaves. Pinch these out as the plant grows, since they will only sap strength from the plant and usually produce no fruit. Do not do this with peppers or eggplants since here this growth will ultimately produce vegetables.

Every two weeks scratch in about one tablespoon of 5-10-5, all-purpose fertilizer around each plant. You can also use fertilizers especially blended for tomatoes, as well as those for peppers and eggplants. If you use your own organic mix, scratch in about two tablespoons around each plant.

As these plants grow, they will need support. When they are about one foot high, hammer stakes (six feet for tomatoes, three feet for peppers and eggplants) into the ground and tie the growing plants to the stakes. If you do not stake your tomatoes, they will flop over on the ground, and many will rot or not ripen properly.

How do I plant the tender vegetables that go into the ground after all danger of frost? String beans are planted in the same manner as the above cold-weather vegetables, but melons, squash, cucumbers, and pumpkins must be planted in mounds. Select seeds of bush or compact varieties, as the vines of standard varieties tend to grow from ten to twelve feet long—much too long for the small or even midsize vegetable garden. Before you plant the seeds, make a mound of earth about six inches high and about eighteen inches across. Dig a well in the center of the mound and fortify with a handful of 5-10-5 fertilizer or two handfuls of your own organic mix. Replace the soil on the mound. Then plant about six or seven seeds in a circle around the mound. When the seedlings are about two inches high, remove all but the three or four strongest.

Feed vine crops every two weeks by scratching one tablespoon of 5-10-5 fertilizer or two tablespoons of your own organic mix into the soil around the plants. Feed beans about one handful of 5-10-5 or two handfuls of your own organic mix per six-foot row. It is important to water these vegetables thoroughly during summer droughts, as a large percentage of vine vegetables is water. If you do not water them sufficiently, your crop may well be inedible.

Harvest summer squash, such as zucchini or yellow squash, when it is young. Sometimes, if you wait even two days, a zucchini can grow to one to two feet long and will be tough. Melons are usually ripe when the fruit separates easily from the vine. Cucumbers should also be picked daily and when young. Winter squash, such as acorn and hubbard squash, as well as pumpkins, should be harvested late in the season, usually after a frost. String beans are best when picked young.

What about pests and diseases? Most varieties of vegetable seeds and most six-pack plants are hybrids and have been bred to resist diseases. However, insect pests will probably strike some of your vegetables. Keep an eye out for holes in leaves or insects on the stems and branches of plants. Tried-and-true rotenone, a traditional insect repellent, is organic, made from a combination of roots of plants that insects abhor. Regular dusting of plants with this powder will help to rid your garden of insect pests. Various herbs, interplanted in your garden, will help to deter insects, as will French marigolds, nasturtium, and garlic. The leaves and flowers of the nasturtium, incidentally, are excellent in salads. If diseases do strike your plants, consult a book on growing vegetables or contact your local County Cooperative Extension Service.

The season is over, and I've harvested my vegetables. Now what? Assess the location of your garden. Is it in the right place from an aesthetic point of view? Is it convenient to your water supply and to the kitchen? Was the fence you installed high enough to keep animals out of the garden? Try to decide where you want to situate the vegetable garden permanently in your landscape. If you can make that decision at this point, prepare the ground, and install your fence. You will save a great deal of precious time in the spring, when you will be busy with other projects.

Besides vegetables, is there anything else I can plant to beautify my property, at least for the time being? Yes, there are the colorful plants that tide you over in summer and fall. They are called annuals.

The Colors that Tide You Over in Summer and Fall: Annuals

Annual flowering plants are indispensable for creating near-instant gratification when landscaping. They live for only one season and grow from seed, flowering with blooms that later turn back into seed, completing their life cycle in this short span of time. With a minimal amount of care, the display they provide is spectacular and very low in price. Annuals are the last of the great bargains, in fact, for they provide not only color in the garden but endless bouquets of cut flowers for the house, all for the price of a few packages of seeds or six-pack containers.

If you are just beginning to landscape your property, annuals will probably be the first plants you install, if only for the satisfaction of adding color and texture to your property. Because annuals live for only one season, there is no need to make permanent decisions about where to plant them. And, they will begin to give you the feel of "painting the canvas" of your property with color. Use them to experiment with colors and color combinations or to test plant areas where you might later wish to install permanent perennial, bulb, and shrub plantings. Annuals will give you some idea of how these beds will look and whether or not the location satisfies you. Or use them simply to dress up the property during the first few years of landscaping while permanent plantings grow to reasonable size and flowering. Beyond that, annuals serve to fill in gaps once your permanent planting is installed and to provide color when planted over spent spring-blooming bulbs. You will find that even five or ten years down the line, there will always be a place in your garden for these very utilitarian plants.

Included in the encyclopedia (pp. 38–55) are annuals that are readily available at garden centers or nurseries in seedling six-packs or packages of seeds. Keep in mind that beyond local sources, there are hundreds of varieties available to you if you avail yourself of mail-order sources. And, if you set up a lighting fixture or two to start seeds indoors before outdoor planting time, the possibilities of even more varieties open up to you. Write for some of the seed catalogues listed in chapter 6 and study them, as they contain a great deal of information that will help you in selecting and growing annuals. There are also many books available on the cultivation of annuals. Ortho's book on annuals is particularly easy to read and helpful. The information included here will help you select, plan, and grow the basic, unproblematical annuals that are right for your garden and area.

Annuals can be purchased in three ways: (1) you can purchase seeds and grow them yourself; (2) you can buy six-packs of plants at garden centers and nurseries (the surest way to secure almost instant color in your garden and to include in your landscape those annuals that must be started indoors under lights long before proper outdoor planting time if they are to bloom by summer); (3) if you are busy and do not have the time to plant seeds, water them, and care for them in their seedling stage, ready-grown annuals, although more expensive than a package of seeds, are the answer.

However, there are drawbacks to these offerings of six-pack annuals. Although more and more varieties become available every year, the industry still offers little more than about a dozen cultivars in a dozen or so varieties of each. These dozen or so represent the most common annuals grown and usually include impatiens, wax begonias, marigolds, petunias, ageratum, geraniums, salvia, asters, zinnias, alyssum, and little else, although of late, lobelia has become more readily available in six-packs. These varieties are generally referred to as "bedding plants," a term that has become anathema to more experienced gardeners. This means that they are suitable for laying down in beds of one or several colors, in various patterns, or in edging of borders. Don't misunderstand me: there is nothing wrong with the above varieties. Indeed, they are easy to grow, require next to no maintenance, bloom profusely, and generally resist drought—in short, a quick and easy fix. And, with careful planning of color selection and leaf texture, attractive plantings can be created.

However, when you restrict yourself to these varieties alone, you have merely scratched the surface of the hundreds of beautiful plants available to you and have sold yourself short in terms of the "adventure" of creating a garden. I was recently in England, visiting renowned horticulturist Rosemary Verey's extraordinary garden at Barnsley House. During the course of our conversation, she remarked more than once, "Why can't Americans be more adventurous when it comes to gardening?" She has a point: too many of us stick to the same old plants, year in and year out—the safe, surefire plants that have become clichés. If the demand for more unusual plants is made, the industry will respond, so as you gain experience and confidence, don't be afraid to ask for more! Eventually, garden centers and nurseries will have to offer greater variety to meet customers' wishes.

Whether you purchase seeds from seed racks in supermarkets, garden centers or nurseries, or from mail-order houses, a much larger variety of plants is available to you in seed form. However, some plants require a great deal of time to germinate and grow to flowering stage. Since seeds of many varieties of annuals should not be planted outdoors until after danger of frost, some will not bloom until very late in the summer, if then.

Furthermore, some seeds should be sprinkled on the soil surface and kept evenly moist at all times because they require light to germinate, while others should be planted and covered with soil, because they require dark conditions to germinate.

So, if you wish to sow seeds directly into the ground, you must limit yourself to those varieties that can be planted outdoors early in spring and sustain late frosts, those that will grow to flowering stage quickly if planted outdoors after all danger of frost, and, unless you have the time and inclination to provide evenly moist conditions for surface-sown seeds, those that should be covered with soil when planted.

Even with these restrictions, there are scores of varieties that you can successfully bring to flower by sowing directly in the soil, either in early spring or after all danger of frost.

A word of warning: If you are going out to buy annual seeds or if you are ordering through a mail-order house, be sure you know *exactly* what the growing conditions of each variety are. Granted this requires some homework, and the encyclopedia of annuals on page 38 will help you in your selection. For example, you may see a packet of snapdragons, with a gorgeous photograph of a rainbow collection of these beautiful flowers, and buy it. You might even be tempted to buy five or six packages of different colored snapdragons. However, snapdragons require a head start of from eight to ten weeks before being planted outdoors after all danger of frost. And, since they need light to germinate, they should be sown on the surface of the soil and kept evenly moist. This means that if you sow the seeds outdoors after frost, around the middle of May in most parts of the country, unless they are surface-sown and kept evenly moist, they probably won't germinate, and if they do, it will be many months down the line before they bloom. Snapdragons are best bought in six-packs at garden centers and nurseries. The same is true for impatiens, wax begonias, ageratum, and petunias.

However, it is a simple matter to avail yourself of varieties that need a head start. If you have a window with a southern exposure, you can place trays of seeds on shelves in the window or on a table in front of it. The problem with this method is that the daylight hours are not really long enough to start strong, vigorous seedlings in midwinter and early spring. You may have some success anyway, but there is a far better way to start seedlings indoors: install a simple fluorescent light fixture. With a small investment of time and money, entire new worlds of plant adventures will open up to you. This assumes, of course, that you do not have a greenhouse or do not wish to buy a seed-starting light unit. (You can build a good-sized structure for about one-quarter the cost of a small manufactured unit.)

It is unwise, incidentally, to accept seeds given to you by well-meaning friends that have come from plants they grew in their gardens. Most annual seeds today are hybrids, that is, they have been developed by crossbreeding two or more cultivars. Thus, plants grown from their seeds will not bloom true to the parent.

How can I build an inexpensive unit to start seedlings under lights? Here's how you do it. Purchase a four-foot-long industrial fluorescent light fixture. Such fixtures cost about $15 in most home improvement centers and usually come with two cool tubes. Substitute one warm tube for one of the cool tubes. The cool tubes radiate the cool colors, blue, green, and violet, necessary for foliage growth, and the warm tubes radiate warm colors, red, yellow, and orange, necessary for blooming. There is no need to buy expensive, special plant-growing fluorescent tubes. Despite manufacturers' claims, results for starting seedlings are just about as good with one cool and one warm tube. Either hang the fixture in a heated basement over a table or workbench, or attach it to the bottom of a shelf in the house. Plug it in and you are ready to start seeds indoors at the proper time. Since fixtures should remain on for about fourteen hours a day, you may want to buy a timer switch to turn lights off and on if you don't wish to be bothered with this daily task. These switches cost less than $10. You can start with one fixture, but even at the beginning, you will probably find that you want at least two. And after several years, you will undoubtedly find that you want three or four to accommodate all the plants you wish to start from seed.

How do I start seeds under lights? You can sow seeds in just about any container imaginable: milk cartons, plastic containers, flowerpots, aluminum trays—in short, anything that will hold a seed-starting soil mixture. Be advised that drainage must be provided, so if you use homemade containers, poke holes through the bottoms so that excess water can escape. You will have reasonable success using these containers. In addition to such homemade containers, there are many products available in garden centers and nurseries that are made specifically for starting seeds.

Every now and then, a product comes on the market that is so exceptional, so easy to use, and results in such total success that it is worth investigating. If you wish to start seeds indoors under lights, it will be well worth your while to write to: Gardener's Supply Co., 128 Intervale Road, Burlington, Vermont 05401, (802) 863-4535. They import seed-starting kits from England called A. P. Propatop, which are made of styrofoam and include a reservoir arrangement and felt, which, by a process similar to wick watering, maintains even moisture for the seed tray included in the kit. This cuts down tremendously on the watering process. The trays each hold about three to four quarts of water, and once filled they need be checked only once a week or so to see if they need refilling. Seedlings are watered from the bottom, so they are not damaged by the force of top watering. A clear plastic top is included to create a minigreenhouse, assuring that humidity is maintained. These units are a godsend to the busy gardener, and the results are impressive: almost 100 percent germination from planted seeds. They are very reasonable in price, can be reused again and again during the season as well as year in and year out, and are also useful for rooting cuttings and watering house plants when you are away from home. In short, they are absolutely indispensable to the home gardener. A four-foot industrial fluorescent light fixture will accommodate three of these self-watering seed-starter trays. Although you will have to invest some money in setting up an indoor light system, consider that a package of six annual plants costs around $3 these days. Each of the A. P. Propatop units contains 40 spaces for growing plants. If you start with three, you can grow 120 plants. These same plants would cost you around $60 at nurseries and garden centers—a substantial savings indeed. In addition, you will have the pleasure of watching seedlings grow during the late winter and early spring months.

Whether you use makeshift containers or avail yourself of the above units, the only other thing you will need to start seeds indoors is the proper soil. Do not purchase potting soil, as it is too heavy in texture to start seeds. Terra-lite or Reddi-Mix, available in garden centers and nurseries, are two products mixed to provide perfect growing conditions for starting seeds. They are sterilized, include vermiculite to lighten soil and retain moisture, and I recommend them. Before placing these products in a container, moisten them thoroughly. Then plant your seeds according to the instructions on the packet; that is, either lightly covered with soil or on the soil surface. If you are using a seed-starting unit that you purchased, plant several seeds in each individual compartment. Insert identifying labels in the proper places. Place the containers under lights for fourteen hours a day with the soil surface about two inches from the light-tube surface. If you are using a homemade container, mist the soil with room-temperature water until it is evenly moist.

If you use the A. P. Propatop unit, the reservoir will provide the proper amount of water. When the seedlings are about one-half inch high, using cuticle scissors, cut off all but the strongest seedlings in each compartment, unless you are growing lobelia, which should be sown heavily and all seedlings allowed to grow. Once a week, feed the seedlings with all-purpose liquid house-plant fertilizer at one-quarter the strength recommended by the manufacturer. About one week before outdoor planting time you must "harden off" your plants in order to acclimate them to the strong sunlight and cool nights of outdoor growing. (This date varies from location to location throughout the country, but if your plants should be set out after "all danger of frost," check locally to find out when it is safe to plant tomatoes outdoors; planting time for these annuals will be the same.) You "harden off" by placing the containers outdoors in a shady spot during the day and bringing them indoors at night. Two days later, place them in a sunny spot for about half a day and a shady spot for the other half. The next day, leave them in the sun for the entire day and bring them indoors only if the night is to be chilly or if rain is predicted. If the plants' leaves start to look bleached, they are receiving too much sun and are not yet accustomed to the strong light. Move them back into shade. After about one week, you can safely plant them in your garden wherever you want them.

The following chart will help you if you wish to start seeds indoors:

VARIETY	WEEKS TO SOW BEFORE PLANTING OUTDOORS	GROWING CONDITIONS*
Ageratum	6–8	Cool; cover seeds with planting medium
Impatiens	6–8	Warm; cover seeds with planting medium
Lobelia	8–10	Cool; sprinkle seeds on top of planting medium
Marigold	2–3	Warm; cover seeds with planting medium
Petunia	6–8	Warm; sprinkle seeds on top of planting medium
Salvia	6–8	Warm; cover seeds with planting medium
Snapdragon	8–10	Cool; sprinkle seeds on top of planting medium
Sweet alyssum	6–8	Cool; cover seeds with planting medium
Zinnia	2–3	Warm; cover seeds with planting medium

*Warm Condition: about 70 degrees F. Cool Condition: about 60 degrees F.

Where on my property can I plant annuals? How should they be grouped?
You can plant annuals anywhere you want summer or fall color. They are suitable for beds, borders, dooryard gardens, in foundation plantings, along driveways, around mailboxes or birdbaths, as edging, along walks, and particularly in window boxes, planters, and containers. Annuals are better suited than perennials and bulbs to container culture. A few varieties prefer

shady conditions, some require reasonable moisture during the season, but most thrive in full sun and ordinary soil, are pest and disease free, and are highly resistant to drought conditions.

Here are a few aesthetic tips for planting annuals:

● Never plant annuals singly since an isolated plant will make little color or texture impact, and do not mix several varieties together willy-nilly, as the effect is a hodgepodge of color. It is best to plant at least five or seven of each variety together in a border or bed grouping. For edging, it is best to plant all of one variety, although with careful selection you can alternate three of one cultivar with three of another, and so forth. However, be very careful about mixing colors and be sure that the colors you select do not clash.

● Although formal beds of annuals in geometric forms can be appropriate for large-scale French-style gardens, as a rule this approach to design has little place in the home landscape. Leave that to your city park administrator, or better yet, several years down the line, try to change his or her approach, since most American park plantings look ghastly. Stick to informal plantings for the most pleasing visual results.

● Annuals are indispensable for covering over the browning foliage of spring bulb plantings. They also fill in the voids of bulb plantings all during the summer and fall.

● Annuals are also valuable in distant parts of the garden, providing splashes of color, helping to define property lines, and adding interest to an otherwise dull part of the landscape. Plant informally to emulate nature. Remember that hot colors—red, yellow, and orange—will make the planting seem closer to the eye, while cool colors—blue, purple, and green— recede and appear to be more distant. If plants with brilliant reds, oranges, and yellows appeal to you, this is the place on your property to plant them. They are too overpowering at close range.

Where in the country can I plant annuals? Annuals will grow in every part of the United States and most of the milder areas of Canada. In some parts of the Deep South, southern Florida, and parts of southern California, some annuals are unsuitable. In these parts of the country, check locally to ascertain which varieties can be grown. As long as some water is provided, annuals even grow in the driest of desert areas.

How do I select a site for an annual planting? Most annuals prefer full sun, so if you are installing a large bed or border, select a sunny location. A few annuals, such as impatiens, lobelia, and wax begonias, thrive in semi-shade and resent full sun. Use these in shady locations. Consult the encyclopedia (pp. 38–55) to see which varieties of annuals are suitable for each light condition. Since most annuals are not fussy about soil, this should not be a problem. However, many will not thrive under very wet conditions, such as in boggy areas or places on your property where water sits for a day or so after rain. Avoid overly wet areas for an annual planting.

How do I plan my annual planting? As always, work out your planting on graph paper. Use a scale of one block on the graph paper to two inches of garden space, and sketch out the area you wish to plant. Be adventurous, for annual plantings are installed for one season only; they are not permanent. Use your annual garden as a practice garden for later perennial and shrub borders or beds. At the same time, enjoy the color they provide for the first few years of your landscape project. When planning your annual planting, be aware of the following:

- You might want to try both a border and an island bed, to decide which is best for your property. Keep in mind that borders, in order to be effective, should be at least six feet deep if you plan on using tall-growing plants as well as shorter varieties. However, if you wish to limit yourself to plants that are about one and a half feet high, a three- or four-foot border will be suitable. Freeform island beds containing taller-growing varieties should be about eight feet across at their widest point. The bed should be about three times as long as it is wide. If you wish to install medium-height and low-growing plants, a five- or six-foot-wide island bed is suitable.
- In a border, place tall plants in the rear, medium-height plants in the middle, and low-growing varieties in front. In an island bed, taller plants go in the middle, surrounded by medium-height plants, with low-growing plants around the edge.
- Always think in terms of color combinations rather than in terms of individual varieties. Try to blend colors pleasingly, avoiding clashing combinations. And remember that combinations such as screaming orange, brilliant red, and sulphur yellow are very difficult to use harmoniously in an annual planting. If you are familiar with a color wheel, you know that continuous segments are the most harmonious: for example, red, red-violet, and violet; blue, blue-violet, and violet; or yellow, yellow-orange, and orange. As a rule, the smaller the bed, the narrower the segment of the color wheel. Complementary (opposite) colors of the basic scheme should be

used very sparingly to highlight the planting. For example, if you decide on a blue-violet, violet, and red-violet garden, a touch of yellow would be useful. A red-orange, red, and red-violet scheme could be highlighted by the opposite color, green, in the form of foliage. This highlighting can be a tricky business, however, so in order to be safe, stick to white as an accent until you get the feel of using colors in landscaping. Occasionally, single complementary colors can be used effectively. For example, golden-yellow dwarf marigolds blend well with the bright blue of lobelia. Always remember that foliage is green and often provides enough of a color contrast. One way to test out your color scheme is to go to a dry goods store and place various colors of silk flowers next to each other. You will be able to see if the colors do or do not clash.

● Despite all warnings to the contrary, most novice gardeners always select a plant because the color of the flower appeals to them. Don't do it! Keep your overall scheme in mind at all times and select your annuals accordingly.

● Plant in groups of five or seven if you are installing a bed or border. Even numbers of plants tend to appear as blocks of foliage and color in the garden.

● Avoid planting in straight lines or in circles around trees, birdbaths, or shrubs. The effect is unnatural and rigid.

● When you are ready to install your annual border or bed, take your chart to the garden with you along with a ruler to measure the spacing of plants. Don't trust your memory.

● As a rule, tall-growing plants should be spaced two feet apart, medium-height plants eighteen inches apart, low-growing plants twelve inches apart, and dwarf miniatures around six inches apart.

How do I install a window-box planting or a large container planting? For these plantings, choose low-growing annuals and those that are relatively drought resistant, since containers often must be watered once, or even twice a day during the hot, dry days of high summer. Keep in mind the color-scheme advice above when selecting. All containers must have drainage holes in the bottom, or the roots of your plants may rot from excess moisture. In addition, drainage material such as pebbles, gravel, or broken flowerpot shards should be placed in the bottoms of the containers. Use a soil mixture that is highly water retentive; that is, either mix a substantial amount of sphagnum peat moss with garden soil, or mix horticultural vermiculite or perlite in a one-to-one ratio with the soil. Before planting, thoroughly soak the planting medium. Annuals are particularly well suited to container and window-box culture. Use window boxes to dress up the facade of the house, on railings at door entrances, on fences, walls, and garden structures, or as planters along the patio or walk. Containers can be used on patios, to dress up shady areas, on porches, stairs, walls, along walks—almost anywhere you might want to add touches of color. Since they do dry out rapidly in hot weather, one way to facilitate maintenance is to fill a large container with sphagnum peat moss, wet it thoroughly, and then place a smaller container planted with annuals in the middle. You can mask the edge of the smaller container with more sphagnum peat moss. During hot dry spells, this method will cut down substantially on watering time.

How do I prepare the soil? Most annuals are not fussy about soil. However, working the soil to a depth of about one foot will help ensure success. If your soil is overly sandy or very clayey, mix in well-rotted compost or sphagnum peat moss in a ratio of about one part additive to two parts soil. The compost or peat moss will help retain moisture during dry spells and make it easier for a healthy root system to form. When you have prepared the planting site, water thoroughly.

When do I plant annuals? Most annuals are planted after all danger of frost. However, there are a few—sweet peas and larkspur, for example— that can be planted in early spring, as soon as the ground is workable. Check the encyclopedia (pp. 38–55) for further information on individual varieties.

How do I plant annuals? First check the encyclopedia to see if the varieties you are planting require rich soil. If this is the case, work about one table-spoon of all-purpose, 5-10-5 fertilizer per square foot of garden space into the soil. Be advised that most annuals do not require rich soil, and feeding may be unnecessary. To plant either small seedlings purchased in six-packs at garden centers or nurseries or those that you have started under lights, dig a hole large enough to contain the small root ball, set the plant in, firm the soil around the plant, and water thoroughly. As explained above, when you plant annuals from seed, some require light to germinate, in which case they must be sown on the soil surface. Others require dark, in which case they should be covered with a light coating of soil. Seed packages usually contain exact instructions about depth of planting, whether or not to cover the seeds with soil, spacing of initial planting, and thinning. Read and follow these instructions for best results.

Should I mulch my annual bed during the summer? It is a good idea to lay down a mulch of one to two inches. Use shredded pine or cedar bark, or compost as mulch. In this way, weeding will be almost eliminated, moisture will be retained, and the bed will look tidy.

What do I have to do to maintain my annual flower planting? Annual plantings are, to a great extent, maintenance free. Pests and diseases rarely attack them, and if you mulch, as suggested above, most weeds will be smothered. However, one thing you must do is *dead-head* spent blooms. This means removing any flowers that have faded. This is done not just for aesthetic purposes but to extend the length of blooming of annuals. The purpose of the flowers is to create seeds. Once seeds have formed, the plant has accomplished its purpose and will thus stop flowering. By dead-heading you frustrate this process and keep the plant blooming until frost. Some varieties of annuals do not require dead-heading, including impatiens, lobelia, and wax begonia, but most do if you wish to obtain the longest possible blooming period. In addition, there are now varieties of annuals that have been bred sterile; that is, they do not set seeds at all, so except for keeping the plant looking attractive, they do not have to be deadheaded. These varieties are called "mules."

What about watering my annual plantings? Although many varieties of annuals are drought resistant, for best results a good deep watering once a week during periods of summer drought is recommended. Water so that the ground is soaked to a depth of about one foot. You can check this by digging a place in the garden where plants do not grow but that has been watered.

Can I plant annuals in a rock garden? Yes, and they are particularly useful there, because the vast majority of plants suitable for rock gardens bloom in spring. Annuals provide color during the rest of the season.

What about pests and diseases? As noted earlier, most annuals are pest and disease resistant, if not free of these problems. However, there are a few that may require care. Zinnia foliage is subject to mildew. To combat this, spray regularly from midsummer to fall with captan or benomyl, available at garden centers and nurseries, according to manufacturer's instructions. For other problems, consult the encyclopedia (pp. 38–55).

Should I save the seeds that form on plants at the end of the season? In most cases no, as most annuals available today are hybrids and will not grow true to their parents.

If I have seeds left over from the previous year, can I plant them? You can, but the results will probably be erratic. To test for germination percentage, place ten seeds on a wet paper towel and place the towel inside a plastic bag. Check after a week or so to see how many have germinated. This figure will approximate the effective germination of the remaining seeds. Since annual seeds are very inexpensive, it is hardly worth taking the chance of using last year's seeds.

The Annual Encyclopedia

Zones are not indicated for annuals since all bloom in all parts of the country for one season only and die after the first hard frost. Some varieties are not suitable for the hottest parts of the country—zones 9 and 10. Check with your local nursery or garden center for specific recommendations in those parts of the country.

Ageratum or Flossflower

Outdoor planting time: After all danger of frost.
Light: Full sun.
Soil: Average, with good drainage.
Moisture: Water regularly during summer drought.
Bloom time: June to killing frost.
Description: Blue, white, or pink blooms in dense heads on tidy mound-type plants.
Height: 6–12 inches, depending on variety.
Tips: Watch for whitefly infestation. To combat this, dust frequently with rotenone, available at garden centers and nurseries, according to manufacturer's instructions. To lengthen display, dead-head faded flowers. Either purchase six-packs of seedlings at garden centers or nurseries, start seeds under lights eight weeks before all danger of frost is over, or sow seeds outdoors after there is no longer any danger of frost.

Plant purchased seedlings or thin planted seedlings 9 inches apart. Use in beds, borders, as edging, in planters, or in window boxes.

Althaea or Hollyhock

Outdoor planting time: After all danger of frost.
Light: Full sun but will bloom in semishade.
Soil: Prefers rich loam but will grow in ordinary soil.
Moisture: Drought resistant.
Bloom time: Midsummer.
Description: Saucer-shaped single, double, or frilled blooms in shades of maroon, red, pink, yellow, salmon, and white.
Height: 5–9 feet, depending on variety.
Tips: Plant outdoors after all danger of frost wherever you wish the plants to grow, as they resent being transplanted. Thin to 18 inches apart. These tall plants can be used at the back of perennial borders, against fences, walls, and houses. They are particularly effective when planted against older houses since they evoke nostalgia for the nineteenth century when they were so popular. Seeds self-sow readily. Foliage can become unsightly if mildew or rust strikes. To combat this problem, spray regularly from midsummer through fall with a fungicide such as captan or benomyl, available at garden centers and nurseries, according to manufacturer's instructions.

Alyssum

Outdoor planting time: After all danger of frost.
Light: Full sun.
Soil: Not fussy; any soil will do.
Moisture: Drought resistant.
Bloom time: Early summer to killing frost.
Description: Violet, rose, or white blooms with low-growing gray foliage.
Height: 3–9 inches, depending on variety.
Tips: Easy to grow and quick blooming. Seeds may be sown directly in the ground after all danger of frost. Follow instructions on seed packet for best results. Also available at garden centers and nurseries in six-packs. Plant purchased seedlings or thin planted seedlings to 3 inches apart. Use as edging or in planters or window boxes.

Anchusa or Summer Forget-Me-Not

Outdoor planting time: After all danger of frost.
Light: Full sun.
Soil: Prefers well-drained soil.
Moisture: Water regularly during summer drought.
Bloom time: Early summer to killing frost.
Description: Clusters of tiny blue or white flowers on medium-sized, dark green, sturdy foliage.
Height: 9–18 inches, depending on variety.
Tips: Easy to grow and quick blooming. Dead-head to lengthen display. Sow seeds in spring after all danger of frost where plants are to bloom. Thin to 6 inches apart. Use in beds, borders, as edging, in window boxes and planters, and for cutting.

Antirrhinum or Snapdragon

Outdoor planting time: After all danger of frost.
Light: Full sun, but will also bloom in semishade.
Soil: Prefers fairly rich, well-drained soil.
Moisture: Water regularly during summer drought.
Bloom time: Early summer to killing frost and beyond.
Description: All colors except true blue in single, double, and butterfly-shaped blooms.
Height: From 6 to 8 inches for dwarf varieties to 5 feet for some standard varieties.
Tips: Dead-head to lengthen display. Start seeds indoors under lights eight weeks before last frost or purchase six-packs at nurseries and garden centers. Using the thumb and the index finger, pinch tips of plants when about 3 inches tall to encourage branching. Then pinch again when new shoots are about 3 inches tall. Snapdragons often winter over in moderate climates. Usually the second year's bloom is even more spectacular than the first. Use in beds, borders, as background, and for cutting. Dwarf varieties can be used for bedding, borders, in window boxes, and planters.

Arctotis or African Daisy

Outdoor planting time: After all danger of frost.
Light: Full sun.
Soil: Not fussy about soil as long as there is reasonable drainage.
Moisture: Drought resistant.
Bloom time: Summer to killing frost.
Description: Brilliant yellow, pink, violet, or rose daisy-type flowers with attractive gray wooly foliage.
Height: 15–24 inches, depending on variety.
Tips: Dead-head to lengthen display. Start seeds under lights indoors six weeks before last frost or sow directly outdoors after all danger of frost. Thin to 1 foot apart. Use in beds, borders, and for cutting.

Aster

Outdoor planting time: After all danger of frost.
Light: Full sun, but partial shade will extend blooming period.
Soil: Prefers rich soil.
Moisture: Keep evenly moist throughout growing season.
Bloom time: Midsummer to killing frost.
Description: Red, pink, purple, blue, and white, varying in size from 1 inch to 6 inches across, depending on variety.
Height: 6–30 inches, depending on variety.
Tips: One of the most popular of all annuals, good for fall gardens. Avoid planting asters in the same place two years in a row, as they will not thrive in the same spot the second year. Start seeds under lights six weeks before last frost, or purchase six-packs at garden centers or nurseries. Sow outdoors after all danger of frost. Set low-growing varieties from 6 to 8 inches apart, taller-growing varieties from 12 to 18 inches apart. Use in beds, borders, and for cutting. Dwarf varieties can be used for edging, bedding, and in planters and window boxes.

Begonia or Wax Begonia

Outdoor planting time: After all danger of frost.
Light: Full sun or partial shade.
Soil: Not fussy about soil.

Moisture: Water regularly during summer drought.

Bloom time: Early summer to killing frost.

Description: White, pink, or scarlet blooms with green or rust-colored foliage.

Height: 6–9 inches, depending on variety.

Tips: Start seeds under lights ten weeks before last frost, or purchase six-packs at garden centers or nurseries. Sow outdoors after all danger of frost, 8 to 12 inches apart. In fall, before killing frost, plants can be potted and grown indoors during the winter as house plants. Use for edging and bedding, in planters and window boxes.

Brachycome or Swan River Daisy

Outdoor planting time: After all danger of frost.

Light: Full sun or semishade.

Soil: Not fussy about soil.

Moisture: Drought resistant.

Bloom time: July to killing frost.

Description: White, blue, lilac, and rose daisylike blooms on a dense foliage carpet.

Height: 9 inches.

Tips: Very easy to grow. For midsummer bloom, start seeds indoors under lights six weeks before last frost, or purchase six-packs at garden centers or nurseries. For later bloom, sow directly outdoors after all danger of frost. Set plants about 9 inches apart. Use for bedding, edging, and in planters and window boxes.

Calendula or Pot Marigolds

Outdoor planting time: Calendulas resist early spring cold. Sow seeds wherever you wish them to grow about four weeks before it is time to set out tomatoes in your area.

Light: Full sun.

Soil: Not fussy about soil.

Moisture: Drought resistant.

Bloom time: Midsummer to killing frost.

Description: Yellow, orange, and apricot blooms on upright brittle plants; single and double varieties available.

Height: 1–2 feet, depending on variety.
Tips: Easy to grow. Dead-head to lengthen bloom. Thin seedlings to 9 inches apart. Flowers are edible and add an attractive touch to salads. Use for bedding, in borders, and for cutting.

California Poppy

Outdoor planting time: California poppies resist early spring cold. Sow seeds wherever you wish them to grow about four weeks before it is time to set out tomatoes in your area.
Light: Full sun.
Soil: Prefers poor, sandy soil.
Moisture: Drought resistant.
Bloom time: June to killing frost.
Description: Orange, red, white, yellow, and pink blooms on finely cut, blue-green leaves.
Height: 18 inches.
Tips: If conditions are ideal, will self-sow year in and year out, to the extent that it can become a nuisance plant in some areas, choking out other cultivars. Thin seedlings to 6 inches apart. For early spring bloom, sow seeds in place where you wish them to grow in early fall. They will winter over. Use in borders, beds, and for cutting.

Calliopsis or Coreopsis

Outdoor planting time: Coreopsis resists early spring cold. Sow seeds wherever you wish them to grow about four weeks before it is time to set out tomatoes in your area.
Light: Full sun.
Soil: Ordinary.
Moisture: Drought resistant.
Bloom time: Early summer to killing frost.
Description: Yellow, orange, red, maroon, and crimson daisylike flowers with dense, medium green, elongated foliage.
Height: 8 inches to 4 feet, depending on variety.
Tips: Very easy to grow. Where winters are mild (Zones 7–9), sow seeds in fall. Sow where plants are to bloom, as Coreopsis resents being

transplanted. Thin to 9 inches apart. Use in beds and borders and for cutting. Dwarf varieties can be used for edging and in rock gardens.

Celosia or Cockscomb

Outdoor planting time: After all danger of frost.
Light: Full sun.
Soil: Light, rich soil.
Moisture: Water regularly during summer drought.
Bloom time: Midsummer to killing frost.
Description: Red, yellow, pink, and rose plumed spikes resembling feathers or velvety fans.
Height: 9 inches to 2 feet.
Tips: Easy to grow. Sow seeds outdoors after all danger of frost, start under lights eight weeks before outdoor planting time, or purchase six-packs at garden centers and nurseries. Set plants about 1 foot apart. Worst enemy is red spider. If this pest strikes, hose down daily during midsummer. Use for bedding, in borders, and for cutting.

Centaurea or Cornflower or Bachelor's Button

Outdoor planting time: Seeds resist cold, so plant where plants are to bloom about six weeks before it is time to set out tomatoes in your area.
Light: Full sun is ideal, but will bloom in semishade.
Soil: Any soil will do.
Moisture: Drought resistant, but regular watering during hot summer months extends bloom.
Bloom time: June to September.
Description: Pink, white, blue, and purple thistlelike flowers in close heads on silver-green foliage.
Height: 2–2½ feet.
Tips: Very easy to grow. Dead-head after bloom to lengthen display. Otherwise, plants tend to bloom themselves to death and become unsightly by midsummer. Useful in beds and for cutting.

Clarkia

Outdoor planting time: Seeds resist cold, so sow where plants are to bloom about six weeks before it is time to set out tomatoes in your area.
Light: Full sun or partial shade.
Soil: Well-drained, slightly rich soil.
Moisture: Water regularly during summer drought.
Bloom time: Midsummer to killing frost.
Description: Purple, rose, clear pink, salmon, and white blossoms on bushy plants.
Height: 3 feet.
Tips: Does not thrive in areas with oppressive heat and humidity during summer. Sow directly outdoors four weeks before last frost. Thin to 6 inches apart. Good cutting flower if placed in water immediately after picking.

Cleome or Spider Plant

Outdoor planting time: After all danger of frost.
Light: Full sun.
Soil: Light, sandy soil.
Moisture: Water regularly during summer drought.
Bloom time: Early summer to killing frost.
Description: Rose, pink, lilac, purple, or white blooms set in lobed foliage.
Height: 3–6 feet.
Tips: Easy to grow. Sow seeds indoors under lights six weeks before outdoor planting time. Or sow seeds directly outdoors after all danger of frost. Although stems grow tall, they are quite sturdy and rarely need staking. Use in borders and beds and for cutting.

Coleus

Outdoor planting time: After all danger of frost.
Light: Full sun or partial shade.
Soil: Not fussy about soil.
Moisture: Water regularly during summer drought.
Bloom time: July to killing frost.

Description: Colorful foliage of amber, brown, bronze, scarlet, green, rich mahogany crimson, yellow, and white. Coleus has no flowers.

Height: Dwarf 8 inches to standard 15 inches.

Tips: Sow in spring after all danger of frost in spot where you wish to grow them. Thin seedlings to 1 foot. Use in beds, borders, window boxes, and planters.

Cosmos

Outdoor planting time: After all danger of frost.

Light: Full sun.

Soil: Ordinary soil that is well-drained.

Moisture: Drought resistant.

Bloom time: Early summer to killing frost.

Description: Bright clear red, rose, pink, yellow, white, and crimson on feathery foliage.

Height: 3–6 feet.

Tips: Start under lights indoors six weeks before last frost or plant where you wish them to grow outdoors after all danger of frost. Thin or plant 18 inches apart. To encourage branching and thus more flowers, pinch tips of plants when they are 1 foot high and then again when they are 18 inches high. Cosmos reseeds readily but does not become a nuisance. Use in beds and borders, for cutting, and as cover for early-blooming bulbs.

Delphinium (Annual) or Larkspur

Outdoor planting time: As early in spring as the ground can be worked.

Light: Full sun.

Soil: Moderately rich, well-drained soil. Compost or well-rotted manure worked into the soil helps them attain maximum growth and flower display.

Moisture: Water regularly during summer drought.

Bloom time: Midsummer.

Description: Spikes of blue, red, white, pink, and purple flowers.

Height: 3–4 feet.

Tips: Sow in place where you wish them to grow in early spring, as soon as the ground can be worked. Larkspur seeds will not germinate in warm weather. Thin to 1 foot apart. Use as background for borders, or as specimen plants. Although bloom period is short, they are so spectacular that they are worth planting, and they are easy to grow. Use in beds, borders, and for cutting.

Dianthus or Pinks or Carnations

Outdoor planting time: After all danger of frost.
Light: Full sun but will bloom in semishade.
Soil: Well-drained, average soil.
Moisture: Water regularly during summer drought.
Bloom time: Midsummer to killing frost.
Description: Brilliant-colored flowers of scarlet, salmon, white, yellow, pink, and crimson on attractive silver-green foliaged plants.
Height: Pinks range from 8 to 12 inches, carnations from 12 to 36 inches.
Tips: Start indoors under lights eight weeks before last frost or sow directly outdoors after all danger of frost. Thin to 6 to 8 inches apart. An old-fashioned flower still as popular as ever, carnations' clove fragrance is very evocative. Use in beds, borders, planters, window boxes, and for cutting.

Helianthus or Sunflower

Outdoor planting time: After all danger of frost.
Light: Full sun.
Soil: Ordinary.
Moisture: Drought resistant.
Bloom time: Midsummer to killing frost.
Description: Yellow.
Height: Dwarf varieties are the only ones recommended for the landscape. These range from 2 to 4 feet.
Tips: Don't overlook some of the lesser-known varieties of this cultivar. Sow seeds where you wish plant to grow after all danger of frost. Thin to 12 to 18 inches, depending on ultimate height of plant. Two-foot-high varieties should be thinned to 12 inches, taller varieties to 18 inches. Use for beds and borders and for cutting.

Impatiens

Outdoor planting time: After all danger of frost.
Light: Partial shade but will bloom in deep shade.
Soil: Ordinary soil enriched with sphagnum peat moss to retain moisture.
Moisture: Evenly moist conditions are best.
Bloom time: Midsummer to killing frost.
Description: White, orange, salmon, red, pink, and purple; single and double varieties as well as bicolored offerings. Foliage is deep green and handsome.
Height: 8–15 inches, depending on variety.
Tips: Start indoors under light eight weeks before last frost or purchase plants from garden centers or nurseries. Set plants about 1 foot apart. You will find that impatiens are among the most trouble free, versatile plants available. They dress up shady nooks in the garden and bloom continuously all during the season. At the end of the season you can pot them up, bring them indoors, and treat them as house plants. Cuttings from plants taken in late fall, before killing frost, will root if placed in water. They can then be potted up, carried over the winter, and replanted in the spring.

Lathyrus or Sweet Pea

Outdoor planting time: As early in spring as the ground can be worked.
Light: Full sun only.
Soil: Rich. Fortify soil to a depth of 18 inches with well-rotted manure or compost.
Moisture: Regular watering essential to survival.
Bloom time: Late spring to midsummer.
Description: Fragrant, pealike flowers in the complete color range, growing on tendril climbing vines.
Height: 2–5 feet, depending on variety.
Tips: Sweet peas must be planted very early in the season, as they need cool temperatures in order to germinate. It is a good idea to soak the pealike seeds overnight in warm water before planting; this helps speed germination. Use on fences, trellises, or walls. Some people grow them in the vegetable garden on supports but use them only for cut flowers. Plants are not that attractive in the landscape.

Lobelia

Outdoor planting time: After all danger of frost.
Light: Full sun or partial shade.
Soil: Ordinary.
Moisture: Prefers evenly moist conditions. Water regularly during summer drought.
Bloom time: Early summer to killing frost.
Description: Intense gentian blue flowers with white eyes, solid dark blue, white, maroon, and light blue flowers. Foliage is either deep green or rust green in small moundlike forms.
Height: 4 inches.
Tips: Start indoors under lights eight weeks before last frost. Set in bunches 4 to 6 inches apart. Lobelia is one of the few annuals that does well in partial shade. The intense blue of some varieties is very rare in annual plants. If summer in your area is very hot, plant lobelia in shady areas for best results. Use in beds and borders, and for edging. Trailing varieties are very suitable for window boxes, planters, and pot culture.

Nicotiana or Tobacco Plant

Outdoor planting time: After all danger of frost.
Light: Full sun but will bloom in partial shade.
Soil: Ordinary.
Moisture: Water regularly during summer drought.
Bloom time: Midsummer to killing frost.
Description: Predominantly white, but also red, pink, yellow, and purple.
Height: 2–4 feet, depending on variety.
Tips: Start seeds indoors under lights six weeks before last frost or sow outdoors after danger of frost. Thin to 18 inches apart. Very fragrant, with a tobacco scent. Some varieties bloom at night. Use in beds and borders and for cutting.

Pelargonium or Geranium

Outdoor planting time: After all danger of frost.
Light: Full sun.
Soil: Not fussy about soil.
Moisture: Drought resistant, although watering regularly during summer drought produces more prolific bloom.
Bloom time: Midsummer to killing frost.
Description: Large blooms in red, white, pink, salmon, and fuchsia, with handsome foliage in green and variegated with white and maroon. Standard as well as cascading and hanging varieties.
Height: 1–2 feet, depending on variety.
Tips: New varieties can be started from seed indoors under lights ten weeks before outdoor planting time. Cuttings can be taken from plants in fall before killing frost, rooted in water, and grown in pots during the winter. Plant out of doors after the last frost in spring. Can also be planted in pots and placed in a cool, dark place over winter, then planted out of doors after the last frost. Six-packs or potted specimens can be purchased at garden centers or nurseries in the spring. Plant outdoors after all danger of frost. Use for bedding, borders, in window boxes, and planters.

Petunia

Outdoor planting time: After all danger of frost.
Light: Full sun.
Soil: Well-drained, ordinary.
Moisture: Drought resistant, although for best results water regularly during summer drought.
Bloom time: Early summer to killing frost.
Description: Red, pink, salmon, crimson, blue, purple, white, and yellow on bushy or trailing foliage.
Height: 6–18 inches, depending on variety.
Tips: Like marigolds, petunias are so readily available and easy to grow that they have become a cliché. Select color combinations carefully to secure a pleasing effect. Start seeds indoors under lights ten weeks before last frost or purchase six-packs from garden centers or nurseries. If you sow seeds after the last frost, bloom time will not be until late summer. Plants tend to become straggly toward midsummer un-

less properly pruned. Be sure to pinch faded blossoms. Don't permit plant to go to seed or display will fade. Use in beds, borders, for edging, in planters, and window boxes. Is not a good cut flower since stems are too short for arranging in containers.

Phlox

Outdoor planting time: After all danger of frost.
Light: Full sun.
Soil: Ordinary.
Moisture: Drought resistant, but regular watering during summer drought results in a more prolific display of bloom.
Bloom time: Midsummer to killing frost.
Description: Clusters of flowers in buff, pink, salmon, red, blue, purple, orange, and yellow.
Height: Dwarf varieties are 7 inches tall; standard varieties are 18 inches tall.
Tips: Do not confuse annual phlox with the perennial variety, although the flowers are similar. Annual phlox is easy to grow and available in a wide color range. Dead-head for continuous bloom. Use in beds, borders, and for edging and cutting.

Portulaca or Rosemoss or Sun Rose

Outdoor planting time: After all danger of frost.
Light: Full sun.
Soil: Prefers poor soil.
Moisture: Drought resistant.
Bloom time: Midsummer to killing frost.
Description: Large double flowers of new varieties come in a rainbow of colors that cover slow-growing, fleshy foliage.
Height: 2–3 inches.
Tips: After danger of frost, sow where you want them to grow. Thin to 3 to 4 inches apart. This self-sewing plant is perfect for places where nothing else will grow. On dull days the flowers close, and on bright days they close around noon. Use for beds, edging, in planters and window boxes.

Salpiglossis or Painted Tongue or Velvet Flower

Outdoor planting time: After all danger of frost.
Light: Full sun.
Soil: Rich.
Moisture: For best results, water regularly during summer drought.
Bloom time: Early summer to killing frost.
Description: Funnel-shaped, velvety flowers in red, purple, brown, yellow, and cream, many veined with gold.
Height: 1–2 feet, depending on variety.
Tips: Sow indoors under lights twelve weeks before last frost. Set outdoors after frost 9 inches apart. Use in borders, beds, or for cutting. Deadhead for longer blooming period. Often self-sows.

Salvia or Sage

Outdoor planting time: After all danger of frost.
Light: Sun or partial shade.
Soil: Ordinary soil with good drainage.
Moisture: Drought resistant, but for best results water regularly during summer drought.
Bloom time: Midsummer to killing frost.
Description: Brilliant red on handsome, dark green foliage.
Height: 1½–4 feet, depending on variety.
Tips: So readily available, it has become a cliché. Colors are so vivid it is difficult to use them effectively in borders. However, if bright red is needed somewhere in the landscape, this plant will certainly provide it and without problems. Sow indoors under lights eight weeks before last frost. Then set outdoors after all danger of frost. Or purchase plants in six-packs from garden centers or nurseries. Set 8 inches apart. When plants are 3 to 4 inches high, pinch tops to encourage branching and thus, more flowers. Use for beds and borders.

Tagettes or Marigold

Outdoor planting time: After all danger of frost.
Light: Full sun but will bloom in partial shade.
Soil: Ordinary, not fussy.

Moisture: Drought resistant, but for best results, water regularly during drought. If plants need water, they will tell you by wilting.
Bloom time: Early summer to killing frost.
Description: Maroon, yellow, orange, and white, on handsome deep green foliage.
Height: 6 inches to 4 feet, depending on variety.
Tips: So easy to grow and readily available that it has become a cliché. You might want to select from some of the more unusual varieties for this reason. Start plants indoors under lights four weeks before last frost or sow seeds where you want them to grow. Thin dwarf varieties to around 8 inches apart, taller varieties to from 18 to 24 inches apart. To lessen the offensive odor of marigolds when using them in cut-flower arrangements, place a tablespoon of sugar in the water. Use in beds, borders, for edging, in window boxes, planters, and for cutting.

Torenia or Wishbone Flower

Outdoor planting time: After all danger of frost.
Light: Full sun, but will bloom in light shade.
Soil: Ordinary.
Moisture: Water regularly during summer drought.
Bloom time: Early summer to killing frost.
Description: Blooms have mauve and violet-blue petals with bright yellow blotches. Plant is compact and bushy.
Height: 8 inches.
Tips: Sow directly outdoors where you wish plant to grow after danger of frost. Thin to 8 inches apart. Valuable for shady locations. Often self-sows. Use for borders, edging, and in containers.

Trapaeolum, Nasturtium, or Indian Cress

Outdoor planting time: After all danger of frost.
Light: Full sun but will bloom in partial shade.
Soil: Ordinary, not fussy.
Moisture: For best results, water regularly during summer drought.
Bloom time: Midsummer to killing frost.

Description: Yellow, orange, and red funnel-shaped flowers on pea-green leaves; standard and climbing varieties.

Height: 6 inches for standard prostrate varieties, up to 5 feet for climbers.

Tips: If soil is too rich, foliage will be lush, but there will be few flowers. The pungent foliage is edible and can be used in salads. Flowers and seeds can be pickled. (Capers, available in food markets, are actually pickled nasturtium seeds.) Use in beds and borders and for cutting.

Verbena

Outdoor planting time: After all danger of frost.

Light: Full sun.

Soil: Ordinary.

Moisture: Drought resistant.

Bloom time: Midsummer to killing frost.

Description: Colorful dwarf plants with flowers borne in large trusses in red, pink, lilac, and white. Often fragrant, and many varieties have white eyes. Has a tendency to spread, with one plant covering a considerable amount of space by the end of the season.

Height: 6–8 inches.

Tips: Sow seeds indoors under lights eight weeks before last frost, as seeds sown directly outdoors after frost won't bloom until late summer. Set seedlings outdoors 9 inches apart. Very easy to grow; a charming plant that should be used more often. Use in beds, borders, and for edging.

Zinnia

Outdoor planting time: After all danger of frost.

Light: Full sun.

Soil: Ordinary.

Moisture: Water regularly during summer drought.

Bloom time: Midsummer to killing frost.

Description: Blooms range in size from miniature to giants in an extraordinary range of colors. Showy, prolific blooms make this one of the most utilitarian of annuals. Foliage is deep green and handsome.

Height: 8 inches to 4 feet.

Tips: After all danger of frost, sow outdoors in place where you wish them to grow. When seedlings are 4 inches high, pinch tips to encourage branching and thus, more flowers. Thin dwarf plants to about 8 inches apart, giants to 18 inches apart. The only problem you may experience is mildew on the foliage, which can make zinnias look unsightly. To combat mildew, spray from early summer to frost with captan or benomyl fungicides (available at garden centers and nurseries) according to manufacturer's instructions or plant only the newly hybridized varieties that resist mildew. Use in beds, borders, and for edging. Dwarf varieties can be used in window boxes and planters.

Attracting Birds to Your Property

What about feeding the birds? This can be one of your most joyous landscaping experiences. Flocks of beautiful songbirds chirping away add a lovely dimension to any garden. What is more, many eat their weight in pesty bugs each week.

What kind of bird feeders should I install? Because there are both birds you will want to attract to your grounds and so-called junk birds, such as starlings, grackles, blackbirds, and English sparrows—unattractive birds that drive away the more rare and beautiful species such as cardinals, bluebirds, goldfinches and orioles—you must be slightly cagey about the kind of feeders you install. Most "junk" birds eat from tray feeders. Hanging feeders, usually long plastic tubes that you fill with various seeds, are equipped with holes and small perches for the birds to rest on while retrieving the seeds. When you purchase a tube feeder, inquire about the perches. Were they designed to make it difficult for the larger "junk" birds to rest on them? Are they specifically designed for the smaller birds? Some tube feeders are made to contain a mix of various kinds of seeds that birds find appetizing, and others are specifically designed to contain thistle. Those for thistle have smaller holes than those for seed mixtures. I have several of both, since thistle attracts goldfinches and pine siskins, very beautiful birds that I want in my garden. To give you some idea of the beauty that can result if you do decide to feed the birds, I feed mine thistle all winter long and continue to do so all through spring and summer. After about five years of feeding, I now attract several dozen goldfinches to my feeders. In spring, when the flowering dogwoods and other flowering trees are in bloom, I hang the feeders in the trees. The contrast of the pink blossoms of the dogwood with the brilliant yellow goldfinches flitting around is a breathtaking sight indeed.

What other kinds of feeders are there? Suet feeders attract chickadees, woodpeckers, nuthatches, titmice, and many other species of birds. This past winter I had three different kinds of woodpeckers at my suet feeder at the same time. These feeders, made of wire screen attached to wood, are quite inexpensive. You fill them with suet, which is available at the meat department of your supermarket or at your butcher. You can even put scraps of steaks or roasts into these feeders.

What about birdhouses? Is there anything I should know about them? Yes. First, hang them out of reach of predators such as cats. Then, be sure to secure them firmly to the object on which you hang them. There is nothing more upsetting to a mother bird (and quite probably to you as well) than to see a birdhouse full of young birds fall to the ground. Birdhouses must be cleaned out each spring before mating season begins, because most birds will not build a nest in a birdhouse that contains an existing nest. Many birdhouses available at retail outlets are not made to facilitate this yearly cleaning process. Don't buy any birdhouse that can't be cleaned out.

Another thing you must be aware of when purchasing a birdhouse is the size of the hole in the house. If you wish to attract desirable birds— that is, chickadees, nuthatches, and wrens—to your house, the hole must be small enough to eliminate entry by pesty English sparrows and starlings. Inquire at your point of purchase about this, or read any printed matter that comes with the birdhouse to be sure the entry hole is the right size for the birds you wish to attract. I do have one birdhouse with a hole that is not the correct size for the small birds, and larger English sparrows live in it all summer long. Rather than fight it, I have attached a small Union Jack to the house, thus turning a rather ordinary birding experience into one with some humor.

What about birdbaths? Not all desirable birds are seed eaters. However, all require water and like to take baths. You will attract many varieties of birds that would not visit your feeders if you install birdbaths.

Where can I learn more about birds? Go to the library and ask for a book about birds. You will probably find your interest will lead you to buying your own bird book, so that you can identify the birds that come to your garden. Roger Tory Peterson is the grand old man of the bird-book world, so consider any of his books. Beyond that, most communities have an active chapter of the American Audubon Society. Inquire at your local library for details.

What else can I do to attract birds to my property? Many kinds of shrubs and flowering trees and plants attract birds to your property. Most of these produce berries in the fall which birds relish. Consult books on birds for more information.

Chapter Two

♦

THE SECOND YEAR

The Superstructure of the Landscape: Trees

Deciduous Tree Encyclopedia

Standard Conifer or Evergreen Encyclopedia

Flowering Tree Encyclopedia

The Backbone of the Landscape: Shrubs

Shrub Encyclopedia

The Lawn or Ground Cover Option

Ground Cover Encyclopedia

The Permanent Vegetable Garden

During the first year of your landscape project you spent a great deal of time assessing your property, taking notes, making rough sketches on graph paper of your design, and eliminating undesirable or unwanted trees and shrubs. You also got your feet wet as a gardener by installing a temporary vegetable garden and secured instant color, as well as gratification, by planting annuals. This year, the second in your landscaping effort, you will plant new trees, establish a permanent vegetable garden, and decide upon the "floor" of your landscape—that is, the "dream lawn," green area, ground cover, or combination thereof. Last year you installed annual flowering plants for summer and fall color. You will do so again this year, and each year thereafter, as annuals are invaluable in filling in voids of color, even after you have installed perennial plantings and spring-blooming bulb plantings. However, be a little more adventurous this year, perhaps starting some seeds under lights so that you can grow some of the more esoteric varieties of annuals.

The Superstructure of the Landscape: Trees

Assuming that you spent the first year of your landscape project assessing your property, it is now time to install trees. By now you should know exactly what varieties of trees you have on your property, either by having consulted books on trees or by having spoken with knowledgeable friends or neighbors. You should know which trees are suitable for your landscape and which trees are "junk" or nuisance trees. "Junk" trees should have been removed during the first year. Overgrown specimens that were too close to the house should also have been removed. If you have no trees on your property, or if you wish to replace those you have removed or plant more trees, now is the time to do so. Trees are the superstructure of your landscape scheme. There are three kinds of trees you need to be concerned with: (1) *deciduous trees,* or those that lose their leaves in the fall; (2) *standard conifer* or *evergreens,* cone-bearing trees with needlelike foliage, which remain green all year long; and (3) *flowering trees,* also for the most part deciduous, which bear flowers in spring or summer and are used primarily for decorative purposes.

The fourth variety of trees, *fruit trees,* is not discussed in this chapter or even in this book, as fruit trees require a great deal of time and effort to maintain. Unless you are willing and able to provide the necessary attention year in and year out, in a short time they become diseased, unsightly messes. They are most definitely *not* recommended for the average homeowner or the average landscape.

- Deciduous trees: Most of these grow to a very large size, some to 100 to 120 feet high at maturity, which can be one hundred years or more. Oaks, maples, beeches, poplars, and birches are included in this category. These trees are used as specimens in the middle of a lawn or ground cover, for shading the house or patio, in distant parts of the property, and sometimes as a windbreak or screen, although standard conifers or evergreens are usually more effective for this purpose. Most deciduous trees bear brilliantly colored foliage in the fall and contrast magnificently with standard conifers or evergreens.

- Standard conifer or evergreen trees: Many of these also grow to over 100 feet in height in around twenty years and live for many years. Yews, pines, spruces, firs, and balsams are included in this category. All bear needles or scalelike foliage and cones and remain green throughout the year. They are best used as screens for privacy, as windbreaks, and occasionally as specimen trees, but because of their tendency to dense growth, they are generally not used for providing shade. Dwarf varieties of conifers are discussed later in this chapter in the section on shrubs, since they are more often used for that purpose.

- Flowering trees: Most of these grow to from 8 feet to 20 feet at maturity, which is from around five to twenty years, depending on the cultivar. They bear beautiful blossoms during spring or summer and often sport colorful foliage in autumn. Some varieties are suitable for providing shade for the house or patio. However, they are generally used as specimen trees to decorate a property with their lovely fragrant blossoms in spring and summer.

How do I select the trees that are suitable for my particular climate zone and environment? By now you should have consulted the Climate Zone Map on page xiv and ascertained exactly which climate zone you live in. This map provides a reasonably accurate division of the United States by temperature zones. It is used by almost everyone in the business of horticulture to instruct customers as to which cultivars are suitable for their particular area. Bear in mind, however, that within each zone, and beyond that, within your particular area and even within your own piece of property, temperatures will vary according to many factors, such as shelter, windbreak, and altitude.

Go through the tree encyclopedias (see pp. 70–95) and eliminate those cultivars that are not suitable for your zone. Notice, for example, that grandiflora magnolias are suitable for zones 7–9 but not for zones 2–6. They require a fairly mild climate and usually do not survive the cold winters of the more northern zones. On the other hand, some varieties, such as some maples, hollies, and flowering crabs, require a cold winter and are thus suitable for northern zones and unsuitable for the warmer climates of the southern zones. You might even wish to make a notation right in the book indicating that one particular cultivar or other is unsuitable for your zone.

Next, assess your property in terms of drainage. If water stands in a particular area for several days after rain, drainage in that area is obviously poor. Of course, drainage conditions are not always this clear, but there is a way you can test drainage on your property. First dig a hole to a depth of about one foot and fill the hole with water. Allow the water to soak in. Repeat this two more times. If water remains after that, drainage is poor and hence unsuitable for some varieties of trees. If the water drains completely, the site is suitable for almost all types of tree *in terms of soil drainage.* Keep in mind, however, that some varieties of trees prefer boggy conditions, so if an area of your property is swampy, there are varieties suitable for it.

If you have no trees on your property, look through the encyclopedia for fast-growing varieties, which will provide shade, shelter, and screen as soon as possible. If you already have trees on your property and wish to add more, you can select from the slower-growing varieties if you wish.

Beyond the Climate Zone Map, how else can I learn which trees are suitable for my area and property? Knowledgeable friends and neighbors in the area can often provide information about which trees are suitable for your property. Your County Cooperative Extension Service can also supply you with suggestions. Beyond the above, local garden-center and nursery personnel are usually informed about appropriate cultivars. And finally, mail-order nursery catalogues contain a great deal of information about which cultivars are suitable for which zones, their growing requirements, and how fast or slowly they grow.

How do I decide which trees I want to plant on my property? Once you have come up with a list of trees suitable for your area in terms of climate, drainage, and growth rate, go through the tree encyclopedias, then consult the catalogues of mail-order nurseries to see which trees they offer, and visit your local garden center or nursery to find out which trees they have in stock. Decide what your needs are. Do you want shade? Do you want privacy? Do you want decorative elements? If shade is your primary objective, it might be best to select from the deciduous trees, although some flowering trees are also suitable for shading the house or patio. For privacy, to screen out ugly views, or to define your property, evergreens are usually the best choice. Flowering trees are perhaps the best choice for use as specimens—that is, trees that are planted in the middle of an area of lawn or ground cover.

As a rule, deciduous trees are best planted on southern, eastern, or western exposures—those parts of the house that face south, east, or west—because their leaves shade the house during the hot days of summer, providing nature's own air conditioning. During winter, these same trees lose their leaves and permit sun to filter into the house, providing a certain amount of heat.

Evergreens are best planted on the northern exposure—the part of the house that faces north—for they retain their leaves in winter and provide insulation from cold and wind in that portion of the house. If prevailing winds in your area are from the west, and in most parts of the country they are, evergreens will serve as a wind block if planted on the western exposure. Evergreens are also suitable as screen plantings to provide privacy.

Flowering trees are far more versatile in terms of planting location and can generally be planted wherever you decide you want a beautiful specimen tree.

Where do I purchase trees? Trees can be purchased from two sources: mail-order houses and local nurseries or garden centers. By now, if you have written to all of the mail-order houses on page 249, you should have their catalogues, detailing what they offer. It is best to order in February; in this way, you will generally be assured that the mail-order nursery won't have run out of a particular cultivar you might want. Go through the catalogues, make your selection(s), and send in your order. Stock purchased from mail-order nurseries is generally much less expensive than that purchased from local garden centers or nurseries. There are several reasons for this. First, mail-order nurseries grow their own stock, thus eliminating the middleman. Second, most stock from mail-order nurseries is shipped *bare root*; that is, the plant is dug from the field, the soil is removed, and then the roots are packed in moistened sphagnum moss and covered with plastic to retain the moisture. This is less costly than shipping or planting in containers (more on this later). Finally, stock from these nurseries is usually either one or two years old, as compared with the three- or four-year-old stock offered at local garden centers or nurseries, so the expense of maintaining the plants has been less. Some mail-order nurseries guarantee their stock for one growing season. That is, if the stock does not arrive in good condition, or if it should not grow during the first year, they will replace it free of charge.

Stock offered at local garden centers or nurseries, as mentioned above, is usually several years older than stock offered by mail-order nurseries and thus has had to be maintained longer. It is usually sold in containers or what is called *b and b* in the horticultural world. *B and b* stands for *balled and burlapped*. When the plant is dug in the field, the soil is shaped into a ball, and it is covered with burlap, which is then tied with twine. All of this entails labor costs, which are added to the price of the stock. Most reliable garden centers or nurseries will guarantee any purchase for one growing season. Be sure to inquire about this before you buy any stock, however. If the nursery does not offer a guarantee, go elsewhere. One advantage to buying locally is that the stock offered is usually appropriate for your particular locale and climate zone. Always consult with nursery personnel about your selection; tell them exactly what you wish to accomplish (provide shade, privacy, decoration, et cetera) by planting a tree and ask which cultivars they recommend. You should also consult with them about tree maintenance, fertilization requirements, susceptibility to pests and disease, pruning requirements—in short, get as much information about the cultivar as possible. If the salesperson doesn't seem very knowledgeable, ask to speak with the proprietor. If he or she doesn't have much information to offer, your best bet is to go elsewhere.

What should I look out for when purchasing trees in any of the three ways they are offered? If you purchase bare-root trees at a garden center or nursery and you have the option of inspecting them there, look to see that the roots are not dried out. If you can inspect the trees without their wrapping, look for a balanced root system, that is, one that does not have all the roots on one side of the plant. Roots should be spread out around the entire plant. If you purchase container-grown stock, buy young, vigorous trees. They are less expensive and accept transplanting and training more easily than older plants, which may have become root bound in the container. Avoid buying container-grown trees whose roots are circled at the root surface, for these may eventually girdle the trunk and provide inadequate support. If a container-grown tree has a stake in it, ask to have the tree untied from the stake. If the tree bends over, it has a weak trunk. Try to find another tree, one that can stand upright. Balled and burlapped plants sometimes have many kinked roots visible at the soil surface. Avoid buying these, because often they are plants that have been balled and burlapped for a number of years, plants that should have been discarded by the seller.

When shall I purchase trees? Although the American Nurserymen's Association is publicizing and promoting fall planting, and there are advantages to planting in the fall, as a novice landscaper you are better off planting trees in the spring. There are several reasons for this: First, the selection available at garden centers and nurseries is much wider in spring than in fall. If you select stock in fall, it may be left over from spring inventory and therefore may be inferior in quality. Second, if you have an unusually severe winter after fall planting, some stock may not survive (although most will). Fall planting advantages include the fact that in most parts of the country rainfall is adequate in fall, so you will not have to irrigate your newly planted trees as frequently as you would if you planted them in the spring. Furthermore, stock planted in the fall will not be subject to the scorching heat of summer. You might wish to consult with local garden center or nursery personnel about fall planting. If they have sufficient stock and guarantee survival of the tree, you may want to purchase and plant in fall.

How do I prepare my trees for planting? Assuming that you have made your selection and purchased your stock, it is now time to plant your trees. The way you treat your stock will differ depending on whether it is bare root, container grown, or b and b (bagged and burlapped).

● Bare-root stock: If you have bought your trees through a mail-order firm and they are bare root, it is important to take steps to ensure their

66

health as soon as they arrive. Unwrap the trees as soon as you receive them. Prune broken roots or branches. Place the roots in a tub of water for several hours, but for no more than twenty-four hours. If possible, plant within a few hours after the soaking. In northern areas, zones 2, 3, and 4, trees may arrive at your door on a cold day, and the roots may be frozen. Allow them to thaw slowly in a cool basement or garage, and then soak them in water.

If planting must be delayed, it is recommended that you *heel-in* bare-root plants. That is, dig a trench in a shady location. Place the roots and about half the trunk inside the trench; cover with soil or peat moss. Keep moist until you are able to plant. Plant as soon as possible, before root growth begins.

● Container stock: Trees sold in containers are often shipped bare root to retail nurseries and potted at the nursery. Sometimes trees are left over from the previous year's stock. After you have purchased a container-grown tree, keep it well watered. Store it in a sheltered location until you are ready to plant. If it is in a metal container, cut the container with shears and gently remove the tree. Plastic containers can be difficult to cut. Water the tree an hour or so before planting, and try to slide the root ball out. Do not bang the tree out of the container; this will damage the root ball. If you have difficulty in removing the plant from the container, cut the plastic away with heavy-duty shears. Once you have removed the root ball from the container, remove all circling or matted roots with pruning shears. This will enable new roots to get a healthy start.

● Balled and burlapped stock: Keep the root ball moist and store the tree in a sheltered location until you are ready to plant it. Avoid bumping or breaking the root ball while handling. If you water the root ball lightly several hours before planting, it will be less likely to crumble. Untie and roll the burlap down the sides of the root ball. You do not have to remove the burlap; it will decay. Sometimes the root ball is bound with a synthetic material. If this is the case, remove this material before planting, as it will *not* decay. After planting, be sure the burlap is completely covered with soil, or it will serve as a wick and siphon off necessary moisture from the newly planted tree.

How do I dig a hole for a tree? When you dig a planting hole, regardless of whether it is for a tree or a small plant, always keep in mind the old adage: "A five-dollar tree deserves and needs a ten-dollar hole." This means you must dig the hole larger than necessary to accommodate the roots or root ball of the fledgling tree. As a guide, the hole should be about twice as wide and twice as deep as the root ball or roots. By digging a large planting hole, a sizeable area of soil will be loosened, allowing the roots to grow more easily than they would in hard-packed soil.

As you dig the planting hole, reserve the top layer of soil, or *topsoil*; this will become your *backfill*. Place it in a pile to the side and use it to refill the hole after planting. Save the lower layers of soil, the *subsoil*, for use in building a watering basin later on.

After you have dug the hole, check the condition of the backfill soil. Light, sandy soil or heavy, clayey soil usually benefit from the addition of organic matter. Make a mixture of about two-thirds backfill soil with one-third compost, rotted manure, or other organic matter. Do not add any chemical fertilizer to the soil at this time, because it can burn the young roots.

How do I plant trees? First set the tree in the hole to determine if you have made the hole large enough. If you have not, enlarge the hole. If you are planting bare-root stock, make a cone-shaped mound of soil in the center of the planting hole. Spread the roots over this mound. Grafted trees (which you probably will not be concerned with, since few trees are grown this way other than fruit trees) may have bud unions, knobby growths just above the root level. If the tree you have selected is grafted and does have a bud union, be sure this union is above ground level when you plant. Then fill the planting hole with the fortified soil. Add the soil in layers of several inches and firm it after each layer. This will help eliminate air pockets, undesirable because soil should be in contact with the plant's roots.

If you are planting a container-grown tree, remove the root ball from the container gently and place it in the hole. Make sure it is at the same level as it was in the container. As with bare-root trees, fill in the planting hole several inches at a time and firm the soil each time.

If you are planting a bagged and burlapped tree, remove the twine, and gently place the tree (and burlap) in the hole. Make sure it is at the same level it was in the burlap. As with bare-root trees, fill in the planting hole several inches at a time, firming the soil after each layer.

My tree is planted. Now what do I do? To facilitate watering, fashion a watering basin around the tree with the subsoil you excavated when digging the hole. Then water the tree thoroughly. Keep the soil moist but not soggy during the first few weeks. Then, throughout the growing season, water regularly during drought, to a depth of about one foot. You can test this by sinking a bamboo stick into the ground to the recommended depth.

If it sinks in easily, you have watered enough. If not, you should probably give the newly planted tree some more water.

It is very important to check the planting depth of a tree after you have installed it and watered it thoroughly. If more soil is needed on top, add it. If the tree is planted too deeply—that is, if the soil line on the tree is beneath the soil level at the planting site—you must raise the tree slightly. Bare-root trees are easily raised. Simply grasp the trunk and pull up gently until the tree is at the proper level; then refirm the soil. With container-grown and bagged and burlapped stock, sink your hands into the ground around the root ball and raise it up. Then add more soil and work it down under the root ball.

How do I prune a newly planted tree? During the process of digging, shipping, and replanting a young tree, some root damage is inevitable. This is evident to the eye in the form of broken or split roots. To compensate for root loss, prune some of the top growth of your young tree. As a rule of thumb, remove one-third of the twig and branch growth. If root damage is severe, that is, more than half of the root system is seriously damaged, you may have to remove up to half of the top growth. Top growth can be pruned either before you plant the tree or after it is in the ground.

How do I stake a newly planted tree? Because of the possibility of unforeseen windstorms, it is a good idea to stake all newly planted trees. Drive two stakes into the ground about eight inches from the tree trunk. They should be perpendicular to the prevailing winds. For example, if the winds in your area usually blow from west to east, your stakes should face north and south. Secure the tree lightly to the stakes with rope fed through a piece of old garden hose or with strips of nylon stocking or cloth. The tree should be free to move on its own so that it will not become dependent on the stakes for support. Check the ties regularly to be sure they are not cutting into the bark of the tree, or they may girdle the tree and kill it. After two years, the tree should be well enough established so that you can remove the temporary support stakes.

How do I protect newly planted trees from the scorching rays of the sun? The bark of young trees is susceptible to sunburn. To avoid sunburn damage, paint the trunk of the tree with white latex paint or purchase tree wrap, available at retail outlets, and wrap it around the trunk for protection. This too can be removed after about two years.

How do I maintain my tree after planting? Each spring, while the tree is still dormant, check for broken limbs, suckers at the bottom of the tree (small shoots that grow from the roots and sap energy from main tree growth), dead branches, and those that crisscross. As the years pass, keep in mind that you want a tree with a single trunk, so remove any secondary trunks that may grow from the roots. Using sharp pruning shears or loppers, a tool about the size of hedge clippers but used for pruning, remove unwanted growth. In the second and subsequent years, it is a good idea to fertilize your tree lightly, although this is often not necessary if your soil is reasonably fertile. To be on the safe side, place a ring of nitrogen-rich fertilizer (20-4-4) on the ground at the outer edge of the tree's leaf canopy—a heavy nitrogen content encourages leaf growth. Do this once in early spring and again in summer. Of course, the amount you use will vary as the tree grows larger. After about five years it will not be necessary to fertilize your tree any longer. You can estimate that about one-half pound of fertilizer should be applied in the circle for every twenty feet of diameter. Beyond this, consult a good book on tree pruning. *All About Trees*, published by Ortho and available in most garden centers, nurseries, home-improvement centers, and bookstores, is a good source of information.

How can I plant some of the more slow-growing varieties of trees that are highly desirable and still have some shade while I wait for them to grow to mature size? Plant the desired cultivar, such as a beech or oak, and about twenty feet away from it plant a fast-growing cultivar such as a poplar. Then, when the beech or oak has reached reasonable size, chop down the poplar or other fast-growing cultivar.

Deciduous Tree Encyclopedia

Acer or Maple, Zones vary

Outdoor planting time: Spring or fall.
Light: Full sun.
Soil: Poor to average, depending on variety.
Moisture: Drought resistant once established.
Tips: These, of course, are the familiar and beloved maples, but some varieties are more suited to the home landscape than others. In the fall,

many maple varieties shed thousands of seed pods, which establish themselves everywhere—in flower beds, shrub borders, and even in drain gutters. It is advisable to plant the monumental varieties—Norway and sugar maples—in distant areas of the property where the seed pods will not create problems. Another problem with Norway and sugar maples is that they are extremely brittle and tend to break in high winds. After Hurricane Gloria passed through eastern Long Island in September 1985, many areas here were practically impenetrable because of fallen maple limbs. In addition, maples are shallow-rooted, with many roots near the surface. These siphon off so much moisture that little, if anything, will grow under them unless one irrigates very frequently. Beyond the above, if you already have a grove of maples or plan on installing one, keep in mind that their heavy shade can cause mildew on the surface of your house and even inside if they are planted too densely and/or too close to the house.

On the plus side, maples grow very fast, are magnificent in fall when their foliage turns to brilliant orange, yellow, or red, and provide deep shade.

Varieties

- *Acer ginnala* or Amur maple, zones 5–8. One of the smaller maples, growing moderately to around 20 feet. Sports fragrant flowers in spring and small, round red fruit in summer. Foliage turns bright red in fall. Useful as a specimen tree on average-sized properties.
- *Acer palmatum* or Japanese maple, zones 6–9. Another small maple, growing slowly to 20 feet. Foliage is often deep red but can also be green or yellow-green, and is delicate, lacy, or feathery. An excellent choice for a specimen tree, particularly when planted near red or white flowering dogwoods or summer-flowering white Kousa dogwood. Most varieties do not drop seed pods.
- *Acer platanoides* or Norway maple, zones 4–9. A fast-growing, very large maple, ultimately reaching a height of 50 to 60 feet and a width of 65 to 75 feet. Because it drops many seeds and its brittle limbs often splinter and fall in high winds there are many other varieties of large shade trees much better suited to the average landscape. See, for example, *Fagus sylvatica.*
- *Acer rubrum* or swamp or red maple, zones 3–7. Fast growing to a height of 50 to 60 feet and a width of 50 to 60 feet. Like the Norway maple, it is not particularly suitable for the average landscape because its limbs break in high winds and it drops seeds everywhere.
- *Acer saccharinum* or silver maple, zones 3–7. Fast growing to 100 feet,

70 feet wide. Silver maples do not cast seed pods all over the place, but they are extremely brittle and suffer heavy damage during windstorms.
- *Acer saccharum* or sugar maple, zones 3–7. Fast growing to 100 feet, 80 feet wide. Like Norway and red maples, sugar maples are not recommended for average-sized properties because their limbs break in high winds and they drop seeds everywhere.

Alnus or Alder, Zones vary

Outdoor planting time: Spring or fall.
Light: Full sun.
Soil: Not fussy. One of the few trees to thrive in waterlogged areas; it will even grow under water.
Moisture: Needs damp soil for best results.
Tips: Plant this tree only if there is a waterlogged area on your property, as there are many cultivars better suited to specimen, border, or screen planting, or for shade.
Varieties
- *Alnus glutinosa* or common, black, or European alder, zones 3–9. Fast growing to 40 to 60 feet. Because it is fast growing, this variety can be planted adjacent to a slower growing, "quality" tree and then removed when the preferred tree reaches reasonable height.
- *Alnus rhombifolia* or white alder, zones 4–9. Fast growing to 60 to 70 feet, 45 to 60 feet wide. Useful for providing fast shade in boggy areas.

Betula or Birch, Zones vary

Outdoor planting time: Spring or fall.
Light: Full sun.
Soil: Average.
Moisture: Normal to wet, depending on variety.
Tips: Some varieties are particularly pest and disease prone, so select carefully. Inquire at a local garden center or nursery or at your County Cooperative Extension Service for recommendations. Plant in clumps for a special effect, rather than spacing at regular intervals.
Varieties
- *Betula maximowicziana*, zones 6–10. Fast growing to 80 to 100 feet. Needs a great deal of space to develop properly.

● *Betula nigra* or river birch, zones 5–10. A native tree, fast growing to 50 to 70 feet. As indicated by its name, this birch prefers very moist conditions. In its native habitat of the South, it grows wild along river banks. Unless you wish to plant on a river bank, *Betula papyrifera* is a better choice.

● *Betula papyrifera* or paper birch, zones 3–8. The best of the birches for the average home landscape; fast growing to 40 to 60 feet. This recommended variety sports catkins in the spring. In spring and summer its white bark contrasts nicely with its medium green leaves, which turn brilliant yellow in fall. Underplant with daffodils for a particularly striking spring effect.

● *Betula pendula* or European white birch, zones 2–10. Fast growing to about 60 feet. The bark is roughhewn and warty as opposed to the smooth-barked paper birch. This variety is prone to many diseases and pests and is therefore not recommended for the average home landscape.

Eleagnus angustifolia or Russian Olive, Zones 1–8

Outdoor planting time: Spring or fall.
Light: Full sun.
Soil: Will grow in any soil.
Moisture: Drought resistant.
Tips: An excellent, fast-growing tree-shrub, useful as a screen or windbreak. Fall berries attract birds and provide food for them throughout the winter. This tree resembles the willowy olive tree, but its bark has thorns and its fruit and leaves can look messy. Best used in distant areas for a screen or windbreak. One of the toughest shrub-trees of all, growing only to 20 to 25 feet.

Fagus sylvatica or European Beech, Zones 5–10

Outdoor planting time: Spring or fall.
Light: Full sun.
Soil: Average.
Moisture: Drought resistant once established.
Tips: Truly the aristocrat of trees. If you have the space for a beech tree, forsake all other endeavors to plant one. But keep in mind that beeches are slow growing, and it will be many years before it assumes its magnificent regal bearing. In the meantime, as it grows, it will serve

as an extremely attractive small and then medium-sized tree. If you are fortunate enough to have one on your property already, give it all the space it needs, nurture it, and cherish it, since, beyond personal enjoyment, you probably paid a premium for the property just because of that particular tree.

Varieties: There are green, purple, and copper-colored beeches in upright and pendulous, or weeping, forms. All grow to around 100 feet high, and often 100 feet wide as well. Most are suitable at maturity only for large properties.

Fraxinus or Ash, Zones vary

Outdoor planting time: Spring or fall.

Light: Full sun.

Soil: Withstands wet soil with poor drainage.

Moisture: Prefers moist conditions.

Tips: Whether you order this cultivar from a mail-order house or purchase it at a local garden center or nursery, be sure to request only a recently hybridized variety that does not bear seeds, as the seedlings on older varieties self-sow everywhere. Because of their lovely leaves, ashes are a good selection as shade trees. Their foliage is feathery, allowing light to penetrate to the ground below. Grass- and shade-loving plants grow well beneath them. This tree also grows moderately fast.

Varieties

● *Fraxinus excelsior* or European ash, zones 4–9. Grows moderately fast to 30 to 50 feet. Leaves remain green in autumn.

● *Fraxinus ornus* or flowering ash, zones 6–8. Grows at a moderate rate to around 35 feet. Fragrant clusters of white-green flowers adorn tree in late spring. Leaves are shiny and turn yellow in fall. Ugly seed pods remain on tree during winter.

● *Fraxinus pennsylvanica* or green (or red) ash, zones 3–8. Grows rapidly to 30 to 50 feet. A good selection for the average home landscape, since it adapts to many soil types, endures cold, and resists drought.

Ginkgo biloba or Maidenhair Tree, Zones 5–10

Outdoor planting time: Spring or fall.
Light: Full sun.
Soil: Average but well-drained.
Moisture: Needs regular watering during first few years after planting or tree will die. Once established, it is drought resistant.
Tips: Select only male plants, as the berries from female plants have an unpleasant odor. An excellent selection for city planting, as it is nearly impervious to pollution and smoke. Pest free.

Gleditsia triacanthos or Thornless Common Honey Locust, Zones 5–9

Outdoor planting time: Spring or fall.
Light: Full sun.
Soil: Average.
Moisture: Drought resistant.
Tips: A very fast-growing tree quite suitable to the average home land-scape. However, be aware of the following. Do not, under any circumstances, dig these trees from the wild or purchase anything but hybrids, as the common varieties are very disease prone. If you select a honey locust at your local garden center or nursery, be absolutely certain that the one you select is a hybrid. On the plus side, grass- and partial-shade-loving plants survive under locusts, and maintenance is low because the small, feathery leaves do not have to be raked up in fall but disintegrate into the soil. Some varieties bear sweet-scented blossoms in spring.

Hybrid Varieties
● Imperial, zones 5–9. Grows moderately to 35 feet. Foliage is bright green.
● Majestic, zones 5–9. Fast growing to 40 to 50 feet. Foliage is dark green.
● Moraine, zones 5–9. Fast growing to 40 to 50 feet. Foliage is medium green.
● Ruby Lace, zones 5–9. Fast growing to 30 to 40 feet. Foliage turns from deep purple to green during season.
● Other hybrids are Shademaster, Skyline, and Sunburst. All are fast growing to 35 to 50 feet.

Liquidambar styraciflua or *American Sweet Gum,* *Zones* 6–10

Outdoor planting time: Spring or fall.
Light: Full sun.
Soil: Prefers rich, loamy soil.
Moisture: Drought resistant once established.
Tips: A medium- to slow-growing tree that reaches a height of 90 feet; prized for its brilliant crimson and purple foliage in autumn. Corky ridges on bark are interesting in winter. However, this tree drops fruit—prickly one- to two-inch balls that are a nuisance. For this reason, avoid planting this tree in your front yard or as shade for a patio.

Platanus acerifolia or *London Plane Tree, Zones* 5–9

Outdoor planting time: Spring or fall.
Light: Full sun.
Soil: Average.
Moisture: Drought resistant once established.
Tips: A fast-growing, nearly indestructible cultivar that tops off at around 50 feet. A good selection for difficult areas. Of the sycamore family, the London plane tree is one of our most disease resistant trees and has attractive bright green foliage and very beautiful green and white bark, which peels from the tree trunk.

Populus or *Poplar, Zones* vary

Outdoor planting time: Spring or fall.
Light: Full sun.
Soil: Average.
Moisture: Drought resistant once established.
Tips: The fastest-growing tree of all—can grow up to 15 feet the first year. Select a spreading rather than a columnar variety for shade. Select a columnar variety for screening.
Varieties
• Imperial Carolina, zones 4–10. Very fast growing to 80 feet. Grass

grows underneath. Pest and disease free. One of the best possible selections for near instant shade.

- *Populus nigra*, zones 4–10. Very fast growing to 60 feet. Columnar in shape, so suitable for screening. To plant a poplar screen, space trees 5 feet apart for very thick screen. Pest and disease resistant.

Quercus or Oak, Zones vary

Outdoor planting time: Spring or fall.
Light: Full sun.
Soil: Average.
Moisture: Drought resistant once established.
Tips: Along with the beeches, the aristocrats of the tree world. There are
   many different varieties, suitable for many types of growing condi-
   tions. Contrary to popular belief, many oaks are reasonably fast
   growing. They are sturdy and rarely splinter in high winds.
Varieties

- *Quercus alba* or white oak, zones 4–9. Grows to 90 feet. Dense foliage is bluish green to reddish brown in fall. A low-maintenance tree, disease resistant, and strong limbed, it suffers little damage from ice or wind.
- *Quercus palustris* or pin oak, zones 4–8. Fast growing to 75 feet. Leaves are fine textured and brilliant red in autumn, remaining on tree until spring, affording an attractive canopy during winter. Excellent selection as a specimen lawn tree.
- *Quercus robur* or English oak, zones 5–8. Grows to 75 feet. Deeply cut, fernlike leaves stay green from spring through fall.
- *Quercus rubra* or red oak, zones 3–7. Grows to 75 feet with dense, lustrous, green foliage that turns deep red in fall. Fastest growing of all oaks. Excellent selection as a shade tree.

Salix or Willow, Zones vary

Outdoor planting time: Spring or fall.
Light: Full sun.
Soil: Requires a lot of moisture.
Moisture: Some varieties thrive under boggy conditions.
Tips: The weeping willow, as it is commonly known, is an extraordinarily

beautiful tree and can be effective on large properties. However, keep the following in mind if you select one for your property. Willows grow very fast but their wood is extremely brittle, subject to ice and wind damage. The roots are shallow, and in high winds these trees can be uprooted. Nothing grows underneath a willow. They are subject to many insect and disease pests. In short, they are a poor choice for an average landscape. If you have a pond on your property, however, nothing is more beautiful than a weeping willow planted next to it.

Ulmus or Elm

Regretfully, because of the prevalence of Dutch elm disease, which is killing off our country's elm trees, this cultivar is not recommended.

Standard Conifer or Evergreen Encyclopedia

Abies or Fir, Zones vary

Outdoor planting time: Spring.
Light: Full sun but will tolerate light shade.
Soil: Resents wet, heavy, clayey soil, so plant only in well-drained locations. Prefers slightly acidic soil.
Moisture: Prefers evenly moist conditions, so water regularly during summer drought until established.
Tips: Firs resist pests and disease but are not suited to polluted city conditions.
Varieties

- *Abies balsamea* or balsam fir, zones 3–6. Flat, shiny, dark green needles from ½ inch to 1 inch long. Grows slowly to 40 to 75 feet, 20 to 25 feet wide. Use as a screen or specimen tree. Loses needles when grown under hot, dry conditions.

- *Abies concolor* or white fir, zones 3–7. Flat, greenish blue needles from 2 to 3 inches long. Slow growing to 30 to 50 feet, 15 to 30 feet wide. Adapts to many growing conditions, including hot, dry regions of the Midwest and upper South. Best used as a specimen tree, as its stiff appearance does not lend itself to use in borders. Should be placed in the distance on large properties, as it can overwhelm smaller landscapes.

● *Abies homolepis* or Nikko fir, zones 5–6. One-inch long, lustrous, dark green needles. Slow growing to 40 to 60 feet, 15 to 25 feet wide. Use in groupings on large properties, as a screen or a specimen. Somewhat more tolerant of heat if provided with light shade.

● *Abies veitchii* or veitch fir, zones 3–6. One-inch long, shiny, dark green needles. Grows moderately to 50 to 75 feet, 25 to 35 feet wide. Perhaps the best choice in most parts of the country, for it is tolerant to dry summer conditions. Use as a screen or in a grouping.

Cedrus or Cedar, Zones vary

Outdoor planting time: Spring.
Light: Full sun.
Soil: Average.
Moisture: Drought resistant, but water regularly until well established.
Tips: Most cedars grow too large for use on average-sized properties. However, if you have room for one large conifer, cedars are among the most beautiful of all evergreens.

Varieties

● *Cedrus atlantica* or atlas cedar, zones 6–9. One- to 1½-inch blue-green needles. Grows moderately to 40 to 60 feet, 30 to 40 feet wide. Very tolerant of drought, but thrives in moist, deep loam. Glauca is the upright form, Glauca Pendula the weeping form.

● *Cedrus libani* or cedar of Lebanon, zones 5–7. One-inch long, shiny, dark green needles. Grows slowly to 40 to 60 feet, 40 to 60 feet wide. Withstands temperatures of −15 to −25 degrees F and is thus the best cedar for northern parts of the country. When mature, it is one of the most majestic cultivars you can select. Requires an estate-sized property for best aesthetic results.

Chamaecyparis or False Cypress, Zones 3–8

Outdoor planting time: Spring or fall.
Light: Full sun.
Soil: Prefers enriched, well-drained, acidic soil.

Moisture: Moist conditions are preferred; however, *Chamaecyparis thyoides,* or Atlantic white cedar, thrives in swampy areas. *C. obtusa,* or Hinoki false cypress, and *C. pisifera,* or Japanese false cypress, tolerate dry conditions.

Tips: Very useful in today's small-scale, informal landscapes, adapting well to average-sized properties.

Varieties

- *Chamaecyparis obtusa* or Hinoki false cypress, zones 4–8. Glossy, deep green, scalelike foliage. Grows moderately to 20 to 30 feet, 5 to 10 feet wide.

- *Chamaecyparis pisifera* or Sawara or Japanese false cypress, zones 4–8. Deep green, scalelike foliage. Grows moderately to 8 to 70 feet, 3 to 20 feet wide, depending on the cultivar. Many cultivars are available, in many sizes and shapes, so inquire at local garden centers or nurseries or at your County Cooperative Extension Service as to which varieties are suitable for your particular area and your needs.

Cupressus or True Cypress, Zones 7–10

Outdoor planting time: Spring or fall.
Light: Full sun.
Soil: Needs good drainage, prefers light soil, but tolerates heavier soils.
Moisture: Dry conditions are preferred.
Tips: Useful in a variety of extreme conditions. See notes below under each cultivar.

Varieties

- *Cupressus arizonica* or Arizona cypress, zones 7–9. Soft green needles on pyramidal structure. Grows moderately to 30 to 40 feet, 10 to 15 feet wide. Useful in areas of excessive heat and drought such as the American Southwest.

- *Cupressus macrocarpa* or Monterey cypress, zones 7–9. Deep green needles on conical form which becomes more open and wide-spreading as it matures. Grows moderately to 40 to 50 feet, 20 to 30 feet wide. The famed California cypress thrives in rocky or sandy soils.

Juniperus or Juniper, Zones vary

Outdoor planting time: Spring.
Light: Full sun.
Soil: Average, but with good drainage.
Moisture: Drought resistant.
Tips: Among the toughest and most diverse of all conifers. A suitable juniper variety exists for almost any conceivable location and growing condition. Check locally at garden centers and nurseries or with your County Cooperative Extension Service for recommended varieties in your area.

Varieties
● *Juniperus chinensis* or Chinese juniper, zones 4–9. Minuscule needles in many shades of green and blue. Medium-sized varieties include Hetzii—upright, spreading to 15 feet; Gold Coast—golden yellow and compact; Kaizuka—green needles with twisted growth habit, upright to 15 to 20 feet; Keteleeri—medium green needles, pyramidal to 25 to 30 feet (useful as a screen) and Pfitzerana—deep green needles, grows to 5 to 10 feet.
● *Juniperus communis* or common juniper, zones 2–6. Sharp, minuscule needles, greenish blue in color. Growth slow to moderate, to 20 feet.
● *Juniperus virginiana* or eastern red juniper, zones 3–9. Native to the United States, this variety can grow to 40 to 50 feet high. Self-seeds in its native areas. Dark green, minuscule needles, which often turn brown in winter. Will grow just about anywhere, under the most extreme growing conditions. However, there are many far more attractive cultivars to select from when landscaping. Harbors cedar apple rust, large ugly growths that do no harm to the juniper itself but do harm adjacent hawthorn or apple trees and currant bushes.

Picea or Spruce, Zones vary
Not recommended for zones 9 and 10

Outdoor planting time: Spring.
Light: Full sun.
Soil: Average. More tolerant to poor soil than most evergreens.
Moisture: Drought resistant once established.
Tips: Many varieties are available. Check locally at garden centers or nurseries and at your County Cooperative Extension Service for cultivars suited to your location.

Varieties

● *Picea abies* or Norway spruce, zones 3–8. Rich, green needles up to 1-inch long. Grows moderately to 40 to 60 feet, 25 to 30 feet wide. Pyramidal in form, but less geometric as tree matures; Pendula is a weeping variety. Use as a specimen or to accent backdrop of property.

● *Picea mariana* or black spruce, zones 2–5. Blue-green needles up to ½ inch long. Grows slowly to 30 to 40 feet, 10 to 15 feet wide. Recommended for colder areas of North America.

● *Picea omorika* or Serbian spruce, zones 4–7. Flat, rich green needles up to 1 inch long. Grows slowly to 50 to 60 feet, 20 to 25 feet wide. Lovely weeping branches form a pyramid. Suitable for moderate climates of the United States but not for very cold or warm areas. Attractive as a specimen tree. Should be more widely known and planted.

● *Picea orientalis* or Oriental spruce, zones 4–7. Rich, dark green needles up to ½ inch long. Grows slowly to 50 to 60 feet, 10 to 15 feet wide. A superb spruce, available in two varieties: Gowdy—narrow, columnar; Pendula—weeping. Thrives in ordinary and poor soil. A fine selection for the home landscape.

● *Picea pungens* Glauca or Colorado blue spruce, zones 3–7. Bluish green needles up to about 1 inch long. Grows rapidly to 30 to 60 feet, 10 to 20 feet wide. Grows in very poor soil, dry conditions, and withstands cold. A cliché, attractive but misused in most landscapes. To my mind, a bad selection because it does not blend well with other plantings but ultimately dominates not only the landscape but the house as well. If you have space in your landscape for a large evergreen, you can select from other cultivars that are far more interesting visually. In other words, if you visit your local nursery or garden center and they try to sell you a Colorado blue spruce, go somewhere else to make your selection.

Pinus or Pine, Zones vary

Outdoor planting time: Spring.
Light: Full sun but will tolerate partial shade.
Soil: Not fussy about soil.
Moisture: Drought resistant.
Tips: Consult your local nursery or garden center or County Cooperative Extension Service for recommendations for your specific area, as many varieties are subject to blight.

Ed Rezek, a world-renowned collector and hybridizer of dwarf conifers, has installed a distinctive foundation planting in front of his house, which is quite different from the run-of-the-mill suburban installation. Notice how Rezek uses the different foliage colors and textures, as well as the shapes of the plants, to create the planting.

The small backyard at Ed Rezek's place, which looks much more spacious than it really is, has been converted into this extravaganza of beauty and tranquillity. By employing clever design and by juxtaposing scores of varieties of dwarf conifers, he has achieved a remarkably harmonious and spacious landscape effect.

Shaded areas of any garden can be a problem to landscape. However, there are many plants which thrive and bloom in the shade. Notice that in this planting the gardener has used annual Impatiens—readily available at garden centers and nurseries—for splashes of color. He has planted them in a large drift, to make a statement, rather than scattering them willy-nilly throughout the shaded area.

Feeding and attracting wild birds to the garden is one of the most gratifying of garden experiences. In my garden I have specially designed thistle feeders, available at garden centers and nurseries, which attract brilliantly colored goldfinches. It has been placed on a flowering nectarine tree, creating this vision of breathtaking beauty. You can move the feeder from tree to tree on your property as they flower, to prolong the glorious visual experience.

Here, a white dogwood called "Snowflake" is underplanted with pink azaleas and pink Darwin tulips, all of which bloom in tandem. And, it is a dazzling combination. When selecting tulips, keep in mind that different varieties bloom at different times of the spring season. The latest to bloom, and those which will flower at the same time as the dogwoods and azaleas, are Darwin tulips. Do not confuse these with Hybrid Darwins, which bloom about three weeks earlier.

I have learned that the severity of a large expanse of patio brickwork or concrete, can be softened with plantings of herbs or annuals. The delicately scented, white blossoms of low-growing Sweet Alyssum self-sows every year in between the cracks of the brickwork, creating this lovely effect.

Above and Right: Most novice gardeners make the mistake of pruning shrubs to look like muffins. Here are two photographs of a popular spring-blooming shrub, Spiraea, or Bridal Wreath, which demonstrates the right and the wrong way to prune shrubs. The proper way to prune is to remove branches at the base of the plant. This allows the plant to grow into a graceful fountain shape, rather than the muffin shape seen in the companion photograph.

Below: Now here's a spectacular planting, and one I'm very proud of! By planting Laburnum, which in nature grows like a tree, and training it to provide a canopy over a small arbor, the yellow hanging panicles provide a lavish, fragrant, show-stopping spectacle every year. It's easy to learn how to prune these and other plants for special effects such as this.

In the foreground of this photograph, taken on my property, are two shrubs: a rare Sergeant's Weeping Hemlock and a columnar English boxwood. Notice the difference in texture and shape between the two. The Hemlock bears needle-like foliage, is of a spreading growth habit, while the boxwood bears small, leathery leaves and is columnar in shape. By contrasting both texture and shape, the planting becomes one of distinction rather than the usual.

Look at this stunning combination of colors on this planting of rhododendrons and azaleas under this Yew tree. I used white azaleas generously in the planting to provide relief from the splashes of color, highlighting each, and separating one from another. This is a very important design principal.

In any landscaping endeavor, one makes mistakes. This approach to a garden gate in my garden is dead wrong. Notice that on the left side, English boxwood is planted, while on the other, some vigorous euonymous has been planted. I recognized this, and removed the euonymous hedge on the right and replaced it with boxwood to match the left hand side. It has created a welcoming pathway to the next garden. To further define the entranceway, the two pineapple finials, ancient symbols of hospitality, have been raised up on modest pedestals.

Left: When you are planting bulbs, try to keep in mind that many early-blooming perennials bloom consequently with them. Use the perennials to soften the stiff look and growth habit of many bulbs. Here, some pink, lily-flowering tulips, are gently enhanced by the somewhat feathery foliage and loosely drooping blossoms of this old-fashioned bleeding heart.

Above: My dooryard garden, which blooms in late winter, was installed in my patio. To make room for the plantings, I simply removed some of the bricks and planted some of the mini bulbs of early spring. Called "minor" bulbs, they are best planted close to the house so that you can see them as you come and go. If they are in a distant part of the garden, since the blooms are quite small, they will most likely go unnoticed.

Left: Climbing roses on a trellis, such as this delicate pink "Constance Spry," provide a focal point as well as lavish and glorious beauty in any garden when they bloom in late spring. Be sure not to overlook these treasures when you plan your landscape.

Here are two ways to prevent moles, voles, chipmunks, and other burrowing creatures from devouring your planted bulbs. Either line the planting area with gutter wire before planting, or place old plastic or rubber flower pots in the ground, with their tops below the soil level, and then plant the bulbs as you would normally. Both work. I have a planting of species tulips, prime treats for nibblers, planted in pots which are sunken into the ground, which is now in its seventh year. Prior to discovering this trick, they rarely made it to the second year.

Interesting looking containers and window boxes, such as this one created by landscape designer, Ken Ruzicka, can be filled with bright blooming annuals and placed wherever you think you might want splashes of color during the season. When you start to design your container or window box planting, think in terms of contrast of blossom and foliage color and texture. If you know anything about arranging flowers, simply apply the same design principals to container or window box plantings.

Varieties

- *Pinus aristata* or bristlecone pine, zones 4–7. Dark green needles up to about 1¾ inches long. Grows slowly to 10 to 20 feet, unpredictable spread. Its slow growth makes this cultivar a good choice for the average landscape. Can be used as an accent in a dwarf conifer and broad-leaved evergreen border.
- *Pinus banksiana* or jack pine, zones 2–7. Dull green needles up to 2 inches long. Grows slowly to 35 to 50 feet, 20 to 30 feet wide. Nearly indestructible, adapting to almost any growing condition. Use as a screen or a windbreak. While there are many cultivars more suitable for the average landscape, consider the jack pine if your soil is very heavy in clay or sand. Trees develop a messy appearance after a few years as cones remain on tree for many years.
- *Pinus bungeana* or lacebark pine, zones 4–8. Rich green needles up to 4 inches long. Grows slowly to 30 to 50 feet, 20 to 35 feet wide. Bark is especially attractive, so lower branches should be cut off as tree grows to expose it. A good specimen tree.
- *Pinus cembra* or Swiss stone pine, zones 4–7. Deep green and bluish white needles up to 3 to 5 inches long. Grows slowly to 30 to 40 feet; columnar in shape. Prefers moist, acidic, well-drained soil. Use as a specimen.
- *Pinus densiflora* or Japanese red pine, zones 4–7. Shiny bright green needles up to 5 inches long. Grows moderately to 40 to 60 feet, 40 to 60 feet wide. One of the best pine trees you can select if you have the space. Pendula is a weeping variety.
- *Pinus flexilis* or limber pine, zones 4–7. Deep green to blue-green needles up to 3 inches long. Grows slowly to 30 to 50 feet, 15 to 35 feet wide. A good specimen tree that adapts well to inhospitable conditions such as drought and poor soil. Glauca Pendula is a weeping variety.
- *Pinus nigra* or Austrian pine, zones 4–7. Deep green needles up to 6 inches long. Grows moderately to 35 to 50 feet, 15 to 25 feet wide. A poor selection in the East because of a blight that has killed off large stands of this cultivar throughout that part of the country.
- *Pinus parviflora* or Japanese white pine, zones 4–7. Soft, blue-green needles up to 6 inches long. Grows slowly to 25 to 50 feet, spread unpredictable. Very attractive in the landscape. A good choice for a specimen tree, as a backdrop, or in borders.
- *Pinus strobus* or eastern white pine, zones 3–8. Medium green to blue-green needles up to 5 inches long. Fast growing to 50 to 80 feet, 20 to 40

feet wide. An excellent selection for the contemporary landscape as it grows quickly, and its feathery foliage has an informal appearance. Blends in well with other trees and shrubs.

● *Pinus sylvestris* or Scotch pine, zones 2–8. Blue-green needles up to 4 inches long. Grows moderately to 30 to 60 feet, 30 to 40 feet wide. Adapts well to many environments. Useful as a screen or windbreak. Somewhat stiff in appearance if used as a specimen.

● *Pinus thunbergiana* or Japanese black pine, zones 5–7. Dark green needles up to 7 inches long. Fast growing to 20 to 40 feet, spread unpredictable. Another cultivar that has been attacked by blight throughout the northeastern part of the country. Because of this it is not recommended in the Northeast. In other coastal regions it adapts well to salt air conditions.

Taxus or Yew, Zones vary

Outdoor planting time: Spring.
Light: Full sun or shade.
Soil: Prefers moist, acidic soil that is well drained. Will not survive under overly wet conditions.
Moisture: Drought resistant once established.
Tips: An excellent selection if you live in recommended zones.
Varieties

● *Taxus baccata* or English yew, zones 6–7. Deep green needles up to 1½ inches long. Grows slowly to 35 to 60 feet, 15 to 25 feet across. An excellent choice for specimen, border, or screen. However, it is limited in its range: it is not tolerant of cold or very hot conditions.

● *Taxus cuspidata* or Japanese yew, zones 4–7. Deep green needles up to 1 inch long. Grows slowly with size varying according to cultivar. More adaptable to heat and cold than the English yew.

Thuja or Arborvitae, Zones vary

Outdoor planting time: Spring.
Light: Full sun.
Soil: Adapts to many soil types.
Moisture: Drought resistant.
Tips: Useful as a screen or windbreak, not as a specimen.

Varieties
- *Thuja occidentalis* or American arborvitae, zones 3–8. Shiny, medium dark green, scalelike foliage. Grows slowly to moderately to 40 to 60 feet, 10 to 15 feet wide. Columnar in shape. A good selection for a screen or windbreak; not suitable as a specimen.
- *Thuja orientalis* or Oriental arborvitae, zones 5–9. Bright green, scalelike foliage. Grows slowly to 18 to 25 feet, 10 to 12 feet wide. Columnar and suitable as a screen or windbreak only. Does not thrive in windy locations.

Tsuga or Hemlock, Zones vary

Outdoor planting time: Spring only.
Light: Full sun or shade.
Soil: Adapts to many soil types.
Moisture: Moderate.
Tips: Another excellent choice, either for a specimen or screen.
Varieties
- *Tsuga canadensis* or Canadian hemlock, zones 3–7. Dark green needles up to ¾ inch long. Grows moderately to 40 to 70 feet, 25 to 35 feet wide. Its soft appearance makes this a good selection as a specimen tree. As the tree matures, its appearance becomes "weeping." With pruning, it adapts well as a screen or hedge.
- *Tsuga caroliniana* or Carolina hemlock, zones 4–7. Sometimes offered in garden centers or nurseries. However, Canadian hemlock is the preferred variety for landscape purposes, because this cultivar has short, stout branches that often are not too attractive to the eye.

Flowering Tree Encyclopedia

Aeschulus carnea or Red Horse Chestnut, Zones 5–7

Outdoor planting time: Spring or fall.
Light: Full sun.
Soil: Average.
Moisture: Drought resistant when established.

Bloom time: Midspring.

Description: 8- to 10-inch-long spikes of pink-to-red blooms on broad, fan-like leaves.

Height: 40 feet, 30 feet across.

Tips: Foliage turns brown when exposed to too much wind or dry heat. Useful as a specimen tree or to provide shade.

Albizia or Silk Tree or Mimosa, Zones 5–10

Outdoor planting time: Spring or fall.

Light: Full sun.

Soil: Average.

Moisture: Drought resistant when established.

Bloom time: Midsummer.

Description: Pink, fluffy blooms on lacy foliage.

Height: 40 feet.

Tips: One of the worst trees you can plant on your property. Tree does not leaf out until mid-June, looking like a hangman's tree until then. Blossoms drop and stain, followed by foliage that tracks everywhere and then by seed pods that sow themselves prolifically. In my opinion and experience, a "junk" tree of the worst order.

Cercis canadensis or Eastern Redbud, Zones 4–9

Outdoor planting time: Spring or fall.

Light: Full sun.

Soil: Average.

Moisture: Drought resistant when established but water regularly during summer drought.

Bloom time: Spring.

Description: Purplish-pink, sweet-pea-shaped blossoms precede 3- to 6-inch, heart-shaped leaves. Also available in white and pink varieties. Irregular in shape; rounded, with one or several trunks. Leaves turn yellow in fall.

Height: 25–35 feet.

Tips: A native species that adapts well to most areas of the country. Forest Pansy sports purple-red foliage.

Chionanthus virginica or Fringe Tree, Zones vary

Outdoor planting time: Spring or fall.
Light: Full sun or partial shade.
Soil: Average.
Moisture: Drought resistant.
Bloom time: Late spring or early summer, depending on variety.
Description: Fluffy clusters of white blossoms, which appear like fringe. Leaves are oval and glossy.
Height: 20 feet.
Tips: Tree leafs out very late in spring, so early spring-blooming flowers planted beneath it can thrive. Slow growing, but there are other flowering trees better suited as specimens because of their more spectacular flowering.

Cladrastis lutea or Yellowwood, Zones 4–9

Outdoor planting time: Spring or fall.
Light: Full sun.
Soil: Average.
Moisture: Drought resistant.
Bloom time: Late spring.
Description: Long, hanging, highly fragrant clusters resembling white wisteria. Bright green foliage turns yellow in fall. Smooth, gray bark provides contrast with foliage.
Height: 35 feet.
Tips: Flowering is erratic with a grand show every two or three years. Wood is brittle and hence subject to wind damage. Growth rate slow to moderate.

Cornus or Dogwood, Zones 5–9

Outdoor planting time: Spring or fall.
Light: Full sun or partial shade.
Soil: Average.
Moisture: Drought resistant when established but water regularly during summer drought.

Bloom time: Spring.

Description: Bracts (technically leaves rather than flowers) of white, pink, or red precede handsome, deep green foliage. Leaves are brilliant red to purple in fall, with red berries that attract birds. Horizontal branching pattern.

Height: 25–30 feet.

Tips: White Cloud and Cherokee, a red variety, are recommended. Unfortunately, this lovely American species is now being attacked by disease. Older specimens are the most vulnerable. Water thoroughly and regularly all during the growing season to stave off disease. If leaves curl and dry, and branch looks dead, remove branch with pruning shears at once. Dispose of branch in garbage or by burning and sterilize shears with rubbing alcohol or household bleach before using again. Spraying regularly with a fungicide such as captan or benomyl (available at garden centers and nurseries) according to manufacturer's instructions may help. One species, *Cornus kousa,* or Japanese dogwood (zones 6–9), is not susceptible to disease. Although not a spring bloomer, this variety sports white flowers that bloom in summer, with orange and red autumn foliage, and small, red, strawberrylike, inedible fruit. Summer Stars is the recommended variety of *Cornus kousa.*

Crataegus or Hawthorn, Zones vary

Outdoor planting time: Spring or fall.

Light: Full sun.

Soil: Average.

Moisture: Drought resistant when established, but water thoroughly during summer drought.

Bloom time: Spring.

Description: Pink or red blossoms on dense, thorny, angular, branched tree. Clusterlike red fruit follows bloom. If birds don't eat it, this fruit provides interesting winter color on bare trees.

Height: 25 feet.

Tips: Can be attacked by aphids, which are easily controlled by hosing down the tree regularly. Thorns on lower branches can injure children, or for that matter, adults, if they bump into them.

Halesia or Snowdrop Tree or Mountain Silver Bell, Zones 5–9

Outdoor planting time: Spring or fall.
Light: Full sun.
Soil: Average.
Moisture: Drought resistant when established.
Bloom time: Spring.
Description: Pendulous, bell-shaped, white blossoms that appear as foliage emerges. Foliage turns yellow in autumn.
Height: Snowdrop tree—30 or more feet; mountain silver bell—60 feet.
Tips: Both of these trees are good for woodland plantings as shade-loving shrubs and flowering plants thrive beneath them.

Koelreuteria or Goldenrain Tree, Zones 5–9

Outdoor planting time: Spring or fall.
Light: Full sun.
Soil: Average.
Moisture: Drought resistant when established.
Bloom time: Late summer.
Description: Spring foliage is salmon color, changing to green in late spring. Blooms with large clusters of yellow blossoms appear in late summer; these become red fruit and then turn to light brown in fall. Autumn foliage display is inconsequential.
Height: 20–40 feet.
Tips: A slow grower appropriate for shading patios. Since roots grow deeply rather than spread out and shallow, many plants survive when planted under this tree. Two columnar varieties exist. They are Kew and Fastigiata.

Laburnum or Golden Chain Tree, Zones 5–7

Outdoor planting time: Spring or fall.
Light: Full sun.
Soil: Average.
Moisture: Drought resistant when established, but water thoroughly during summer drought.
Bloom time: Spring.

Description: Hanging yellow blossom clusters up to 20 inches long, followed by medium green leaves. When grown as a tree it is vase-shaped; however, *Laburnum* can be trained as an espalier against walls or on arbors or trellises. The classic English garden Laburnum walk is an arbor festooned with this plant, trained and pruned to grow in such a manner.

Height: As a tree, to 20 feet.

Tips: Although *Laburnum* can be effective as a specimen tree, it is a magnificent spectacle grown on a trellis or an arbor. The seed pods that follow bloom are poisonous, and since they sap energy from the tree, they should be removed as they form.

Liriodendron tulipifera or Tulip Tree, Zones 4–9

Outdoor planting time: Spring or fall.
Light: Full sun.
Soil: Average.
Moisture: Drought resistant when established.
Bloom time: Late spring.
Description: Two-inch-long green and gold tulip-shaped blossoms appear after tree is about ten years old. Medium green foliage turns to soft yellow in fall.
Height: 60–90 feet.
Tips: Although a charming tree, it is not generally recommended for average-sized landscapes, since it grows to towering heights. It is better suited to larger plots of ground, where it can be used as a specimen tree or as a backdrop.

Magnolia grandiflora or Southern Magnolia, Zones 7–10

Outdoor planting time: Spring or fall.
Light: Full sun.
Soil: Average.
Moisture: Drought resistant when established, but water thoroughly during summer drought.
Bloom time: Late spring to autumn, depending on variety and zones.
Description: Huge (10-inch), strongly fragrant white blooms followed by cone-shaped seed heads that bear bright red seeds. Leaves are broad,

oval, and leathery. Rust-colored fuzz often covers undersides of leaves. This is the classic southern magnolia.

Height: 100 feet (but only after 50 years).

Tips: Many think *Magnolia grandiflora* is hardy only in the South. However, in protected areas of zone 7 and even zone 6, it often not only survives but thrives. Because this tree is so magnificent when in bloom, it is surely worth a try if you feel your property offers sufficient protection in the form of windbreaks, shelter, or a screen of sturdy evergreens.

Magnolia soulangiana or Saucer Magnolia, Zones 4–10

Outdoor planting time: Spring or fall.

Light: Full sun.

Soil: Average.

Moisture: Drought resistant when established, but water thoroughly during summer drought.

Bloom time: Early spring.

Description: Chalice-shaped, 6-inch flowers in white, pink, or purplish red, followed by medium green, oval, velvety foliage. Deciduous with gray bark, which is attractive during the winter.

Height: 25 feet.

Tips: In zones 6–8 it is best not to plant this cultivar in a spot with southern exposure, as late frosts can discolor blossoms forced into bloom by this protected environment. Eastern, western, or northern exposures are preferred. In zones 4 and 5, southern exposure is acceptable.

Malus or Crab Apple, Zones 4–10

Outdoor planting time: Spring or fall.

Light: Full sun.

Soil: Average.

Moisture: Drought resistant when established, but water thoroughly during summer drought.

Bloom time: Spring.

Description: A vast variety of cultivars is available. Blossoms range from white, to pink, to deep red on deep green foliage that turns brilliant red in fall. Many varieties bear small red crab apples, ranging from berry size to small apple size in summer and fall. This fruit is edible.

Height: 25 feet.

Tips: Dwarf and semidwarf varieties are available for use in patios and small gardens. Standard-sized trees can be used as specimen trees, in borders, or as backdrops. It is a good idea to check at a reliable local nursery for the names of varieties recommended for your particular area. *Malus* American Beauty, one of the most popular and finest examples of a specimen tree, is an excellent red-flowering crab from a foliage point of view. Don't overlook this variety in planning your scheme. In fact, if you have room for only one flowering tree, *Malus* or *Prunus* (see below) are perhaps your best choices, in light of the fact that dogwoods now are subject to a blight.

Melia azedarach or Chinaberry, Zones 7–10

Outdoor planting time: Spring or fall.
Light: Full sun.
Soil: Average.
Moisture: Drought resistant when established.
Bloom time: Late spring to early summer.
Description: Clusters of lavender blossoms produce yellow fruit that remains on the tree well into winter. Foliage is large, divided into smaller leaflets. Fall color is yellow.
Height: 30–50 feet.
Tips: A fast-growing flowering tree that is very undemanding and unproblematical. However, since limbs are brittle they are subject to high wind damage.

Oxydendrum arboreum or Sourwood or Sorrel Tree, Zones 5–9

Outdoor planting time: Spring or fall.
Light: Full sun.
Soil: Average.
Moisture: Drought resistant when established.
Bloom time: Midsummer.
Description: Clusters of creamy white, bell-shaped blossoms hang along 5 to 10-inch branches. Foliage is bronze in spring, becoming shiny green in summer and turning to brilliant red and bronze again in fall.
Height: 25–40 feet.

Tips: A slow-growing tree that has something to offer all year round. Pyramidal in shape, it serves as a fine shade tree for patio or garden.

Paulonia tomentosa or Empress Tree, Zones 5–10

Outdoor planting time: Spring or fall.
Light: Full sun.
Soil: Average.
Moisture: Drought resistant when established.
Bloom time: Spring.
Description: Lavender-blue clusters bloom before or during leaf-out. Foliage is heart-shaped and 12 inches across.
Height: 50 feet.
Tips: A shallow-rooted tree that casts very dense shade. Little will grow beneath it, so it is best used in distant parts of the garden.

Prunus or Flowering Cherry, Peach, Plum, Apricot, and Almond Trees, Zones vary according to variety

Outdoor planting time: Spring or fall.
Light: Full sun.
Soil: Average.
Moisture: Drought resistant when established, but water thoroughly during summer drought.
Bloom time: All bloom in spring.
Description: Cherry, peach, and plum trees sport spectacular spring bloom but are, with the exception of the latter, fruitless, thus largely eliminating constant maintenance, pest and disease control, fruit drop, and other complications of fruit trees. Flowering cherry has single or double blossoms in white or pink, some in pendent clusters. The bark is a lustrous mahogany when young, similar in appearance to paper birch. Flowering plum has smaller blossoms in white or pink. Its leaves are purple, red, or coppery red. Some varieties produce a small fruit that can be a nuisance if planted near a walk or patio. Although flowering peach and apricot are very beautiful, they are subject to many of the pests and diseases of their fruit-bearing cousins and therefore are generally not recommended for landscape planting.
Height: Most grow to 20 feet, some to 40 feet.

Tips: The selection is vast, and it is perhaps best to consult a local nursery or your local County Cooperative Extension Service for varieties recommended for your area. Along with *Malus* or flowering crab apple, varieties of *Prunus* are perhaps your best selection if you have room in your landscape for only one or two flowering trees.

Sophora japonica or Japanese Pagoda Tree, Zones 5–8

Outdoor planting time: Spring or fall.
Light: Full sun.
Soil: Average.
Moisture: Drought resistant when established.
Bloom time: Mid to late summer.
Description: Foot-long clusters of cream-colored, sweet-pea-like blossoms on medium green, small, oval leaves. Limbs are smooth and green.
Height: Grows moderately to 20 feet, then very slowly to 50 feet.
Tips: Flowers can stain when they drop. Offers moderate shade, so it is suitable for patios and gardens.

Sorbus aucuparia or European Mountain Ash or Rowan, Zones 3–7

Outdoor planting time: Spring or fall.
Light: Full sun.
Soil: Average.
Moisture: Drought resistant when established.
Bloom time: Blossoms in spring, berries in fall.
Description: Small white blossoms cover tree in spring, with hanging clusters of orange or red berries in fall. Leaves are small and oval and turn to yellow or orange-red in fall.
Height: Larger varieties grow to 50 feet; however, the smaller American ash grows to around 15 feet and is well suited to the average-sized landscape.
Tips: Especially attractive when planted in front of evergreens, which set off the berries during fall and winter.

Styrax or Snowbell, Zones 5–9

Outdoor planting time: Spring or fall.
Light: Full sun.
Soil: Average.
Moisture: Drought resistant when established.
Bloom time: Late spring.
Description: White, bell-shaped flowers hang from strongly horizontally patterned framework. Leaves turn yellow in fall.
Height: 30 feet.
Tips: An excellent tree for shading patios and gardens because its root system is noncompetitive and its growth habit is compact. Highly recommended for average-sized properties.

The Backbone of the Landscape: Shrubs

If trees are the superstructure of the landscape, shrubs—deciduous, dwarf conifers, and broad-leaved evergreens—are its backbone. Deciduous shrubs lose their leaves in the winter like deciduous trees. Forsythia is an example of a deciduous shrub. Very often, however, they offer landscape interest throughout the season. Most bloom in spring, but some bloom in summer and fall. Many sport vividly colored foliage in fall, before the leaves drop, and some are even of interest in the winter because of bark coloration or texture.

Dwarf conifers are actually trees. Their foliage is evergreen and needlelike, but their scale and landscape usage are the same as shrubs, so they are included in this chapter. Some examples are dwarf spruce, low-growing juniper, and other dwarf varieties of standard evergreens. They do not sport blossoms or berries, but texture and color variation are substantial, ranging from near-blue through many shades of green, to yellow. They retain needle color all year long.

Broad-leaved evergreens retain their leaves throughout the year. They differ from dwarf evergreens or conifers in that their foliage is not needlelike but leaf-shaped. Rhododendrons and evergreen azaleas are examples of broad-leaved evergreens. They also offer interest at different times of the year. Many bloom in spring, but some bloom in summer, and some offer brilliant red, orange, or yellow and subtle blue, black, and white berries after bloom or later, in summer or fall. In most cases, the berries remain on the shrub during the winter, contrasting colorfully with the green foliage. These berries also attract birds to the garden and provide food for them. No landscape is complete without a substantial planting of shrubs.

There are shrubs to fit every landscape. They range in height from low-growing six-inch plants to towering 15- to 20-foot-high bushlike plants. Blooms come in every color of the rainbow; foliage ranges from feathery to leathery in every conceivable shade of green.

Where can I buy shrubs? Included in the encyclopedia (see pp. 104–26) are shrubs that are generally available throughout the country, if not at garden centers or nurseries, through mail-order houses.

Local garden centers or nurseries are often the best source for shrubs if you are just starting out with your landscape scheme, as generally speaking, they offer only varieties that are recommended for your area. And, if they are reliable and know their business, they can also offer you help with any special problems you might encounter with a particular variety or provide you with special planting instructions. Often they offer free landscape advice and even complete plans for foundation plantings or shrub borders (this, of course, in exchange for your business). As always, be sure to ask lots of questions *before* you purchase stock. Get as much information as you can from merchants about their offerings. If the salesperson does not seem to know the business, ask to speak to the proprietor. If the proprietor fluffs you off with a shrug, or tells you that a particular shrub is appropriate locally without offering further information upon being asked, go somewhere else.

To save yourself grief, it is a good idea to ask friends or neighbors who live in the area about their experience with various nurseries. If they have had a bad experience, they will surely tell you about it. Often they know of nurseries that may be further away from your home but offer very special cultivars. As mentioned above, reliable nurseries usually guarantee their stock for one growing season and will generally take your word for it if you inform them that one of your spring purchases died over the summer. And if you purchase in the fall, most nurseries will now offer the same guarantee over the winter, if they have recommended the plant for fall planting. Keep in mind that as with all plants, you will have to water shrubs on a regular basis, particularly during the first summer, until they are established. If you do not do so, it is not only unfair but somewhat dishonest to report failure and expect a replacement from your nursery.

Some garden centers and nurseries also offer bare-root plants. These can be a good buy *if* the plants are dormant. Inspect them closely and never buy a bare-root plant with leaves, white sprouts, or other signs that indicate they are no longer dormant.

As with trees, the shrubs offered through mail-order houses are almost always less expensive than those you might purchase locally, and the selection is far more varied. There are many reasons for this. First, most planting material sold at garden centers or nurseries is container grown. If not grown locally, it has been shipped in the containers, a far more expensive proposition than the bare-root stock usually offered by mail-order houses. However, if you follow instructions carefully, there is no reason why the bare-root stock, shipped without soil (the roots are usually packed in wet sawdust or spaghnum peat moss enclosed with plastic wrap), should not grow as successfully as container-grown stock. Most likely, the bare-root stock you order from a mail-order house will be a younger plant, sometimes only a year or two old. Container-grown plants are usually at least three years old, sometimes older. However, after several years, the bare-root will catch up to the container-grown in size and vigor.

To begin with, read the rest of this section. Then write for some of the catalogues listed on page 249. Do this early in the season—January or February at the latest. When they arrive, study them carefully to see what is offered. After you've made a preliminary selection, double-check the catalogues to make sure that the varieties you are interested in are recommended for your particular zone. For example, there are many varieties of rhododendrons, in fact, varieties that grow in just about every zone except for the far northern areas. Some may be recommended for zone 7 or 8 and will not survive in zones 5 and 6, while others may require colder temperatures and not survive in the warmer zones. The same can be said of other cultivars. When you've made your decisions, it is a good idea to phone your County Cooperative Extension Service. Ask to speak to the agricultural division and tell them that you want advice on cultivars suitable for your planting area. This is a free service offered all over the country (you pay indirectly through your taxes). Then order your plants. Almost all mail-order nurseries ship at the proper planting time and include all instructions for immediate care, planting, and care through the season.

Friends, family, and neighbors are also sources of shrub planting material. In this case, accept whatever is offered. Find out the name of the shrub, inquire about planting, maintenance, and ultimate height, and then decide where you wish to install the plant. If a friend or relative offers you a gift certificate for a garden center or nursery, accept with enthusiasm: that one special, extravagant plant that may have been beyond your budget at the moment can be yours by redeeming it.

How do I go about planning my shrub planting? Which shrubs are suitable for which purposes? Planting shrubs is considerably more complicated than installing bulbs, perennials, or annuals, primarily because they are a permanent installation. Once planted and growing to maturity, they require a great deal of effort to move, with the exception of some of the smaller cultivars, such as azaleas, potentilla, and other dwarf plants. These shrubs should be moved only in early spring or early fall. For our purposes here, consider your plans as permanent. This doesn't mean you won't make mistakes; all gardeners do. It is quite likely that several years down the line you will have to take an ax and chop down this or that shrub because it is in the wrong place or has overpowered its surroundings. But with proper planning, you can minimize these errors.

Since you have already planned and planted the superstructure of your landscape, the trees, it is time now to install the backbone of your landscape, the shrubs. Shrubs have many uses. They can be used in foundation plantings, as hedges, and in borders along the sides, back, or front of your property or dividing one area of your property from another. If you mix deciduous shrubs, dwarf conifers, and broad-leaved evergreens, you can attain a planting that offers interest throughout the season.

As with any planting, work your scheme on graph paper. Using a scale of one block on the graph paper to two inches of planting space, sketch out the area you wish to plant. Then go outdoors to the area and try to visualize the planting. One way you can help yourself visualize the ultimate height of the various cultivars you wish to use is to insert bamboo sticks or poles equal in height to the mature height of the selected plants in the spots where the plants will grow. Experiment on paper with various shapes (conical, round, horizontal, fountain-shaped) until you find one (or a combination) that suits you. Then study the encyclopedia to determine which shrubs fit your needs. Here are a few dos and don'ts to bear in mind when planning a shrub planting:

• Never select a shrub simply because you happen to like the color of its flowers. Consider the other aspects—shape, height, growth, habit, and foliage—and be sure it is in keeping with the scheme you have in mind.

● Although it would seem only common sense to take note of windows when planning a foundation planting, many people neglect to do so. Do not plant tall shrubs in front of windows, for they will block the view outside and prevent sunlight from shining into the house.

● Also, take note of the doorway. Avoid shrubs that overgrow their bounds and would impede passage to and from the house. Further, avoid planting shrubs with thorns close to the entrance of the house.

● When you are ready to install your foundation or shrub border planting, take your chart with you to the garden for reference and bring a yardstick to measure distances properly.

Here are some tips to help you select the shrubs that will best suit your purposes:

● If you wish to provide a screen or hedge for privacy throughout the year, select either dwarf conifers or broad-leaved evergreens, as both retain their foliage and green color all year long. Deciduous shrubs are not recommended for screens since they lose their leaves in winter. Further, if you want a hedge effect rather than an informal look, choose a broad-leaved evergreen with small leaves, such as one of the various *Ilex* listed in the encyclopedia. These can be kept to the desired height and width by annual trimming. If you decide that you wish to soften the formal effect of a screen, you can install deciduous shrubs and dwarf conifers as well as perennials, annuals, and spring-blooming bulbs in front of it.

● If a less formal shrub border is what you have in mind, select from all three categories: flowering deciduous shrubs, flowering broad-leaved evergreens, and dwarf conifers. When you design your border, keep in mind that the deciduous shrubs will lose their leaves in the winter, so space the evergreen varieties you select throughout the planting so the border will not look spotty during the winter.

● When installing a foundation planting, assuming that you are starting from scratch—that is, you've either disposed of the old foundation planting or there was none there to begin with—think in terms of using all three kinds of shrubs. *Do not, under any circumstances, select standard-sized conifers for your planting. Although they will be of manageable size when you purchase them, a few years down the line they will outgrow the planting, requiring expensive removal. Consider that a Norway spruce may be only four feet high when you install it, but ten years down the line it can tower to more than thirty feet. Select only dwarf conifers for that segment of your planting.*

● Avail yourself of advice from garden center and nursery personnel. Keep in mind, however, that their recommendations for foundation plantings are sometimes uninventive—restricted to a few rather common vari-

eties, particularly those they have in stock. Better nurseries usually offer more imaginative recommendations and selections. Although you will be tempted to take their advice, investigate the availability of varieties yourself and then confer with the nursery personnel to make your final selection.
• The all-dwarf conifer foundation plantings commonly installed in front of residences in this country are monotonous in that they usually include little or no variety in color and texture. And they rarely include flowering deciduous shrubs. A foundation planting of nothing but deciduous shrubs will look barren and ugly during the winter. The best way to approach this planting is to consider the texture of foliage, the color of the foliage in different seasons, the color of the blossoms, and the ultimate height of the plant, and then select from the three types of shrubs. Once you've decided which plants you want to use, if you want an informal look to your planting, design your scheme in an informal manner. That is, do not make it symmetrical. For example, place two conical-shaped dwarf conifers on either side of the doorway or at either end of the planting. If, however, your house is very formal in design, you may wish to install a symmetrical formal planting.

What about the aesthetics of shrub planting when you are installing a foundation planting or shrub border?
When installing a foundation planting or shrub border, keep in mind the following:
• Vary the height of the planting.
• Avoid installing a foundation planting in a straight line. Space some plants close to the foundation and others farther out. In other words, create a garden in front of your house, in much the same way that you would plant a perennial border.
• If you are selecting from small, low-growing plants, consider planting three of each variety together in one area rather than one of three different varieties. This will tie the planting together and give it a unified appearance.
• Perhaps most important, allow enough space to accommodate the mature size of the plants. If you do not, in a few short years the foundation planting will look overcrowded and overgrown and may even have to be yanked out and replaced. If you have installed your planting properly, it should look just a bit sparse for the first year or so. In a few years the planting will fill out and be appropriate for the landscape.
• For variety, select from conical-shaped dwarf evergreens, horizontal low-growing cultivars, fountain-shaped deciduous flowering shrubs, mound-

shaped dwarf evergreens, and informal, loosely shaped broad-leaved evergreens.

● Finally, once you've installed your foundation planting or your shrub border, dress it up with an assortment of spring-blooming bulbs, perennials, and annuals.

Where in the country can I plant shrubs? Consult the zone designations included in each entry of the shrub encyclopedia (pp. 104–26) to determine which varieties are suitable for your particular location. You will find that there are varieties suitable for every area of the United States and Canada, regardless of how cool or warm the climate may be.

How do I select a site for a shrub planting? As far as light requirements are concerned, most shrubs can be planted in either full sun or partial shade, with some thriving in shade or even deep shade as well. Consult the encyclopedia for specific recommendations. Although some varieties will thrive in areas with poor drainage, most prefer a reasonably well-drained location. As explained in the tree section above, to test a site for drainage, dig a hole to a depth of about one foot and fill the hole with water. Allow the water to soak in. Repeat this two more times. If water remains after that, drainage is poor and may not be suitable for some varieties of shrubs. If all of the water drains, the site is suitable for almost all varieties of shrubs *in terms of soil drainage.*

How do I prepare the soil? Although many shrubs are not particularly fussy about soil, it is a good idea to prepare the shrub border bed or foundation planting bed before installing the plants. This will create the proper growing conditions for the young plants and give them a good start in their new home. After you've selected the site for a particular plant, dig a hole about one and a half feet deep by three feet in diameter. (This is in accordance with the old rule of thumb: a five-dollar plant requires a ten-dollar hole.) If the plant you have selected is acid loving, as is the case with most broad-leaved evergreens, mix the soil with organic matter such as spagnum peat moss or well-rotted compost in a ratio of about one part soil to one part organic matter. If the plant does not require acid conditions, mix about one part organic matter to two parts soil. Replace the mixture into the hole and water thoroughly. Do this about a week before you install your plants.

When do I plant shrubs? Although spring has traditionally been the recommended time for most shrubs, recent research shows that early fall is actually as good a time for most varieties, sometimes better. The reason for this is that young plants do not have to withstand the high temperatures or prolonged dry spells of summer. If you do install a fall planting (after the first heavy frost), cover the entire planting with a six-inch mulch of salt hay, a commonly used mulch of hay and salt available at garden centers and nurseries. This will prevent plants from heaving that results from alternate freezing and thawing of soil during the course of the winter, and that can expose surface roots to the elements. Check with your local garden center or nursery about the advisability of fall planting in your area and be sure that they offer a guarantee on any plants you purchase on their recommendation.

How do I plant shrubs? Once you've prepared the soil, dig a hole about twice as wide and deep as the root ball in the case of container or bagged and burlapped stock, or twice as wide and deep as the root structure of bare-root plants. Position the plant in the hole at the level at which it was grown at the nursery. With bare-root stock you can almost always see where the soil level was on the bark of the plant. Fill in soil beneath, around, and on top of roots. Tamp down firmly. Water thoroughly. When the water has drained, tamp again and firm the soil. Water thoroughly again. Check the encyclopedia and add fertilizer only if recommended. Keep in mind that very few shrubs require fertilizer at planting time if you have fortified the soil before planting.

Should I mulch shrubs after planting? If you plant in the fall, it is a good idea to lay on a six-inch layer of mulch to prevent heaving. If you plant in spring, mulch also, as the mulch will help keep weeds down and retain moisture.

Should I water my shrubs during the summer? Although many shrubs are drought resistant, during the first year, while they are establishing themselves in the earth, they require regular watering, particularly during summer drought. In subsequent years, it is a good idea during prolonged periods of summer drought to water to a depth of 1½ feet at least once a week.

How do I maintain my shrub plantings after the first year? Although most shrubs will survive and even thrive without an annual feeding, for best results, each spring before growth commences, work about one cup of all-purpose 5-10-5 fertilizer into the soil around the plant. It is not necessary to dead-head (remove spent blossoms from) shrubs.

What if my deciduous shrubs begin to grow too large or become dense with twigs? Prune the shrubs to control their size. To do this, you will need pruning shears or loppers, and quite possibly a small saw. As a rule, most deciduous shrubs should be pruned immediately *after* bloom. If you prune *before* bloom, you will remove the blossom buds and end up with few or scattered blooms on the bush. Most deciduous shrubs should be pruned at soil level. Remove some of the older flowering wood and the plant will send up new, vigorous growth, which usually blooms the following season. Try to maintain the natural shape of the shrub rather than imposing a "muffin" shape on the bush. Nothing looks more contrived and ridiculous than a shrub with a naturally graceful, fountainlike form that has been pruned into a round ball or an inverted triangle. After you've removed old and dead wood, you can prune individual branches back if you wish, but again, try to retain the natural form of the plant. With very old and overgrown shrubs, it may be necessary to saw off old or dead wood. Again, always do this at the base of the plant, removing the entire branch.

What if my broad-leaved evergreen shrubs begin to grow too large? This is a serious problem. If you selected the shrubs, then you chose the wrong variety for the location you had in mind. If the shrubs were on the property when you purchased it, they probably should be yanked out and replaced. There are some things you can do to rejuvenate ungainly rhododendrons, the cultivar most likely to grow out of bounds, but this is a complicated matter and is best left to professionals.

Are there any varieties of shrubs that I can plant in a woodland garden or in a shady spot? Yes, there are many. Check the encyclopedia (pp. 104–26) for recommendations.

Are there any varieties of shrubs that I can count on to grow if I don't have time to water regularly during the summer? Yes. Most shrubs, with the exception of some of the broad-leaved evergreens, are highly drought resistant once established. Consult the encyclopedia (pp. 104–13 and pp. 122–26) for further information.

After a number of years some of my shrubs no longer bloom very profusely. What should I do? The reason deciduous shrubs sometimes decrease in bloom is that they are overgrown. See the section on pruning, above, to rectify the situation. Acid-loving plants such as azaleas and rhododendrons sometimes decrease in bloom because they are not receiving the acidic food they require for vigorous growth and blooming. Apply Miracid, available at garden centers and nurseries, in early spring and then again in late fall according to manufacturer's directions.

What about pests and diseases? Most shrubs resist pest and disease infestation. You may encounter one or more of the following problems, however, although chances are you won't:

Powdery mildew. Leaves become disfigured by a white fuzz. Spray with captan or benomyl, according to manufacturer's instructions, from midsummer until early September to control this problem. Lilac is most susceptible.

Scale. Minuscule hard-shelled parasites attach themselves to the undersides of leaves of some broad-leaved evergreens and to the bark of some deciduous shrubs such as pussy willow. They suck the juices of the plant, and if not controlled, can eventually kill the plant. Dormant oil spray, available at garden centers and nurseries, applied very early in the spring will smother the parasites and control the problem.

Red spider. This is a mite that causes plants to become yellow and weak and the undersides of leaves to appear dirty in its advanced stages. In early stage of attack, webs appear, near the ribs or margins of leaves and then over the entire surface. If the trouble is in the early stages use tedion; if it is fairly advanced, apply kelthane—both are available at garden centers and nurseries. Use according to manufacturer's instructions.

Shrub Encyclopedia

DECIDUOUS SHRUBS

Azalea or Exbury, Ghent, or Mollis Azalea, Zones 4–8

Outdoor planting time: Spring or fall, but will survive summer planting.
Light: Full sun or partial shade.
Soil: Rich, slightly acid.
Moisture: Provide sufficient moisture during summer. Plant will tell you if it needs watering by wilting visibly.

Bloom time: May or June.
Description: Spectacular cluster blooms in brilliant red, purple, orange, yellow, pink, salmon, coral, white, and combinations thereof.
Height: 3–5 feet.
Tips: Foliage tends to become mildewed during summer. This does no harm to the plant. If the unsightly look of this bothers you, spray from early summer to fall with captan or benomyl fungicides, according to manufacturer's instructions. Azalea is certainly among the most beautiful of all shrubs. Look for deciduous purple varieties that bloom very early in spring. They make lovely companion plantings for yellow forsythia, which blooms around the same time. Since deciduous azaleas require slightly acidic soil, scratch in one tablespoon of Miracid, available at garden centers and nurseries, around the plant each spring before bloom. Remove spent blooms with fingers after bloom to ensure a spectacular bloom the following year.

Buddleia davidi or Butterfly Bush, Zones 5–9

Outdoor planting time: Spring or fall.
Light: Full sun.
Soil: Thrives in almost any soil.
Moisture: Drought resistant once established, but water regularly during summer drought for best results.
Bloom time: Summer.
Description: Purple, orchid pink, dark wine, or pure white lilaclike fragrant flowers on medium green foliage.
Height: 4–6 feet.
Tips: This plant is often referred to as summer lilac and attracts butterflies. Foliage dies down to the ground in the winter, growing again to mature height in spring.

Chaenomeles japonica or Japanese Scarlet Quince, Zones 4–9

Outdoor planting time: Spring or fall.
Light: Full sun or partial shade.
Soil: Prefers sandy loam.

Moisture: Drought resistant once established, but water regularly during summer drought for best results.
Bloom time: Later winter to early spring.
Description: White, pink and white, pink, salmon, orange, or red blossoms appear when almost no other shrub blooms. Some varieties sport thorns.
Height: 5–10 feet, depending on variety.
Tips: Easy to grow, unproblematical.

Cornus or Red Twig Dogwood, Zones 4–8

Outdoor planting time: Spring or fall.
Light: Full sun or partial shade.
Soil: Thrives in almost any soil.
Moisture: Drought resistant once established, but water regularly during summer drought for best results.
Bloom time: Later winter or early spring.
Description: Creamy white or yellow flowers, depending on variety, and bright green leaves. Waxy white berry clusters appear in fall and are relished by birds. Twigs turn brilliant red in winter and are prized for this reason, as they add color to the landscape at that time of year.
Height: 10–12 feet, depending on variety.
Tips: Careful pruning can restrict height; Sibirica is a shorter variety that grows less rampant.

Deutzia gracilis rosea or Pink Deutzia, Zones 5–10

Outdoor planting time: Spring or fall.
Light: Full sun or partial shade.
Soil: Thrives in almost any soil.
Moisture: Drought resistant once established, but water regularly during summer drought for best results.
Bloom time: May or June.
Description: Delicate pink flowers cover branches during bloom period.
Height: 3 feet.
Tips: Useful in foreground areas of shrub borders, in foundation plantings, or interplanted with perennials in a herbaceous border because of its tidy, low-growing tendency.

Euonymus alatus compactus or Burning Bush, Zones 3–9

Outdoor planting time: Spring or fall.
Light: Full sun and partial shade.
Soil: Thrives in almost any soil.
Moisture: Drought resistant once established, but water regularly during summer drought for best results.
Bloom time: Spring and fall for foliage.
Description: This cultivar sports inconspicuous yellow flowers in spring followed by orange fruits, but is grown primarily for its brilliant red autumn foliage. It is also attractive in winter because of its decorative corky bark.
Height: Compact variety grows to 6 feet, standard variety to around 10 feet.
Tips: Autumn foliage is spectacular. Prune annually in fall to encourage bushy growth.

Forsythia intermedia, Zones 5–9

Outdoor planting time: Spring or fall.
Light: Full sun or partial shade.
Soil: Thrives in almost any soil.
Moisture: Drought resistant once established, but water regularly during summer drought for best results.
Bloom time: Early spring.
Description: Yellow flowers cover plant in early spring. Foliage is bright green throughout summer.
Height: 6–8 feet.
Tips: Avoid weeping versions, as they require annual pruning to keep them under control once established. Upright varieties such as Linwood Gold are recommended. Prune after flowering rather than in spring for the most profuse display each season. Some people use forsythia as a hedge, clipping it in early spring. Avoid doing this, as a twiggy plant, half-covered with flowers, is an ugly sight. Branches can be cut in early spring before bloom, brought indoors, placed in water, and the bloom forced for indoor displays. Northern Lights is a variety recommended for zones 3 and 4, and although it does not bloom as profusely as cultivars suitable for warmer climates, tests at the University of Min-

nesota after winter temperatures of −30 degrees F have proven that bloom is respectable.

Hydrangea macrophylla or French Blue Hydrangea, Zones 5–10

Outdoor planting time: Spring or fall.
Light: Full sun or partial shade.
Soil: Rich soil with some acidity.
Moisture: Drought resistant, but water regularly during summer drought for best results.
Bloom time: July or August.
Description: Large blue, white, or pink blooms on handsome, deep green foliage.
Height: 3–6 feet, depending on variety.
Tips: For blue blooms, scratch in one tablespoon of acid fertilizer such as Miracid when shoots first emerge in the spring. For pink blooms, add one tablespoon of garden lime when shoots first emerge in the spring. You can propagate hydrangeas easily by taking foot-long cuttings in the fall and planting them in a pot of soil. Place the pot in an unheated garage or cellar and keep the soil evenly moist during winter. In spring, plant the rooted cuttings. *Hydrangea arborescens* and *paniculata*, Grandiflora, are hardy to zone 4.

Kerria japonica pleniflora or Double Globe Flower, Zones 4–9

Outdoor planting time: Spring or fall.
Light: Full sun or partial shade.
Soil: Thrives in almost any soil.
Moisture: Drought resistant once established, but water regularly during summer drought for best results.
Bloom time: May or June.
Description: Attractive, buttonlike golden blossoms cover the plant in spring. Foliage is dark green, remaining attractive throughout the year.
Height: 3–5 feet.
Tips: Each spring prune off brown tips only. This low-maintenance plant is tidy, does not grow rampantly, and rarely needs major pruning.

Lagerstroemia indica or Crape Myrtle, Zones 6–10

Outdoor planting time: Spring or fall.
Light: Full sun only in northern climates.
Soil: Thrives in almost any soil.
Moisture: Drought resistant once established, but water regularly during summer drought for best results.
Bloom time: August or September in the North, July or August in the South.
Description: Soft, fringed flowers in red, pink, white, or purple grow during the summer.
Height: 4 feet.
Tips: Purchase only those plants recommended for hardier districts. Crape myrtle used to be found only in the warm climates of the South, but hardy versions have been hybridized. The tops of the plant die down during the winter but grow again to full size in spring.

Magnolia stellata or Star Magnolia, Zones 5–9

Outdoor planting time: Spring or fall, although fall is best.
Light: Full sun.
Soil: Fertile, well-drained soil.
Moisture: Water regularly during summer drought.
Bloom time: Very early spring.
Description: Star-shaped white flowers appear before leaves.
Height: Can grow to nearly 12 feet, but usually grows to 6 feet.
Tips: One of the earliest of the blooming shrubs. Very hardy. Never needs pruning. Centennial is a hybrid that has larger flowers and more petals than the ordinary variety. Leonard Messel is a dark pink form, a European hybrid sometimes available in the United States.

Philadelphus virginalis or Mock Orange, Zones 4–8

Outdoor planting time: Spring or fall.
Light: Full sun or partial shade.
Soil: Any soil will do.
Moisture: Drought resistant, but water during summer drought for best results.
Bloom time: May or June.

Description: Pure white, scented, semi-double flowers cover branches in spring.
Height: Can grow to 8 feet.
Tips: Once established, annual pruning is recommended or shrub will become a messy thicket. Prune old flowering wood at soil level after shrub has bloomed. Do not cut young shoots, as they will be the flower bearers the following year.

Potentilla fruticosa or Gold Drop or Buttercup Shrub, Zones 4–10

Outdoor planting time: Spring or fall.
Light: Full sun or partial shade.
Soil: Any soil will do.
Moisture: Drought resistant once established, but for best results water regularly during summer drought.
Bloom time: Spring to summer.
Description: Bright, golden yellow flowers resembling buttercups on dense, fernlike foliage.
Height: 3 feet.
Tips: Effective in borders and as a hedge when planted on 12-inch centers.

Prunus glandulosa rosea or Flowering Almond, Zones 4–9

Outdoor planting time: Spring or fall.
Light: Full sun or partial shade.
Soil: Any soil will do.
Moisture: Not as drought resistant as most shrubs; should be watered regularly during summer drought.
Bloom time: April to May.
Description: Double pink flowers emerge first, followed by satiny green leaves.
Height: 3–4 feet.
Tips: A large planting of this charming shrub will scent the air with almonds in spring.

Salix discolor or French Pink Pussy Willow, Zones 5–9

Outdoor planting time: Spring or fall.
Light: Full sun or partial shade.
Soil: Any soil will do.
Moisture: Drought resistant once established.
Bloom time: Early spring.
Description: The familiar silvery gray catkins of pussy willows precede green foliage.
Height: Average mature height is 10 feet.
Tips: Use for screen or background planting. Very hardy plant. This variety is a vast improvement on the common pussy willow, which is very subject to scale.

Spiraea prunifolia or Bridal Wreath, Zones 4–8

Outdoor planting time: Spring or fall.
Light: Full sun or partial shade.
Soil: Thrives in almost any soil.
Moisture: Drought resistant once established, but water regularly during summer drought for best results.
Bloom time: May to June.
Description: Graceful arching branches completely covered with pure white flowers on medium green foliage. Useful as a specimen, border, or hedge planting. Pink and red varieties are also available.
Height: 5–6 feet.
Tips: Prune in fall every few years to maintain vigor. Do this by removing branches at soil level, not by cutting branches halfway down. Vanhouteii, a fountain-shaped plant, is the most commonly planted variety. *Spiraea japonica*, Goldmount, forms a low-mounded plant with pink flowers in May and golden leaves throughout the growing season. However, this variety is suitable only for cool climates—its leaves become badly sunburned in the South.

Syringa or Lilac, Zones 3–9

Outdoor planting time: Spring or fall.
Light: Full sun or partial shade.
Soil: Prefers fertile, well-drained soil.

Moisture: Drought resistant once established.

Bloom time: Late spring.

Description: Clusters of pink, white, lilac, pale lilac, or deep purple flowers on medium green leaves.

Height: 5–20 feet, depending on variety.

Tips: There are many hybrids available that grow to a manageable height: Persian lilac, with its deep purple blooms, grows to only 6 feet and is useful as a shrub border. Korean lilac, with pink blooms, grows to only 5 feet. Most varieties, however, are too tall for borders but can be used as screens or planted in a grove in distant parts of the landscape. The leaves tend to host mildew during summer. Although harmless to the plant, if this bothers you, spray with captan or benomyl fungicide beginning in early summer, according to manufacturer's instructions. Dead-head flowers for a more profuse bloom the following year.

Viburnum carlesi or Flowering Snowball, Zones 3–10

Outdoor planting time: Spring or fall.

Light: Full sun or partial shade.

Soil: Thrives in almost any soil.

Moisture: Drought resistant once established, but water regularly during summer drought for best results.

Bloom time: Early spring.

Description: Waxy white, pink-tinged, highly fragrant blossoms on gray-green foliage that turns a handsome bronze red in fall.

Height: 6 feet.

Tips: Requires little care and has a good, uniform, shapely growth habit.

Viburnum dentatum or Arrowwood, Zones 5–9

Outdoor planting time: Spring or fall.

Light: Full sun or partial shade.

Soil: Thrives in almost any soil.

Moisture: Drought resistant once established, but water regularly during summer drought for best results.

Bloom time: Late spring.

Description: Attractive white flowers on deep green foliage, which becomes bright red in the autumn. Berries, which begin to appear after flowering, are blue.

Height: 8–14 feet, depending on variety.

Tips: Little pruning required.

Weigela eva rathke or Red Flowered Weigela, Zones 5–9

Outdoor planting time: Spring or fall.

Light: Full sun or partial shade.

Soil: Thrives in almost any soil.

Moisture: Drought resistant once established, but water regularly during summer drought for best results.

Bloom time: Late spring to summer.

Description: Scarlet, trumpet-shaped flowers on medium green leaves.

Height: 5–6 feet.

Tips: Requires little care, but after a few years old flowering wood should be pruned at soil level after blossom time.

BROAD-LEAVED OR EVERGREEN SHRUBS

Arctostaphylos uva-ursi or Kinnikinnick Bearberry, Zones 2–10

Outdoor planting time: Spring or fall.

Light: Full sun or partial shade.

Soil: Prefers well-drained soil and will grow in sand.

Moisture: Drought resistant once established, but water regularly during summer drought.

Bloom time: Spring.

Description: Small pink flowers followed by red berries on creeping, matlike plant with small (1-inch-long) shiny leaves, which turn bronze in fall.

Height: 8 inches.

Tips: Does not transplant well, so once planted leave in place.

Azalea; see Rhododendron

Berberis julianae or Wintergreen Barberry, Zones 5–9

Outdoor planting time: Spring or fall.

Light: Full sun or partial shade.

Soil: Well-drained light loam.

Moisture: Drought resistant once established, but water regularly during summer drought.

Bloom time: Spring.

Description: Yellow flowers followed by blue-black berries in fall. Leaves are spiny-toothed, growing to 3 inches long. Foliage turns red or yellow in fall.

Height: 6 feet, but can be trimmed to shorter heights.

Tips: Most varieties have small thorns. Some varieties are banned in grain-growing areas because they harbor a disease called black rust of wheat, which attacks wheat plants.

Buxus microphylla or Little Leaf, Japanese, or Korean Boxwood, Zones 5–10

Outdoor planting time: Spring or fall.

Light: Full sun or partial shade.

Soil: Average, loamy soil.

Moisture: Requires regular watering during summer drought.

Bloom time: There are no flowers.

Description: Attractive, small, round-tipped leaves. Some varieties sport white or black berries in fall.

Height: 1–3 feet, depending on variety.

Tips: These cultivars are hardier and less problematic than English boxwood and are a fine substitute in areas too cold for the popular English variety.

Buxus sempervirens or Common Boxwood, Zones 5–10

Outdoor planting time: Spring or fall.

Light: Full sun or partial shade.

Soil: Average, loamy soil.

Moisture: Requires regular watering during summer drought.
Bloom time: There are no flowers.
Description: Attractive, small, round-tipped leaves. Common boxwood does not sport berries.
Height: 1–25 feet, depending on variety and age of plant.
Tips: Height can be controlled by annual trimming in spring. Check locally to see if this cultivar is hardy in your area.

Calluna vulgaris or Heather, Zones 4–10

Outdoor planting time: Spring or fall.
Light: Full sun or partial shade.
Soil: Light, sandy, acidic soil that is not rich. If soil is rich, plant will become leggy, that is, grow much taller than is healthy for plant, and die.
Moisture: Requires regular watering during summer drought.
Bloom time: Summer.
Description: Very small blossoms in showy spikes 6 to 8 inches long. Most varieties are purple, but some are red and white. Leaves are minute and green, turning bronze in fall in some varieties.
Height: 6 inches to 3 feet, depending on variety.
Tips: Although heather will grow in shade, it must have sun to bloom. The closely related *Erica* (heath) is similar in appearance and culture.

Camellia japonica or Common Camellia, Zones 7–10

Outdoor planting time: Spring or fall.
Light: For best results plant in partial shade, although plant will survive in full sun.
Soil: Requires rich loam, so fortify at planting time with substantial quantities of rotted compost or sphagnum peat moss in a ratio of about one part additive to one part soil.
Moisture: Requires regular watering during summer drought.
Bloom time: Late winter to early spring, depending on zone.
Description: Spectacular blooms in pink, white, red, and combinations thereof set on handsome, deep green foliage.
Tips: Camellias are much hardier than is generally thought. Although most people think they grow only in the South, they can thrive even in

protected areas of zone 6, although a very severe winter may kill all foliage. Camellias grow in zone 7, where I live, and although a severe winter did kill their foliage to the ground, it has come back dramatically and after three years has reached its former height. Full sun tends to burn and brown camellia blossoms in early spring, so a partially shaded location, perhaps an eastern or even a northern exposure, is preferable. Southern exposure in full sun is not the best location for camellias, though they will survive there. They are particularly dramatic espaliered against a wall.

Camellia sasanqua, Zones 7–10

All information is the same as for *Camellia japonica* except that this cultivar is slightly less hardy and probably will not survive in zone 6 or 7. It is exceptionally beautiful, however, and for that reason is certainly worth trying to grow in a sheltered location.

Cotoneaster, Zones 5–10 depending on variety

Outdoor planting time: Spring or fall.
Light: Full sun or partial shade.
Soil: Ordinary.
Moisture: Water regularly during summer drought.
Bloom time: Spring flowers and fall berries.
Description: Small pink to white clusters of flowers in spring followed by red berries in fall, which often last through the winter. Foliage on evergreen varieties is deep green and handsome.
Height: 2–20 feet, depending on variety.
Tips: Select carefully from the many varieties available, keeping in mind how you wish to use the plant. Small, low-growing cultivars can be used for ground cover; taller varieties can be espaliered against the house or a fence. Very versatile plants with many uses.

Daphne cneorum or Garland Flower, Zones 4–10

Outdoor planting time: Spring or fall.
Light: Full sun or partial shade.
Soil: Any soil will do.

Moisture: Water regularly all during the growing season.
Bloom time: Spring.
Description: Clusters of small, rose pink, fragrant flowers on a low-growing shrub with small (1-inch-long) leaves.
Height: Less than 6 feet.
Tips: Roots should be kept cool and moist, so a heavy mulch of shredded pine bark or rotted compost is recommended.

Euonymus fortunei or Winter Creeper, Zones 5–9

Outdoor planting time: Spring or fall.
Light: Full sun or partial shade.
Soil: Ordinary.
Moisture: Drought resistant, but should be watered regularly during summer drought.
Bloom time: Flowers insignificant; grown for foliage.
Description: Many varieties have glossy, dark leaves; some bear red or orange fruit.
Height: 1–5 feet, depending on variety.
Tips: Subject to scale. Spray with dormant oil spray, available at garden centers and nurseries, according to manufacturer's instructions in early spring, before new growth starts.

Ilex acquifolium or English Holly, Zones 7–8

Outdoor planting time: Spring only.
Light: Full sun only.
Soil: Sandy loam.
Moisture: Water regularly during summer drought.
Bloom time: Flowers are inconspicuous; grown for foliage and fall and winter berries.
Description: Glossy green or blue-green foliage, and brilliant red, white, or orange berries.
Height: Can grow to 40 feet but can be kept in bounds by yearly pruning.
Tips: Although beautiful, English holly doesn't adapt to either the colder or hotter regions of our country. The plant may survive in the warmer areas of zone 6 if planted in a sheltered spot and is worth a try because of its beauty.

Ilex cornuta or Chinese Holly, Zones 6–10

Outdoor planting time: Spring only.
Light: Full sun.
Soil: Sandy loam.
Moisture: Water regularly during summer drought.
Bloom time: Flowers are inconspicuous. Bright red berries last through the winter.
Description: Dark green, shiny leaves.
Height: 9 feet.
Tips: Good as a substitute for English holly in areas too cold or hot for that cultivar.

Ilex crenata or Japanese Holly, Zones 6–10

Outdoor planting time: Spring only.
Light: Full sun.
Soil: Sandy loam.
Moisture: Water regularly during summer drought.
Bloom time: Flowers are inconspicuous. Black berries last through the winter.
Description: Small, round, dark green leaves.
Height: Can grow to 20 feet, but can be kept in bounds by shearing.
Tips: Used in northern areas as a substitute for English boxwood. A useful hedge or shrub plant.

Ilex glabra or Inkberry, Zones 4–10

Outdoor planting time: Spring only.
Light: Full sun or shade.
Soil: Sandy loam.
Moisture: Water regularly during summer drought.
Bloom time: Flowers are inconspicuous and are followed by small black berries in fall.
Description: Dark green, lustrous leaves, 1 to 2 inches long.
Height: Can grow to 10 feet, but can be kept in bounds by shearing.
Tips: Useful as a substitute for hollies as far north as Minneapolis. Use as screens, specimens, in foundation plantings, or shrub borders.

Ilex opaca or American Holly, Zones 5–10

Outdoor planting time: Spring only.
Light: Full sun.
Soil: Sandy loam.
Moisture: Water regularly during summer drought.
Bloom time: Flowers are inconspicuous and are followed by red berries.
Description: Dark green, lustrous, spiny leaves.
Height: Can grow to 50 feet, but can be kept in bounds by pruning.
Tips: Used in northern areas in place of English holly.

Kalmia latifolia or Mountain Laurel, Zones 4–9

Outdoor planting time: Spring or fall.
Light: Full sun or partial shade.
Soil: Needs acidic soil, so work one tablespoon of acid fertilizer such as Miracid into the soil each spring before growth begins.
Moisture: Water regularly during summer drought.
Bloom time: Late spring to early summer.
Description: Pink and white flowers in clusters on shiny, handsome, 5-inch-long leaves.
Height: Can grow to 10 feet or more, but can be kept under control by judicious pruning.
Tips: Although *Kalmia* will grow in shade, the more sun it gets the showier the display of flowers.

Leucothoe fontanesiana, Zones 4–10

Outdoor planting time: Spring or fall.
Light: Full sun, or shade.
Soil: Light, peaty, acidic soil.
Moisture: Water regularly during summer drought.
Bloom time: Late spring.
Description: Small white flowers in attractive, 3-inch-long, drooping clusters grow on dark green, lustrous foliage about 7 inches long.
Height: Can grow to 6 feet.
Tips: Use in borders or foundation plantings but not as specimen plants, as they are too short. If plant becomes lanky and invasive because of

suckering, reshape by cutting stems back to the base of plant in spring to force new, compact growth.

Mahonia aquifolium or Oregon Holly Grape, Zones 5–10

Outdoor planting time: Spring or fall.
Light: Partial shade.
Soil: Not fussy about soil.
Moisture: Water regularly during summer drought.
Bloom time: Spring.
Description: Small, yellow, fragrant flowers grow in spikes with edible, blue-black, grapelike berries in summer on glossy, dark green, com-pounded foliage which may turn purple in fall.
Height: 3–4 feet.
Tips: Needs protection from heavy winds. Has been known to thrive in southern areas of zone 4, in southeastern Nebraska, and near Chicago.

Mahonia bealei or Leatherleaf Mahonia, Zones 6–10

Outdoor planting time: Spring or fall.
Light: Partial shade.
Soil: Prefers slightly acidic soil.
Moisture: Water regularly during summer drought.
Bloom time: Spring.
Description: Clusters of lemon yellow flowers followed by blue-black fruit. Leaves are compound, that is, consist of many small leaflets, and up to 16 inches long.
Height: To 12 feet.
Tips: A handsome plant that should be more widely grown.

Pieris floribunda or Andromeda, Zones 4–10

Outdoor planting time: Spring or fall.
Light: Partial shade.
Soil: Light soil.
Moisture: Water regularly during summer drought.
Bloom time: Spring.

Description: Small, white, erect clusters of flowers on shiny, 3½-inch-long leaves.

Height: 6 feet.

Tips: Handsome and very easy to grow—a good all-purpose cultivar for foundation planting or shrub borders.

Pieris japonica or Japanese Andromeda, Zones 5—10

Outdoor planting time: Spring or fall.

Light: Partial to heavy shade.

Soil: Prefers acidic soil.

Moisture: Drought resistant but water regularly during summer drought.

Bloom time: Spring.

Description: Small, creamy white flowers in drooping clusters up to 5 inches long on dark green, lustrous foliage up to 3½ inches long.

Height: Can grow to 10 feet.

Tips: Plant in heavy or semishaded areas, as full sun makes plants susceptible to lacebug infestation.

Pyracantha coccinea or Scarlet Firethorn, Zones 6—10

Outdoor planting time: Spring or fall.

Light: Full sun or partial shade.

Soil: Not fussy about soil.

Moisture: Drought resistant when established, but water regularly during summer drought.

Bloom time: Flowers early in summer; berries in fall and winter.

Description: Clusters of small white flowers with abundant, showy, inedible, red or orange berries in fall and winter. Small leaves may fall late in season in northern parts of growing range.

Height: Can grow to 20 feet or can be contained and used as espalier against walls.

Tips: Lalandei has been found to be hardy as far north as Minneapolis. A splendid plant for autumn and winter berry color. Works well with hollies and other berry-bearing plants to brighten winter landscapes.

Rhododendron and Azalea, Zones 3–10 *depending on variety*

Outdoor planting time: Spring or fall.
Light: Full sun or partial shade.
Soil: Prefers rich soil on the acidic side.
Moisture: Water regularly during summer drought.
Bloom time: April to June, depending on variety.
Description: Bloom colors encompass the entire color wheel in large and small clusters—a near endless variety.
Height: 1–40 feet, depending on variety.
Tips: Since the selection available throughout the country is so vast, and since various cultivars are suitable for different areas, it is best to consult with local nurseries or your County Cooperative Extension Service as to which varieties thrive in your area.

Viburnum rhytidophyllum or Leatherleaf Viburnum, Zones 5–9

Outdoor planting time: Spring or fall.
Light: Full sun or partial shade.
Soil: Rich, well-drained.
Moisture: Water regularly during summer drought.
Bloom time: Spring.
Description: Small white or pink flowers in flat clusters followed by small red to black berries on 7-inch-long, shiny, dark green foliage that is wooly underneath.
Height: To 9 feet.
Tips: May not be totally evergreen in northern part of range.

DWARF CONIFERS

These are miniature varieties of the standard evergreen trees. Every year, more and more varieties of dwarf conifers are being offered in garden centers and nurseries. This makes a great deal of sense, because standard evergreen trees, although magnificent when fully grown, are far too large for the average landscape. Although this encyclopedia includes a reasonable selection of dwarf conifers it would be almost impossible to cover all the new varieties appearing on the market each year. For more information, I suggest you write for some of the catalogues listed on page 249. Also, check local retail outlets for their offerings. Zones are not included in this section of the encyclopedia, as all varieties thrive in most areas of the country.

Arborvitae or Thuja

Outdoor planting time: Spring or fall.
Light: Full sun or partial shade.
Soil: Ordinary.
Moisture: Drought resistant once established, but water regularly during summer drought.
Description: Pyramidal, conical, globular, or columnar in shape, with gold, and light to dark green foliage, depending on variety.
Varieties
● *Thuja occidentalis* or American arborvitae: compact, pyramidal; can be dwarfed by vigorous pruning.
● *Thuja occidentalis*, Woodwardii or Woodward globe arborvitae: globular, bushy, compact; can even be used in window boxes.
● Hetz's Midget or dwarf globe arborvitae: slow growing, globular, with medium green foliage.

Chamaecyparis or False Cypress

Outdoor planting time: Spring or fall.
Light: Full sun or partial shade.
Soil: Ordinary.
Moisture: Drought resistant once established, but water regularly during summer drought.
Description: Globular, pyramidal, or spreading in shape, with silver blue, green, or gold foliage, depending on variety.
Varieties
● *Chamaecyparis*, Fletcheri Nana or Fletcher cypress: narrow, columnar, green.
● *Chamaecyparis nootkatensis*, Pendula or weeping Nootka cypress: branchlets hang vertically in long, graceful streamers.
● *Chamaecyparis obtusa*, Aurea Nana or gold dwarf Hinoki cypress: heavy, gold foliage.

- *Chamaecyparis obtusa*, Compacta Nana: flat form of Hinoki cypress (see below).
- *Chamaecyparis obtusa*, Gracilis Nana: deep green foliage, upright growth.
- *Chamaecyparis obtusa*, Kosteri Nana: lacy foliage with broad growth habit.
- *Chamaecyparis obtusa*, Torulosa Nana or dwarf twisted-branch cypress: Branches are twisted and filamented, growing compactly into an irregular pyramidal form.
- *Chamaecyparis pisifera*, Argentea Nana or dwarf silver cypress: dense globe with soft-plumed, silvery blue foliage.
- *Chamaecyparis pisifera*, Argentea Variegata Nana or variegated dwarf silver threadleaf cypress: silvery, variegated foliage.
- *Chamaecyparis pisifera*, Aurea Pendula or dwarf gold thread cypress: low, compact, with bright golden, pendulous filaments. Does not burn in sun.
- *Chamaecyparis pisifera filifera*, Aurea Variegata Nana or dwarf gold variegated cypress: gold, variegated foliage.
- *Chamaecyparis pisifera*, Minima or dwarf threadleaf cypress: compact, with green foliage.
- *Chamaecyparis pisifera*, Sulphuria Nana or dwarf sulphur cypress: bright, sulphur-colored broad, moundlike growth habit.

Juniperus or Juniper

Outdoor planting time: Spring or fall.
Light: Prefers full sun, but will grow in partial shade.
Soil: Ordinary.
Moisture: Drought resistant.
Description: Creeping, low, and spreading; vase-shaped or columnar.
Varieties

- *Juniperus chinensis*, Blue Vase or Blue Vase juniper: intermediate in height (around 5 feet); vase-shaped.
- *Juniperus chinensis*, Old Gold or Old Gold juniper: golden yellow in color.
- *Juniperus chinensis*, Pfitzerana Aurea or gold tip juniper: bright golden color in spring and summer.
- *Juniperus horizontalis*, Bar Harbor or Bar Harbor juniper: low, creeping, steel blue foliage with a fernlike appearance.

- *Juniperus horizontalis,* Blue Chip or Blue Chip juniper: silvery blue foliage; spreading, low-mounding habit.
- *Juniperus horizontalis,* Glauca or blue creeping juniper: blue foliage, creeping.
- *Juniperus horizontalis,* Plumosa or Andorra juniper: low-spreading habit, summer foliage silvery green, turning purple after frost.
- *Juniperus japonica,* Compacta or Japanese juniper: semiupright in habit; foliage is heavy and ranges in color from slate to green.
- *Juniperus procumbens,* Nana or dwarf Japanese juniper: short, stiff branches forming a carpet up to 6 feet across, mounding to 10 inches in the center.
- *Juniperus rigida,* Pendula or weeping needle juniper: narrow, tall, and pendant in habit.

Picea or Spruce

Outdoor planting time: Spring or fall.
Light: Full sun or partial shade.
Soil: Ordinary.
Moisture: Drought resistant when established, but water regularly during summer drought.
Description: Blue or green foliage; moundlike, conical, pendulous, or columnar in form.
Varieties
- *Picea,* Alberta or Alberta spruce: conical dwarf with medium green needles.
- *Picea mariana nana* or nest black spruce: mound-shaped with short, light gray-green needles.
- *Picea pungens* or dwarf blue spruce: conical dwarf with blue needles.
- *Picea pungens globosa* or dwarf globe blue spruce: globe-shaped dwarf, with silvery blue needles.

Pinus or Pine

Outdoor planting time: Spring or fall.
Light: Full sun or partial shade.
Soil: Ordinary.
Moisture: Drought resistant when established, but water regularly during summer drought.

Description: Various shades of green and blue-green, mound-shaped, colum-nar, pendulous, or conical.

Varieties

• *Pinus pumila* or dwarf Siberian stone pine: spreading habit; needles light blue-green to blue.

• *Pinus strobus,* Nana or dwarf white pine: feathery needles.

• *Pinus strobus,* Ontario or dwarf Ontario white pine: irregular-shaped, spreading habit.

• *Pinus sylvestris,* Waterei or dwarf Scotch pine: Compact, slow-growing form of scotch pine; conical when young, becoming rounded with age.

Taxus or Yew

Outdoor planting time: Spring or fall.

Light: Full sun or partial shade.

Soil: Ordinary.

Moisture: Drought resistant when established, but water regularly during summer drought.

Description: Medium to deep green needles on columnar, moundlike, or globular plants.

Varieties

• *Taxus,* Aurea Nana or golden dwarf yew: bright yellow-green foliage.

• *Taxus densiformis* or spreading Japanese yew: mound-shaped, with me-dium green needles.

• *Taxus fairview* or Fairview yew: globular and compact in growth habit.

Tsuga canadensis or Sargent Weeping Hemlock

Outdoor planting time: Spring or fall.

Light: Full sun or partial shade.

Soil: Ordinary.

Moisture: Drought resistant when established, but water regularly during summer drought.

Description: Fine needles of medium green color.

Tips: Pendula or Sargent weeping hemlock is one of the most beautiful of all evergreens; with a graceful pendulous growth habit, reaching around 4 feet in height and spreading to 6 or more feet.

The Lawn or Ground Cover Option

Next to selecting permanent trees for your landscape, choosing the material for and determining the extent of your lawn are probably the most important decisions you will have to make regarding your property. Of course we've all seen photographs of vast sweeping lawns in England and Ireland—emerald greenswards, cooling to the eye, the perfect setting for outdoor living and entertaining, adding untold elegance to any property. And we've probably all dreamed of having such lawns surrounding our houses. Keep in mind, however, that the climate in Britain is ideal for growing lawns. Summers are not too hot, and there is usually sufficient rainfall to keep the grass a rich green all summer long. Furthermore, many of those lawns are scores, if not hundreds of years, old. The grass is so thick that weeds simply do not grow.

Be advised right from the start that a "dream lawn" is very expensive to install and to maintain. Here's what is involved:

● It must be *dethatched* each spring; that is, raked vigorously to remove dead grass and other organic matter. If thatch is thick, this entails either buying or renting a dethatching machine.
● It must be reseeded in spring, and often in fall as well, to fill in bare spots.
● Almost all lawns become acidic and must be treated with lime each spring to lower a high acid rate, inhospitable to growing a beautiful lawn.
● The lawn must be treated with preemergent weed killers, most of which are toxic. It must also be fed with chemical fertilizers. To treat your lawn with these, you must purchase a spreader to scatter the chemicals properly.
● The lawn must be mowed at least once a week, and sometimes twice a week, from the end of April to the end of October. This, of course, involves purchasing a mower, or in the case of larger lawns, a small tractor, which will cost at least $1,000. You must have this machine serviced regularly, and these days, some mowers are so complex that only trained (i.e., expensive) mechanics can fix them if they break down. And they will break down, just as surely as your automobile will. If you don't have the time or inclination to mow yourself, you will have to hire someone to do this for you, if you can find someone who shows up on a regular basis. This can cost you up to four or five hundred dollars a season.
● Leaves must be raked from the lawn in the fall.

● During summer drought, it must be watered regularly, often entailing the expense of installing a sprinkler system.

And that is just the beginning! All of the above additives ultimately may *poison*, yes *poison*, the pure water table, perhaps nature's most precious gift to us. In environmental terms "dream lawns" make no sense at all in this country.

Before you consider installing a "dream lawn," please write to the Bio-Integral Resource Center, a group formed in 1979, which publishes information on many aspects of environmentally sound pest control. A recent bulletin, "Least Toxic Lawn Management," contains a collection of published articles on the subject. It costs $5.75, postpaid. Another organization that is monitoring pesticide use is the National Coalition Against the Misuse of Pesticides, 530 Seventh Street, S.E., Washington, D.C. 20003. Membership costs $10 and includes a subscription to a newsletter published five times a year. Included is information on nontoxic lawn control.

So then, there are the facts. Think once, think twice, think ten times about whether or not you really want to spend all of that time and money maintaining your "dream lawn," and, more to the point, whether or not you wish to assume the responsibility of helping to pollute the environment.

I do have a lawn—more precisely, a green area—which I am slowly but surely, year in and year out, transforming into gardens and borders and replacing with ground covers. As far as I am concerned, if what I have left is green, that's fine with me, crabgrass and weeds notwithstanding. I don't panic when a dandelion grows in the grass; in fact, I rather enjoy their bright yellow blossoms here and there in my green area. I do fill in bare spots with grass seed in spring, but I add nothing to the soil. I do have to have it mowed, but less and less each year. My ultimate aim is to do away completely with the lawn, installing more ground cover, more borders, and more brick, stone, and wood chip–mulched surfaces. I know people of substantial means who employ armies of lawn experts to help maintain their lawns. After a few years, even they generally throw up their hands and begin to convert to low-maintenance ground cover and various natural surfaces other than grass.

In addition to all of the negative aspects of lawns just described, think of the time you will save by planning a very small lawn, reducing the size of your existing lawn, or doing away with your lawn altogether. All of this extra time can be applied to maintaining perennial borders, vegetable gardens, and other aspects of your landscape. And don't let anyone tell you that a beautiful lawn is more gratifying than a magnificent border of flowers, or homegrown, flavor-filled, fresh vegetables. It isn't, believe me. In summary, you have four options:

1. Install a "dream lawn." This is extremely expensive, time consuming, and potentially harmful to the environment.
2. Install a "green area." This is quite inexpensive, minimally time consuming, and safe for the environment.
3. Install substantial amounts of ground cover and natural surfaces such as brick, stone, slate, and wood chips. This is moderately expensive, but once installed, these materials are virtually self-maintaining and are safe for the environment.
4. Install a very small "dream lawn" or a small "green area" along with substantial areas of ground cover and natural surfaces.

I recently bought a new house and there is no lawn planted or I bought an older house and the lawn, or what is left of it, needs complete replanting. What should I do? Assuming that you have made a decision about how much lawn, if any, you need or want, and assuming that you want either a play area for children or a green area for adults, you have two options. For instant gratification, you can install sod. Sod is sold in the form of rolls or pieces of earth with grass growing from them. To install sod, you prepare the soil and then lay the sod on top of it, watering it regularly while the roots of the grass grow from the pieces of sod into the soil. Sod is generally not sold in retail outlets but is available only through landscape contractors. This usually means you must hire a landscape contractor to install it. (This is advisable in any event, as landscape contractors have the experience and expertise to install sod properly.) You will save yourself a great deal of time, energy, and ultimately money if you take this route. You can do this at any time during the growing season, as long as you maintain a regular watering schedule as the sod becomes established.

The other option is to prepare the soil surface and plant grass seed. This also takes a great deal of time, energy, and expertise and is also best left to professional landscape contractors. It is a very complicated task involving aerating, and probably rototilling the soil, feeding it with fertilizer, applying preemergent weed killer, spreading the seed, and tamping the soil with a heavy roller. All of the implements essential for installation must either be purchased or rented to plant grass seed properly. New lawns should be installed in spring or fall, not in summer.

What if you are determined to install a new lawn yourself? It is impossible to advise you about which kind of grass-seed mixture you can plant, since there are scores of blends, or combinations, of grasses that are custom mixed for the various climatic regions of the country. I suggest you go to your local garden center or nursery and ask for free pamphlets offered by the various lawn seed companies. These pamphlets offer complete installation instructions. Also ask the proprietor for advice about your project. Then call or visit your County Cooperative Extension Service and ask their advice about which kinds of grass mixtures are best for your area. You can also ask their advice about how to prepare the soil for seeding.

My property already has an established lawn that is in reasonably good shape but in need of some renovation. What should I do? Renovating an established lawn is a task you can take on yourself, but do this in *spring* or *fall* only! The procedure is as follows:

- Deeply scratch all bare spots with a cultivator—a long-handled garden tool that you can purchase at nurseries or garden centers and that is essential for doing all kinds of tasks around the garden.
- Work well-rotted compost, or dried cow or sheep manure, available at garden centers and nurseries, into the scratched areas.
- Seek advice from your local garden center or County Cooperative Extension Service about which grass blend is appropriate for the area of your property you wish to reseed.
- When you have selected the appropriate seed, hand sprinkle it on the scratched surface at the rate recommended on the package.
- Tamp the soil firmly with your feet or with a homemade tamper. You can make this tool by nailing a flat piece of wood about one foot square to a four-foot-high two-by-four.
- Water the area thoroughly with your hose set at spray or misting level. Do not water with the full force of the hose or the seed will wash away or gather in little grooves of the soil.
- Rope off the area of newly planted seed so that you won't step on the seedlings as they germinate.
- Keep the area evenly moist during the germination period. If a spring downpour of rain is predicted, it is a good idea to throw large bed sheets over the planted area to keep the seed from washing away. The sheets may get soiled, but they can always be laundered.
- Do not mow the area until the newly planted seed is at least 1½ inches high.
- Keep the area well watered during summer drought.

What should I do each year to maintain my lawn? You can hire a lawn maintenance service to tend to feeding, aerating, removing thatch, and killing weeds. If you do, be sure to check with them to find out exactly what chemicals they use in the process. Then call your County Cooperative Extension Service to ascertain whether or not these chemicals can be harmful to the environment. If you want to avoid using harmful chemicals to maintain your lawn, start by mowing high—that is, set the mower so that it cuts the grass two and a half to three inches high. The tall grass will smother out the weeds. Here are some other things you can do to maintain your lawn without the use of dangerous chemicals:

- Each spring, using a metal lawn rake or a strong bamboo rake, available at garden centers and nurseries, remove thatch (dead grass and other organic matter that has gathered on the soil surface during fall and winter) from lawn.
- Reseed bare areas as described above, in both spring and fall.
- Water thoroughly during drought periods to keep grass growing strongly, thus choking out weeds.
- Rake all leaves off the lawn in fall.
- Learn to enjoy the dandelions and buttercups that will inevitably grow in your lawn during spring.

What are ground covers? Where should I use them? Ground covers are plants that are low-growing, perennial (that is, they come up year in and year out, surviving winter cold), and virtually maintenance free. They cover bare areas, rapidly eliminating almost all possibility of weed growth. There are many varieties of ground cover that you can use instead of lawn. They are ideal for hilly slopes that are difficult to mow, for shady areas, where grass often won't grow, for filling in between shrub plantings, and for providing large green areas in lieu of grass.

How can I extend the use of ground cover, thus cutting down on lawn area? There are many ways you can do this. Here are just a few:

- Make foundation plantings and shrub borders twice the width as usual.
- Create islands of shrubs surrounded by ground cover in the middle of your lawn.
- Create large, informal beds of ground cover greenery under trees.
- Convert your front yard to a garden of shrubs, trees, and ground cover without any lawn. You probably don't use your front yard for

leisure or entertaining, so why not eliminate the lawn here? Install stepping-stone paths throughout the area to provide for strolling or maintenance.

- In short, use ground cover in any area of your property. If you wish to use a given area for outdoor living, simply install a flagstone, brick, or shredded cedar or pine bark surface and surround it with ground cover and other plantings.

Read through the ground cover encyclopedia that follows and select various plants appropriate to the areas you want to cover. Purchase plants either from a local nursery or garden center or from a mail-order nursery. Consult with friends and neighbors and ask if they have supplies of ground covers that they can give you. Many varieties, such as pachysandra and ajuga, are so widely planted that you will probably find someone who will let you thin out their plantings and take what you wish. Then prepare the soil. Dig to a depth of about six to eight inches, and work in about a bushel of rotted compost, sphagnum peat moss, or well-rotted sheep or cow manure for every one hundred square feet of area. Dig holes, plant ground cover, and keep them well watered until established. Then sit back, enjoy the planting, and forget about mowing and maintaining those areas of your property for the rest of your life.

Ground Cover Encyclopedia

Ajuga reptans or Carpet Bugle, Zones 4–10

Outdoor planting time: Spring or fall.
Light: Sun or shade.
Soil: Ordinary.
Moisture: Drought resistant, but water regularly during summer drought.
Bloom time: Spring and summer.
Description: Evergreen foliage with small, violet-blue blossoms.
Height: Foliage about 6 inches, flower spikes 6–9 inches.
Tips: Spreads rapidly and vigorously by runners underground. There are many varieties, including a variegated variety with white and deep green foliage. A good selection for deep shade.

Arctostaphylos uva-ursi or Bearberry,
Zones 3–7

Outdoor planting time: Spring or fall.
Light: Sun or partial shade.
Soil: Ordinary.
Moisture: Drought resistant, but water regularly during summer drought.
Bloom time: Midspring.
Description: Evergreen foliage is dark green, leathery, and dense. White to light pink clusters of urn-shaped blossoms.
Tips: Grows densely, spreading to about 15 feet and rooting along branches. Foliage turns red in winter. Ideal for flat areas or slopes.

Cotoneaster conspicuus, Decorus or Necklace Cotoneaster,
Zones 6–10

Outdoor planting time: Spring or fall.
Light: Full sun.
Soil: Ordinary.
Moisture: Drought resistant.
Bloom time: White or pink blooms in spring, with red berries in fall, often lasting well into winter.
Description: Low-spreading evergreen foliage close to the ground.
Tips: An excellent choice for sunny areas.

Cotoneaster dammeri or Bearberry Cotoneaster,
Zones 5–10

Outdoor planting time: Spring or fall.
Light: Full sun.
Soil: Ordinary.
Moisture: Drought resistant.
Bloom time: White or pink blooms in spring with red berries in fall, often lasting well into winter.
Description: 6-inch-high evergreen foliage.
Tips: Spreads rapidly. A good selection for a new landscape.

Cotoneaster horizontalis or Rock Cotoneaster, Zones 5–9

Outdoor planting time: Spring or fall.
Light: Full sun.
Soil: Ordinary.
Moisture: Drought resistant.
Bloom time: White or pink blooms in spring with red berries in fall, often lasting well into winter.
Description: May grow to a height of 3 feet, spreading to 15 feet.
Tips: Spreads rapidly. An excellent choice for slopes, but because of its ultimate height, not recommended for areas where low-growing ground covers are required.

Euonymous fortunei radicans or Common Winter Creeper, Zones 5–9

Outdoor planting time: Spring or fall.
Light: Sun or shade.
Soil: Ordinary.
Moisture: Drought resistant.
Bloom time: Grown for foliage only.
Description: Glossy, deep green leaves, sometimes variegated, depending on variety.
Tips: An excellent choice for deeply shaded areas. Will attach itself to trees and climb the trunks, forming a dense mat of foliage.

Hedera baltica or Baltic Ivy, Zones 5–10

Outdoor planting time: Spring or fall.
Light: Sun or shade.
Soil: Ordinary.
Moisture: Drought resistant.
Bloom time: Grown for foliage only.
Description: Quick spreading foliage.
Tips: Hardier than *Hedera helix* and recommended for zone 5.

Hedera helix or *English Ivy, Zones* 6–10

Outdoor planting time: Spring or fall.
Light: Sun or shade.
Soil: Ordinary.
Moisture: Drought resistant.
Bloom time: Grown for foliage only.
Description: There are many varieties available, in many shades of green, some variegated with white and yellow coloration.
Tips: Most ivies need winter protection from zone 5 northward, so do not select this ground cover if you live in these areas.

Iberis sempervirens or *Candytuft, Zones* 4–10

Outdoor planting time: Spring or fall.
Light: Sun or shade.
Soil: Ordinary.
Moisture: Drought resistant, but water regularly during summer drought.
Bloom time: May.
Description: Evergreen, needlelike foliage covered with 1-inch clusters of white blooms in spring. A large planting can be a beautiful spectacle.
Tips: An excellent selection because of its blooms, which provide a lovely backdrop for spring-blooming bulbs and shrubs. Can be grown from seed.

Juniperis or *Juniper, Zones* 3–10 *depending on variety*

Outdoor planting time: Spring or fall.
Light: Sun or shade.
Soil: Ordinary.
Moisture: Drought resistant.
Bloom time: Grown for foliage only.
Description: Evergreen in various green or blue shades.
Tips: Many varieties are suitable for ground cover. Almost indestructible: resists disease, drought, and neglect. See the evergreen encyclopedia (p. 81) for further recommendations.

Lonicera japonica, Halliana or Hall's Honeysuckle, Zones 4–10

Outdoor planting time: Spring or fall.
Light: Sun.
Moisture: Drought resistant.
Bloom time: June.
Description: The familiar honeysuckle, with its lovely fragrant blooms on deciduous vines bearing small green leaves.
Tips: Honeysuckle is invasive, spreading everywhere by underground runners. Not recommended unless you want a completely wild area on your property.

Pachysandra, Zones 5–8

Outdoor planting time: Spring, summer, or fall.
Light: Shade.
Moisture: Water regularly during summer drought. Leaves will tell you if the plant needs water, as they wilt.
Bloom time: Midspring.
Description: Evergreen foliage up to 12 inches long with insignificant clusters of white flowers in spring.
Tips: Always one of the best ground covers for shade. Not invasive, evergreen, blends perfectly with broad-leaved evergreens. Spring-blooming bulbs can be underplanted for a lovely green carpet background to their color. Despite the fact that some consider it a cliché, for my money pachysandra is still the best of the shade ground covers. Once established, it requires no maintenance whatsoever.

Potentilla or Cinquefoil, Zones 4–8

Outdoor planting time: Spring or fall.
Light: Shade.
Moisture: Water regularly during summer drought.
Bloom time: Late spring, early summer.
Description: Shiny, toothed, evergreen leaves spread rapidly by strawberrylike runners. Small yellow blooms.
Tips: Plant under trees or shrubs or as a ground cover for bulb plantings.

Sedum, Zones 4–10 depending on variety

Outdoor planting time: Spring or fall.
Light: Full sun.
Moisture: Drought resistant.
Bloom time: Spring to fall, depending on variety.
Description: Low-growing succulent plants in many varieties. Blossoms range from white, to yellow, orange, pink, or red.
Tips: Recommended for difficult full-sun areas.

Vinca or Creeping Myrtle, Zones 4–10

Outdoor planting time: Spring, summer, or fall.
Light: Sun or shade.
Moisture: Drought resistant.
Bloom time: Early to late spring.
Description: Deep green evergreen foliage with purple or white flowers in spring.
Tips: My pet hate. If planted in sun, it will take over the entire garden. Weeds grow through it, necessitating constant weeding. In desperation, I finally dug out a large planting of creeping myrtle and disposed of it. It is less rampant in shade, and weeds tend not to grow through it under this light condition.

The Permanent Vegetable Garden

Last year you installed a vegetable garden in a temporary location. If the location was suitable, it is time to install it there permanently. If not, select the spot that you now feel is appropriate for convenience and aesthetics. If the original location was suitable, you need not prepare soil or install fencing, as you have already done these tasks, although you might decide that you want to install a more permanent type of fence. You might have discovered that your garden was not large enough to accommodate all that you wished to grow. If so, now is the time to enlarge it. If it was too large, make it smaller.

If the original location was not suitable, you will have to reread the vegetable section in chapter 1 and once again fortify the soil and install a fence. Whether or not you relocate your vegetable garden, be a little more adventurous this year in selecting which vegetables you grow. Try something you've never grown or eaten before.

Asparagus

Now that you've decided on the permanent location for your vegetable garden, it is time to plant asparagus, a perennial vegetable. Asparagus, considered by many to be the king of vegetables, is among the first of the spring vegetables to appear. Top-quality asparagus requires a climate with winters cold enough to freeze at least several inches of the ground, so the Northeast, Mid-Atlantic, Midwest, and Rocky Mountain areas of the country are suitable, while the Deep South, Southwest, and southern California are not. In the South, asparagus is likely to grow in areas such as the mountainous regions of Virginia, the Carolinas, Georgia, Alabama, and Kentucky.

For a family of five or six, a fifty- to seventy-five-foot row, two rows thirty to thirty-five feet, or a twenty-by-twenty-foot plot is large enough for a good supply of the vegetable. For two or three people, use rows or plots half as large as the above. It takes two years to bring a new asparagus bed to maturity. Here's how you do it.

Where do I buy asparagus plants? Although you can start asparagus plants from seed, you'll get quicker and more satisfactory results if you buy one-year-old plants from a garden center or a mail-order nursery. Plants are usually available from mid-March to late April. When you purchase plants, check to see that the roots and crowns, the part of the plant where roots originate, are not dried out. Good-quality plants should have a root spread of fifteen inches or more. If you buy plants through the mail, order by February, since March is the proper planting time in many parts of the country.

Which varieties of asparagus should I buy? For years, Mary Washington and Waltham Washington, both of which have been bred to resist asparagus rust, a fungus disease that can severely cripple plants, were the old standbys. However, in the past few years some new hybrids have been introduced. These produce larger crops of the vegetable and are even more rust resistant than the two Washington varieties. Jersey Centennial is one of the newer varieties recommended.

How do I install an asparagus bed? The initial preparation is the most important part of putting in asparagus. It requires a lot of work, but once in place, your asparagus bed will produce for fifteen to twenty-five years. Select a spot in full sun with well-drained soil. In the spring, as soon as the soil can be worked, dig a row eighteen inches wide by fifteen inches deep. Since asparagus requires a very fertile loam, fortify the excavated soil by mixing it with organic matter (compost, well-rotted manure, leaf mold, sphagnum peat moss, dried cow manure, or a combination) in a ratio of about three parts soil to one part organic matter. Also mix in a complete fertilizer such as 5-10-5, using one pound of fertilizer per seven feet of row. If you opt for an organic mix (see p. 19), incorporate about two pounds per seven feet of row. Refill the trench until it is eight inches below ground level. Leave the remaining fortified soil beside the trench for later use.

Next, place the crowns of the plants one and a half feet apart in the rows, and spread the roots around. Cover the crowns with two inches of fortified soil. Press the soil firmly over the plants, and water thoroughly. As the plants grow, gradually add fortified soil around them every week or two. In about three months, the trench should be filled.

Can I cut asparagus the first year after planting? Although for years it was thought that you could not cut asparagus the first year after planting, recent research at a number of universities has indicated that, in fact, it is a good idea to do so, but only for two weeks—from the time the first spears appear. It has been found that early cutting actually spurs strong growth. To cut asparagus, wait until the spears are about eight inches high; then, using a razor-sharp knife, cut every spear, even those that are not of edible size.

How do I maintain my asparagus bed the first year? During the first year, keep the bed well watered during hot, dry, summer weather. Also, be sure to weed from the beginning. At the end of the growing season, remove and dispose of the tops of the plants that have been nipped by frost, since they may harbor the spotted or common asparagus beetle (a metallic blue or black insect with orange or yellow markings). Adult beetles gnaw on plants and shoots, and larvae often attack crowns and berries. If asparagus beetles attack your plants, pick the bugs off or spray the plants thoroughly with 5 percent rotenone WP (five tablespoons to one gallon of water). One or two applications are usually sufficient.

What do I do to my asparagus bed the second year? In early spring, before growth starts, clean up any debris on the surface of the soil. Then fertilize by gently scratching into the soil surface either one pound of 5-10-5 fertilizer per seven feet of row or two pounds of homemade organic fertilizer. Top the bed with a two-inch mulch of organic matter such as well-rotted compost. During hot dry spells, water plants thoroughly. Remove any weeds and cut off all stalks that produce berries just below the berry line, so that the energy of the plant will go into developing a strong root system. At the end of the season, remove and dispose of any tops that have been nipped by frost.

How long can I cut asparagus the second year after planting? Here again, new information reveals that you can cut during the entire season, from mid- to late-April, when the spears first appear above ground, until July fourth, the usual cut-off date for asparagus picking.

How do I maintain my asparagus bed after that? Keep it well watered during summer drought, feed it in early spring as described above, and remove weeds as they grow. Watch for asparagus beetles and take steps to eliminate them. Cut and dispose of tops that have been nipped by frost at the end of the season. If you maintain your asparagus faithfully, you should be able to harvest asparagus for the next twenty years or so.

Chapter Three

◆

THE THIRD YEAR

Patios

The Near Foolproof Jewels of Spring: Dutch Bulbs

The Early-Blooming Bulbs

Last year you installed the trees and shrubs you decided you wanted, selected a permanent location for your vegetable garden, and installed your lawn area or ground cover. This spring, if any of your trees or shrubs failed to live through the winter, you will have to replace them. If your stock was guaranteed through the winter by either a mail-order source or a local nursery or garden center, contact them for replacement. If not, you will have to seek advice about whether or not the tree or shrub was appropriate for your climate zone, and then determine whether the stock was unhealthy or whether you did not provide proper maintenance. In any case, replace those trees or shrubs that did not survive the winter.

If possible, prepare your vegetable garden as early in the spring as possible by turning over the soil and working in compost. Reseed bare spots on your lawn or green area. By now you should have a good idea about where you want to install your patio or outdoor living area. If not, decide upon it now, as this is a third-year project. Continue to think in terms of annual flowering plants for color during the course of the year, as the installation of perennial plants will not be scheduled until next year. And all during the spring or summer, start taking notes on where you might want to plant spring-blooming bulbs such as daffodils and tulips, for this is a third-year project you will do in the fall.

Patios

Assuming that you have moved chairs and tables around for two years and determined exactly where you wish to place your patio or outdoor living area, it is time to make decisions about how and when to do it. As far as the installation goes, you have two options: do it yourself or hire a landscape contractor to do it for you. Certainly one factor in creating a successful landscape is knowing your limitations; that is, knowing what you can handle and what you can't. When it comes to patios, this decision is largely determined by what kind of materials you wish to install on the ground. Some types of outdoor flooring are easy to install; others require the expertise of an experienced carpenter or mason.

What is the first thing I should do when deciding upon installing a patio? First, read this section. Then, because there are so many different kinds of flooring you can put down, and because the instructions for installing each are complicated, requiring one or more books on that subject alone, buy a book on patios and their installation or take one out of the library.

From a purely practical point of view, what is the most important thing I should consider? Drainage is the most import aspect of patio installation. Some materials, such as brick laid in sand, wood decking, gravel, or stones or slate laid in sand, allow water to seep through to the ground. This is particularly important if you have a lovely flowering or shade tree near the patio, since the roots of the trees will have access to necessary moisture. Other materials, such as concrete, brick laid in mortar, or tile laid in mortar, do not allow water to seep through to the ground. In addition, water will gather on such a surface after it rains unless the surface is sloped to provide drainage.

What is the easiest kind of flooring to install if I plan on doing it myself? Brick, stones, or slate in sand are the easiest materials to install and require no special expertise. However, you must provide a bed of sand for the surface and install heavy-gauge plastic to prevent weeds from growing through. This is easily done. I include brief instructions here for installing a brick-in-sand patio, so that you will have some idea of how to do it. However, you should consult a book on patio surfaces for further information. First, dig to a depth of about eight inches and lay down heavy-gauge plastic (available at garden centers, hardware stores, and nurseries) over the entire surface you wish to pave. Then spread about four inches of builder's sand on top of the plastic. Moisten the sand thoroughly, then tamp it down using a two-by-four. Using a level placed on top of the two-by-four, make sure the sand surface is absolutely level. It is best to install the edges of the flooring first to create a framework within which you can work. By doing this you avoid laying too many bricks in any one course. You can use half bricks set on end to do this. Lay these bricks on the bed of sand so that the tops will be one inch above the horizontal brick flooring.

Completely enclose the flooring area with the edging. Then set the bricks horizontally in place on top of the bed of sand, leaving about one-quarter inch between each one. There are many patterns of brickwork you can use. The most common are herringbone (which is somewhat complicated for a nonprofessional bricklayer to achieve), running bond, Flemish bond, and basket weave. Consult a book on patio installation for further information on various brick patterns. Once you have laid down the bricks pour dry sand on top. Then, with a broom, sweep the sand into the grooves between the bricks. Water it down with a fine spray from a hose until all the sand in the grooves has settled. Then fill in low spots with more sand if necessary.

What other kinds of flooring are easy to install? Any kind of flooring set in sand is fairly easy to install. Wooden decking is somewhat more complicated, but if you have had some experience with building things out of wood, you may find you can handle it. If you decide on this kind of flooring, you must use *treated* lumber, available at lumberyards.

What kinds of surfaces are difficult for an amateur to install? Any kind of surface set in concrete is complicated; installation of such surface is best left to a professional mason. Consult a book on patio installation for further information.

If I decide to install a brick- or stone-on-sand flooring, what can I do about weeds growing in the cracks between the bricks or stones? There is a new weed killer on the market that is nonhazardous to the environment. It is called Roundup and is manufactured by the Monsanto Chemical Company. It is available in garden centers and nurseries, and next to compost and mulch it is probably the homeowner's best friend. You must purchase a spraying unit to use this product, but in terms of hours spent weeding, it is still worth every penny. This weed killer can be used all over your property—in driveways, between plants in borders, between rows in vegetable gardens—without fear of poisoning the environment.

What about selecting a patio flooring that is aesthetically pleasing and harmonizes with the architecture of my house? This, of course, is a matter of personal taste. However, there are some rough guidelines as to which surfaces go with which architectural styles. Generally speaking, wooden decking is most in harmony with contemporary architecture. Brick or stone in sand or mortar work well with traditional architecture, either American

Colonial, or Victorian. Concrete must be used very carefully and should be combined with other materials in order to be attractive. Nothing, but nothing, is uglier than a large slab of bare concrete sitting in the middle of your landscape. Do not trust the judgment of a landscape contractor if you opt for concrete, but consult patio books for further information about using concrete with pebbles, stones, or other materials.

Once I've installed my patio, how can I dress it up? Surround your patio with a shrub border, with flowering trees, with a specimen shade tree, with annuals in the summer, with a perennial border, or with flowering bulbs in the spring. Flowering plants in containers and planters can be placed here and there as well as small specimen trees in containers. When you select furniture for your patio, try to make it blend in with the architecture of the house. For example, redwood furniture does not work well with an American Colonial or Victorian house. Very sleek, modern outdoor furniture works best with contemporary architecture. Until you install a permanent outdoor grill or barbecue pit (which you might wish to do a year or so down the line), a simple hibachi, very inexpensive and available at home improvement centers and discount stores, is perfectly adequate for outdoor cooking. More complicated units that work on bottled gas or electricity are also available.

I did as you said and planted a tree for shade near my patio area, but it is not big enough to provide shade. What should I do? Purchase a table with a large umbrella over it. These tables are attractive, dress up the grounds, and provide the necessary shade.

The Near Foolproof Jewels of Spring: Dutch Bulbs

Among the most foolproof plantings you can install in your landscape are spring-blooming Dutch bulbs, both the well-known "major" bulbs—daffodils, tulips, hyacinths, and crocuses—and the often overlooked "minor" bulbs —scilla, muscari or grape hyacinth, galanthus or snowdrop, species tulips and crocuses, minidaffodils, chionodoxa or glory-of-the-snow, and others.

These bulbs are virtually insect and disease free, and they require little maintenance beyond soil preparation at fall planting time and some annual feeding. And every year, from the first spring on, most bulbs reward you with a dazzling display of glorious color. What is more, most multiply freely, so that after five years, should you care to create more bulb displays on your property, you can do so simply by digging after bloom, dividing the bulb clump, and replanting.

Where can I buy bulbs? Toward the end of summer and into the fall, nurseries, garden centers, and many supermarkets sell bulbs. However, their selection may be limited. Many mail-order nurseries offer a wider selection. Simply write for their free catalogues (see p. 248) and then order. It is a good idea to write for catalogues by June and to place your order by the end of July or early August. In this way, you will be assured of getting what you want, avoiding the disappointment of desired varieties being sold out. Most mail-order nurseries deliver bulbs at the proper planting time.

Where can I plant bulbs? You can install a bulb planting virtually anywhere you want spring color: in flower beds and borders, interplanted among foundation plantings, along driveways and walks, around mailboxes and bird baths, naturalized (planted informally, as in nature) in fields, under deciduous trees, or in the woods. Use your imagination and install them anywhere you want, but keep the following aesthetic guidelines in mind:

- Always plant at least twelve of the major bulbs together, preferably all the same color. It is best to plant twenty-four if your budget permits. In this way, your planting will make a statement. Fewer bulbs tend to get lost in the landscape. "Minor" bulbs should be planted in groups of no less than fifty, preferably one hundred, or they too will be lost.
- Never buy a rainbow mixture of bulbs. The result at bloom time will be a hodgepodge of color, ineffective and often messy looking.
- Avoid planting in a straight line or in a single circle around a tree or bush, for the result will look unnatural.
- When planning a bulb scheme, concentrate on two or three colors in each location, but do not mix them together. For example, a cluster or drift of violet-colored tulips next to a drift of yellow and a drift of white tulips looks more harmonious than one cluster each of violet, orange, red, pink, yellow, and white.
- Decide whether you want a formal or informal looking bulb garden and then stick to your decision. Keep in mind that an informal garden is asymmetrical and is thus more appropriate for the majority of res-

idences. Few of us live in houses so stately that a formal planting is called for.

- Remember that hyacinths and certain tulips—tall Darwin, Lily-Flowering, Cottage, Triumph, and Darwin Hybrid—are stately, formal, and somewhat rigid in appearance, so use them sparingly unless you want a very formal look. Species tulips, daffodils, and the "minor" bulbs are often better suited to an informal planting.
- Consider the landscape not only from the outdoor point of view, but from indoors, through windows. Since bulbs begin blooming in late February and continue on through the spring, plan your outdoor plantings of early-blooming bulbs so that you can enjoy them from inside as well as outside. Chances are that with late winter and early spring cold and rain, you won't be spending too much time outdoors enjoying your garden.
- For displays in distant parts of your property, plant large groups of a single variety of bulbs in drifts rather than in symmetrical beds. The effect is more natural looking and creates an eye-catching display.
- Although not of an aesthetic nature, this tip will prove invaluable: Beware of bargains. Bulbs are quite inexpensive, and bargain collections are usually of inferior quality. As a rule, with almost all planting stock, you get what you pay for. There are, however, two exceptions to this rule. Many mail-order bulb suppliers offer mixtures of daffodils for naturalizing at reduced prices. These are certainly worth the money *if* you plan to naturalize them in meadows, woods, or under deciduous trees. The other exception is end-of-season sales at nurseries and garden centers. Individual varieties of bulbs are often reduced in price toward the middle of November. Since there is still time to plant, you might wish to consider buying some of these to fill in your landscape several years after your initial planting. But don't avail yourself of these bargains when installing your initial bed, as the selection is usually quite limited and has been picked over by others earlier in the season.

Where in the country can I plant bulbs? Consult the Climatic Zone Map on page xiv to see which zone you live in. Then refer to the zone indications at the beginning of each individual bulb entry below to see if that particular bulb is recommended in your region. Note that the very warm and very cold areas of the United States and Canada are often inappropriate for some bulb varieties. Most bulbs need a period of cold to develop roots, while others are too tender for extreme cold.

How do I select a site for a bulb planting? Your first consideration is light. Most bulbs require either full sun or partial shade in order to perform well. Very few thrive in deep shade, so avoid areas under evergreen trees, foundation plantings with northern exposures, and other areas of little sunlight. The next thing to consider is drainage. All bulbs require good drainage to grow properly. Beyond the obvious—that is, swampy soil or areas where water gathers and remains after rain—you can easily test a planting site for proper drainage. Dig a hole to the depth at which the bulbs will be planted—usually eight to twelve inches. Fill the hole with water. Allow the water to soak in. Repeat this two more times. After the third time, let the water sit for six to eight hours. If it remains after that, drainage is not sufficient for growing bulbs, and you should select another site for the planting. Unless there is air in the soil, bulbs will rot, and there is no air in waterlogged soil.

How do I plan my bulb planting? As always in planning a landscape, it is best to work out your scheme on graph paper. Using a scale of one block on the graph paper to two inches of garden space, sketch out the area you wish to plant. Now let your imagination have free reign. Here are a few points to remember:

- Tall-growing varieties are generally best placed to the rear of the bed, with shorter varieties to the front.
- Consult the bloom sequence chart (p. 152) to see if the varieties you wish to plant bloom at the same time or in sequence. For example, you will see on the chart that *muscari* or grape hyacinths bloom at the same time as most daffodils. The deep blue of the grape hyacinths and the yellow of the daffodils are very beautiful in combination. Purple crocuses on the other hand, would bloom well in advance of the yellow daffodils, so that combination would be impracticable. In mail-order bulb catalogues you will often see photographs of a wide variety of bulbs all in bloom at the same time. These photos are misleading: the growers force some later-blooming varieties to bloom early. Regardless of what you may see in a photograph, crocuses do not bloom at the same time as Darwin tulips, but from six to eight weeks earlier.
- One way to ensure an effective bloom sequence in the same location is to overplant. You do this by planting two varieties that bloom in sequence together, one on top of another. Early-blooming bulbs are smaller in stature and bloom than most later varieties and require

149

shallower planting. Thus, if you are installing some standard daffodils or May-flowering tulips, for example, plant them first at the recommended six-inch depth. Fill in the excavation to a depth of two inches, and then plant crocuses, snowdrops, scilla, or other early-blooming bulbs at that level. Finally, fill in to the surrounding soil surface.

- If you are planning on mixing vivid colored tulips, you might invest in a child's paint box and paint in the colors on your graph-paper scheme. This will help you avoid clashing colors and achieve a more pleasing final effect.

- When you are ready to plant, take your chart to the garden with you to use as a guide. Avoid last-minute changes, for they are almost always dead wrong.

How do I prepare the soil? Soil types range from very sandy and light to very heavy and clayey, not only from one part of the country to another, but even within a given property. If any given soil lacks organic matter, and thus nutrients for plants, success will be limited. For this reason, whenever you install a planting of any kind, it is a good idea to fortify and prepare the soil. This holds true for bulbs as well as other planting material. While soil fortification does require some work, it will definitely help ensure results. And, considering that you are planning your landscape for years to come, the effort will soon be amortized.

First, excavate the bed to a depth of one foot. Then mix the excavated soil with organic material such as sphagnum peat moss and/or well-rotted manure or compost, in a ratio of two parts soil to one part organic material. Never use fresh manure, as it can burn tender roots. Then replace the mixture into the excavated bed. Water thoroughly. It is best to do this several days in advance of your planting schedule.

How do I plant bulbs? Assuming that you have designed your scheme, ordered the bulbs, selected the appropriate site, and fortified the planting bed, it is time to plant your bulb garden. When you go to the garden to plant the bulbs, be sure to bring a ruler with you so that you can measure the appropriate depth and spacing of bulbs. Be sure you have your design scheme with you as well. Aside from the bulbs, you will need fertilizer. For many years it was universally thought that all-purpose 5-10-5 fertilizer and bonemeal were the best foods for bulbs. However, recent research conducted by the bulb industry has revealed that adding bonemeal is a waste of time and money. It is now believed that a fertilizer with a 9-9-6 ratio of nitrogen, phosphorus, and potassium secures the best results. This fertilizer, called Holland Bulb Booster, is available at many nurseries and garden centers, as well as from mail-order supply houses. As a general rule, before planting, dig a hole twice as deep as the recommended depth for a particular bulb. Mix the fertilizer with the soil in a ratio of one tablespoon per square foot, three-quarters cup per ten square feet, and four cups per fifty square feet. Replace the soil to the recommended planting level. Then flatten out the bottom of the planting hole by patting it gently with your hand. This will ensure an even surface for the bulbs so they won't fall on their sides in the hole when you fill it in with soil. Set the bulbs in place with the pointed ends up and gently press them into the soil. Cover the bulbs with the rest of the soil, tamp down lightly, then water thoroughly. If there are dry spells in your area during the fall, be sure to water the planting thoroughly at least once a week. That's all there is to it.

Should I mulch my bulb planting to protect it from winter cold? In most areas of the country, a winter mulch is not necessary for bulb plantings. However, in far northern climates, zones 2 and 3, it is a good idea to apply a six-inch layer of salt hay, available at garden centers and nurseries, over the planting after the first deep frost. Remove this mulch in late winter or early spring, when the bulbs first begin to emerge from the ground.

What if there is a warm spell and my bulbs start coming up in January or February? What should I do? Nothing. The bulbs are hardy and will not be damaged by subsequent cold.

What if my early-blooming bulbs bloom and then there is snow? What should I do? Nothing. The flowers are hardy and will not be hurt by snow.

How do I maintain my bulb planting after the first season's bloom? In late winter or early spring, when the bulbs begin to emerge from the ground, apply a dusting of 9-9-6 fertilizer (Holland Bulb Booster) in the amounts recommended above. Sprinkle the fertilizer evenly on the soil surface of the bulb planting.

After the bulbs bloom, remove spent blossoms by cutting the stalks of tulips, daffodils, hyacinths, and scilla. Other bulb blossoms will wither and drop off naturally. Do *not* cut off foliage of any bulb variety, the leaves contain substantial amounts of nutrients that are needed for next year's bloom. These nutrients seep down to the bulb, replenishing it. If you cut the foliage, you will rob the plant of its natural food supply. Allow the foliage to wither and dry naturally; then you can remove it. If you find the foliage unsightly, you can either tie it up in bundles with string or rubber bands, or overplant bedding annuals in the area to hide the withering foliage and provide color during the summer. (See also the bulb overplanting section of chapter 4.)

After several years I have a lot of foliage but few flowers. What is wrong? Overcrowding is probably the reason, except in the case of tulips (see the section on tulips, pp. 167–72). If bloom is sparse, simply dig up the clump

Bloom Sequence Chart

Below is a chart of approximate blooming dates for various bulbs in the warmer areas of zones 5 and 6 and the colder areas of zone 7. If you are in zone 4, add one week; in zone 3, add about two weeks. In zone 8, subtract one week. Although you should bear in mind that these dates are approximate, they will help you in planning a sequence of bloom.

VARIETY	BLOOM TIME
Snowdrops *(Galanthus)*	March 1–20
Crocus (species)	March 1–20
Crocus (Dutch)	March 10–25
Chionodoxa (glory-of-the-snow)	March 25–April 10
Puschkinia (Lebanon squill)	March 25–April 10
Tulip (species)	April 1–30
Scilla siberica (squill)	April 10–25
Muscari (grape hyacinth)	April 10–25
Daffodils and Narcissi	April 10–30
Hyacinths	April 15–30
Tulip: early	April 15–30
Tulip: Mendel	April 25–May 10
Tulip: Triumph	April 25–May 10
Tulip: Double Peony	April 25–May 10
Tulip: Darwin hybrid	April 25–May 10
Tulip: lily-flowering	April 25–May 10
Tulip: Darwin	May 5–20
Tulip: Cottage	May 5–20
Tulip: Parrot	May 5–20
Scilla campanulata	May 15–30

after bloom, separate the bulbs, and replant them immediately in the same or other beds. See individual entries for further information.

What about pests and diseases? Although spring-flowering bulbs are virtually insect and disease free, most are not animal or rodent proof, with the exception of all daffodils and narcissi and most scilla. The bulbs and foliage of these cultivars are poisonous to animals and rodents, so they do not nibble either above or below ground. However, all other spring-flowering bulbs are taste treats for deer, racoons, rabbits, chipmunks, and burrowing creatures such as moles and voles.

If deer and racoons are a problem, about the only thing you can do is to sprinkle dried blood meal on the shoots when they emerge. Blood meal is available at garden centers and nurseries and also serves as a fertilizer for emerging bulbs. Rabbits and chipmunks find tulips and crocuses delectable. I have found that dried blood meal deters these creatures too. Remember that you must apply blood meal after every rain. Beyond this, I have found that placing a piece of one-inch-mesh chicken wire over the entire planting helps keep rodents away. Once the emerging shoots are several inches tall, the rodents don't seem to savor them. I remove the chicken wire at this point.

Moles burrow beneath the ground and eat bulbs. They are attracted to your lawn by grubs that live beneath the surface, eating the grass roots. If you can rid your lawn of grubs, the moles will probably go away and not bother your bulb plantings. There are insecticides available at garden centers and nurseries that you can apply to your lawn to kill grubs. Check with your local County Cooperative Extension Service for information about which insecticides are recommended and/or permitted for use in your area.

Recently, there have been plagues of vole infestations in various parts of the country. These rodents eat not only bulbs but the roots of fruit trees, azaleas, evergreens, and other trees. At present, there is little that can be done to rid your property of these creatures, except keeping one of their natural enemies, cats, in and around your garden.

Inquire locally at nurseries and garden centers or from neighbors about the vole and mole problem in your area. If it is serious, run a trial planting of a few bulbs to see if the burrowing rodents are present and hungry before you install a large and expensive planting. Or plant only daffodils and scillas, which are impervious to animal and rodent damage.

When do I plant bulbs? Spring-flowering bulbs are planted the previous fall. If you order from a mail-order nursery, most will ship your bulbs at the proper planting time for your zone. If you purchase them at a nursery, inquire as to when to plant. In zones 5–7, the best time to plant is from mid-October through late November. In zone 8, you can plant into the beginning of December. In zones 4 and northward, early September through early October is a good time to plant.

What if, for some reason, I have not been able to plant my bulbs at the recommended time? Although it is not recommended for best results, as long as the ground can be dug, you can still plant bulbs. Should hard freezes be forthcoming, cover your planting area with salt hay to keep the ground from freezing hard, and plant at your earliest convenience.

The Early-Blooming Bulbs

Planting crocuses, snowdrops, scilla, chionodoxa, and other early-blooming, small-flowering bulbs is something you really do to please yourself. Viewed from a distance by passersby, these bulbs present an inconsequential display, perhaps with the exception of Dutch crocuses clustered here and there. But what a wonderful lift even a small planting next to the entrance of your house or within window view gives as it speaks brightly of spring during the dreary late February and March days. Plant all of these bulbs near the house, where you can enjoy them.

Galanthus or Snowdrops, Zones 3–9

These, along with species crocuses, are among the earliest blooming of all bulbs, appearing in late February or March in most parts of the country. The blossoms are translucent, with three green-tipped inner petals and three longer, pure white outer petals on six- to eight-inch-high stems. Slender foliage, from three to eight inches long, ripens and withers away by late spring.

Since the flowers are small and quite inconspicuous, plant snowdrops near your dooryard or in a spot where they can be seen through the window. Because of their gracefully arching stems, they are particularly effective if planted in perhaps eight to ten clusters of ten to fifteen bulbs each, with the clusters placed from four to six inches apart. In this way, each cluster resembles a small, fountainlike display. Another effective way to plant snowdrops is to naturalize the bulbs beneath deciduous trees (not under evergreens, as the shade is too dense). To create any kind of naturalized display you will need at least several hundred bulbs. Eventually they should cast their own seeds about and produce a more prolific display.

Snowdrops can generally be left undisturbed for years. If one day they should become very crowded with little bloom, dig the bulbs shortly after flowering, divide them, and replant immediately. Snow, ice, and freezing temperatures do not affect the blossoms or foliage.

HOW TO PLANT: Select a site with good drainage in full sun or partial shade. If planting in clusters, prepare soil as described above (see p. 150). Excavate to a depth of two to three inches; do *not* add fertilizer. Pat down the soil, set the bulbs in place about one inch apart, cover them with soil, tamp the soil surface, and water thoroughly. If you are naturalizing the bulbs under deciduous trees, toss the bulbs gently on the ground and plant them where they land simply by digging a hole two to three inches deep for each, covering them with soil, tamping it down, and watering thoroughly.

MAINTENANCE: After bloom, allow the foliage to ripen and wither before removing. It is not necessary to fertilize snowdrops.

TIPS: After bloom, cover bare spots with annuals or refer to chapter 4 for recommended permanent bulb overplanting varieties.

Species Crocus, Zones 3–10

This is a very early-blooming, low-growing crocus, sometimes called "snow crocus" or "early-bunching crocus," and is available in a wide range of colors: white, yellow, gold, cream, blue, lavender, purple, bronze, and combinations thereof. It blooms earlier than the more widely planted Dutch or giant crocus, and its blossoms are smaller. Along with the Dutch crocus, it is perhaps the only bulb that can produce an effective display if colors are mixed when planted. However, I feel species crocuses produce a more dramatic display when planted in irregularly shaped drifts of one variety next to a drift or several drifts of other varieties.

Keep in mind that species crocuses bloom at the end of February or the beginning of March in most areas of the country. Since the weather at this time of year does not lend itself to strolling or sitting in the garden, plant your crocuses so that they can be viewed from indoors through a window; or plant them near entrances to the house so that you and others can enjoy their welcome early color as you come and go in and out of the house. For an even earlier bloom, install species crocuses in a sheltered spot with a southern exposure, preferably in front of the wall of the house or a garden wall, should you have one. These little jewels are native to mountainous areas and are quite hardy. Do not worry if a hard frost is expected or even if there is a snowfall. Cold and ice usually will not injure the foliage or blooms.

Unless they are planted in groups of several hundred or a thousand, species crocuses generally do not produce an effective display in a distant part of the garden; the blooms are too small. Even at close range, in order to make a "statement," be sure to plant a minimum of fifty corms of each variety. (Corms are similar to bulbs, however they reform totally beneath soil during the season.) One hundred or one hundred and fifty is better. (They are relatively inexpensive.) Fewer than fifty will produce a meager display, not worth the effort of planting or the cost.

The usual recommended planting distance is two to six inches apart, but species crocuses provide the most effective display when bunched very close together, providing a cluster of color. For this reason, I suggest planting them one inch apart. I came to this conclusion through trial and error and only recently had my findings reinforced when reading Louise Beebe Wilder's *Hardy Bulbs*, first published in 1934 and to my mind still the finest book available on the aesthetics of bulb planting. Ms. Wilder recommended installing crocuses in closely planted clusters or drifts. Consider that at one inch apart you will need close to 150 bulbs to produce a display a mere one foot square. Even if you do plant species crocuses two or more inches apart, you will eventually have a cluster effect, as they multiply readily. However, it may take five years or so before the planting reaches maximum effectiveness.

Some suggest planting species and even Dutch crocuses willy-nilly, or naturalized in the lawn. This is a bad idea for two reasons: first, the display is too spotty to be effective; and second, as with all bulbs, crocus foliage must be allowed to ripen and brown in order for the bulbs to survive. Therefore, you should not mow your lawn until the crocus foliage browns. Inevitably, however, your grass will be overgrown before this happens and you will want to mow. If you do, your crocuses will die within a year or two.

Five years or so down the line, when your crocus plantings have become very crowded and bloom diminishes, it is time to dig up the bulbs after the foliage browns, separate them, and replant. You can replant immediately or store the bulbs in mesh bags or old nylon stockings in a cool, dry, shady place until fall, and replant them. At this time you can enlarge your current clusters or drifts or plant the excess bulbs in other parts of your garden.

HOW TO PLANT: Select a site with good drainage in full sun or partial shade. Do not plant in deep shade under evergreens. However, since deciduous trees do not leaf out until late spring or early summer, you can plant under these trees. Prepare the soil as described above (see p. 150). Excavate to a depth of six inches and mix in one tablespoon of 9-9-6 fertilizer (Holland Bulb Booster) per square foot of planting area. Fill in the hole to within two to four inches deep. Pat down the surface, place the bulbs one inch apart, cover them with soil, tamp the soil surface, and water thoroughly.

MAINTENANCE: Each spring, when shoots emerge, scratch in one tablespoon of 9-9-6 fertilizer (Holland Bulb Booster) per square foot of planting area. Once bloom is over, do not cut the foliage but allow it to ripen and brown before removing it.

TIPS: Since foliage browns by late spring, there will be a bare spot in your garden where species crocuses have bloomed. You can either fill in the area with annuals or select from perennials recommended as permanent bulb overplantings in chapter 4. Crocuses are relished by rabbits, chipmunks, and burrowing rodents. Refer to the section on pests and disease above (see p. 153) for information deterring these creatures.

Some Available Species Crocus Varieties

VARIETY	DESCRIPTION
Ancyrensis or Golden Bunch	Very early flowering; deep golden-yellow, clustered blooms
Chrysanthus Advance	Inside lemon yellow; outside shaded purple
Chrysanthus Blue Pearl	Delicate blue
Chrysanthus Canarybird	Orange-yellow cup with bronze spots on exterior of flower
Fuscotinctus	Yellow with plum-colored stripes
Hubert Edelsten	Delicate soft lavender
Lady Killer	Striking violet purple, edged in white
Moonlight	Lovely cream colors; one of the most beautiful of the crocuses
Sieberi Violet Queen	Amethyst violet
Susianus or Cloth of Gold	Deep golden yellow, tinged with bronze
Tomasinianus	Pale lavender with silver-gray outside
White Triumphator	Pure white outside, blue veins

Dutch or Giant Crocus, Zones 3–10

These bloom after the species crocuses and are from two to three times the size of the latter. They are available in white, gold, deep purple, lilac, and light blue with silvery stripes. They are effective when mixed, though I feel they produce a more effective display when planted in drifts of one variety next to a drift or several drifts of other varieties.

Like species crocuses, giant crocuses are most effective when clustered together in groups of no less than twenty-five, preferably fifty or one hundred. They should also be planted with window views or dooryard displays in mind, they bloom very early. Like other early-blooming bulbs, they are quite hardy and are usually not harmed by freezing temperatures, snow, or ice.

For an effective cluster display the first spring after planting, plant corms about two inches apart instead of the recommended three to six inches apart. As with species crocuses, planting them randomly in the lawn produces a spotty display, and since their foliage must be allowed to ripen before cutting, early lawn mowing will eventually kill Dutch crocuses.

After five years, when your plantings become very crowded, dig the corms up after the foliage browns, separate them, and either replant them immediately or store them in mesh bags or old nylon stockings in a cool, dry, shady place until fall.

HOW TO PLANT: Select a site with good drainage in full sun or partial shade. Do not plant in deep shade under evergreens. However, since deciduous trees do not leaf out until foliage is well along the way to ripening, you can plant under these trees, despite the deep shade they cast in summer. Prepare soil as described above (see p. 150). Excavate to a depth of six inches and mix in one tablespoon of 9-9-6 fertilizer (Holland Bulb Booster) per square foot of planting area. Fill in the hole to within two to four inches deep. Pat down the surface, place corms two inches apart, cover them with soil, tamp the soil surface, and water thoroughly.

MAINTENANCE: Each spring, when shoots emerge, scratch in one tablespoon of 9-9-6 fertilizer (Holland Bulb Booster) per square foot of planting area. Once bloom is over, do not cut the foliage, but allow to ripen and brown before removing it.

TIPS: Since foliage browns by late spring, there will be a bare spot in your garden where Dutch crocuses have bloomed. You can either fill in the area with annuals or select from perennials recommended as permanent bulb overplantings in chapter 4. Crocuses are relished by rabbits, chipmunks,

Some Available Dutch Crocus Varieties

VARIETY	DESCRIPTION
Giant yellow	Deep gold-yellow
Jeanne d'Arc	Pure white
Queen of the Blues	Lilac or light purple
The Sultan	Deep purple
Striped Beauty	Light purple streaked with silvery white

and burrowing rodents. Refer to the section on pests and diseases above (see p. 153) for information on deterring these creatures.

Muscari or Grape Hyacinth, Zones 2–10

Muscari or grape hyacinth blooms at the same time as most daffodils and makes an ideal contrast to them, with its yellow, cream-colored, and white blooms. Lesser-known varieties sport blooms in feathery sky blue, purplish green, and various shades of purple. Many varieties are available, but the common grape hyacinth, with its sweet-scented, deep sky blue blooms on six- to eight-inch stems, is the most popular. Some object to the fact that *Muscari* foliage appears in fall, winters over, and looks somewhat untidy in spring. However, as a companion planting to daffodils, planted at some distance from close-range viewing, grape hyacinths offer a dazzling display. And in any event, soon after bloom the foliage withers and dies. Plant in drifts of at least fifty in front of a daffodil planting and leave undisturbed for years. Or dig, divide, and replant after bloom if planting becomes crowded. Muscari can also be naturalized in meadows or under deciduous trees.

HOW TO PLANT: Select a site with good drainage, in full sun or partial shade. Prepare the soil as described above (see p. 150). Excavate to a depth of six inches and work in one tablespoon of 9-9-6 fertilizer (Holland Bulb Booster) per square foot of planting area. Fill in the hole to around three inches deep, pat down the soil, set the bulbs in place about three inches apart, cover with the soil, tamp the surface, and water thoroughly. If you are naturalizing them under deciduous trees or in a meadow, gently toss the bulbs on the ground and plant them where they land simply by digging

Some Available Muscari Varieties

VARIETY	DESCRIPTION
Armeniacum early giant	Deep coba.: blue with white rim
Armeniacum Blue Spike	Soft blue; double
Armeniacum Cantab	Bright, clear Cambridge blue
Botryoides Album	Pure white
Comosum or tassel hyacinth	Greenish purple; this variety blooms at the end of May and early June

a hole two to three inches deep for each, covering the bulb with soil, tamping it down, and watering thoroughly.

MAINTENANCE: After bloom allow the foliage to ripen and wither before removing it. It is *not* necessary to fertilize *Muscari* after the initial planting. TIPS: Since the foliage disappears by late spring, there will be a bare spot in your garden where *Muscari* has bloomed. You can either fill in the area with annuals or select from the perennials recommended as permanent bulb overplantings in chapter 4. Burrowing pests relish *Muscari* bulbs. Refer to the section on pests and diseases (p. 153) for information on combatting these pests. Rabbits and chipmunks tend to disregard *Muscari* foliage in spring.

Scilla sibirica or Squill, Zones 1–8

This is the most popular and, for your purposes, the most useful of the small *Scillas*. Its deep, electric, gentian blue color blends effectively with the sulphur yellow of miniature daffodils, most of which bloom at the same time. As with other early-blooming bulbs, plant in drifts of fifty to one hundred, either interspersed with mini-daffodil-drifts or in front of them. Place them within close view of windows or entrances. Several hundred bulbs planted in drifts will be noticeable in distant parts of the garden, should you care to go that route. *Scilla* naturalizes well under deciduous trees and can be left undisturbed for years.

HOW TO PLANT: Select a site with good drainage in full sun or partial shade. Prepare soil as described above (see p. 150). Excavate to a depth of three inches, pat down the soil, do *not* fertilize, set the bulbs in place about three inches apart, cover them with soil, tamp the surface, and water thoroughly.

If you are naturalizing them under deciduous trees or in a meadow, gently toss the bulbs on the ground and plant them where they land by digging a hole two to three inches deep for each, covering the bulb with soil, tamping it down, and watering thoroughly.

MAINTENANCE: If you do not wish *Scilla* to throw seedlings, remove its blossoms when spent. Allow the foliage to ripen and wither before removing it. It is not necessary to fertilize *Scilla*.

TIPS: After bloom, cover bare spots with annuals or refer to chapter 4 for recommended permanent bulb overplanting varieties.

Puschkinia or Lebanon Squill, Zones 3–10

These bloom around the same time as *Chionodoxa* or glory-of-the-snow and sport one-half to one-inch-long bluish white or pure white blossoms on four- to eight-inch stalks. When spottily planted here and there, their effect is insignificant, but as with all small bulbs, planted in drifts of fifty or one hundred, they produce a cloudlike display of subtle color. A drift of *Puschkinia* planted in front of or behind a drift of *Chionodoxa* is particularly effective. *Puschkinia* can also be naturalized under deciduous trees, where it multiplies readily.

HOW TO PLANT: Select a site with good drainage in full sun or partial shade. Prepare soil as described above (see p. 150). Excavate to a depth of three inches, pat down the soil, do *not* fertilize, set the bulbs in place about three inches apart, cover them with soil, tamp down the surface, and water thoroughly. If you are naturalizing them under deciduous trees or in a meadow, gently toss the bulbs on the ground and plant them where they land by digging a hole two to three inches deep for each, covering it with soil, tamping it down, and watering thoroughly.

MAINTENANCE: If you do not wish *Puschkinia* to throw seedlings, remove its blossoms when spent. Allow the foliage to ripen and wither before removing it. It is not necessary to fertilize *Puschkinia*.

TIPS: After bloom, cover bare spots with annuals or refer to chapter 4 for recommended permanent bulb overplanting varieties.

Chionodoxa or Glory-of-the-Snow, Zones 3–10

Blooming slightly later than crocuses and snowdrops, around the same time as *Puschkinia* and before *Scilla siberica*, these small flowering bulbs bear lovely, sky blue, white-eyed blossoms on six-inch stems. Since the blossoms are small, they should be planted in drifts of no less than one hundred and situated where they can be viewed from windows or near the house entrance. *Chionodoxa* is particularly effective when planted under deciduous trees, where it naturalizes readily. There is a well-established planting under a stately beech tree in my neighborhood which is a breathtaking sight in spring. Once planted, *Chionodoxa* can remain undisturbed for years, the display becoming more beautiful with each passing year.

HOW TO PLANT: Select a site with good drainage in full sun or partial shade. Prepare the soil as described above (see p. 150). Excavate to a depth of three inches, pat down the soil, do *not* add fertilizer, set the bulbs in place about one inch apart, cover with the soil, tamp the surface, and water thoroughly. If you are naturalizing them under deciduous trees, toss the bulbs gently on the ground and plant them where they land simply by digging a hole two to three inches deep, covering it with soil, tamping it down, and watering thoroughly.

MAINTENANCE: After bloom, allow the foliage to ripen and wither before removing it. If you do not wish *Chionodoxa* to throw seedlings, remove its blossoms when spent. It is not necessary to fertilize *Chionodoxa*.

TIPS: After bloom, cover bare spots with annuals, or refer to chapter 4 for recommended permanent bulb overplanting varieties.

Narcissus or Daffodils (standard height), Zones 4–10

Daffodils are probably the most universally grown and loved of all the spring-flowering bulbs, for practical as well as aesthetic reasons: they are not only pest and disease free, but rodent proof as well. Most varieties perform well over a period of five, ten, or even fifteen to twenty years, though some do not. After the first three years, some form thick clumps of foliage but steadily produce less flowers. In some instances, the bulbs die out completely. In 1972, at the Planting Fields Arboretum on Long Island, a daffodil planting trial was installed in which two hundred different varieties of daffodils, representing twenty classifications, were planted in groups of six bulbs each. They were left undisturbed, and the number of flowers produced was tabulated each year. After ten years, some varieties were strong and still flowering to perfection. Others had fewer flowers, while still others had disappeared completely. The varieties that consistently produced a lavish display were: Arctic Gold, Binkie, Broughshane, Cantabile, Carlton, Cherie, Dove Wings, Duke of Windsor, February Gold, Flower Record, Ice Follies, March Sunshine, Mrs. R. O. Backhouse, Red Rascal,

Spellbinder, Sweetness, Sun Chariot, Thalia, Trevithian, and Winifred Van Graven. This is not to say that other varieties won't perform well for you. However, the above varieties are proven performers.

Plant daffodils in drifts of at least twelve rather than in clumps, or naturalize them in a meadow, woodland garden, or under deciduous trees. The deep cobalt blue grape hyacinth is particularly effective as a companion planting, as it blooms at the same time. Be sure not to overlook the white varieties, Mount Hood and Thalia, as these can add a subtle touch to your plantings, toning down the sulphur yellows and oranges of many varieties. You may find the pink or apricot varieties to your liking. However, I feel they are novelties and tend to have a somewhat washed-out appearance. If you are fortunate enough to have a stand of white birch trees on your property or are planning to plant some, daffodils planted underneath are a beautiful sight in spring. The sunshine yellow of the flowers and the white bark of the birches are very effective together.

The one fault many find with daffodils is that in order to assure continued bloom, their foliage must be allowed to ripen and wither, looking somewhat unsightly for six to eight weeks after the bloom period is over. There are a number of ways you can minimize this messy look. You can overplant with perennials or annuals. You can gather the foliage together, fold it over, and secure it with a rubber band or string. You can plant your daffodils in the distance, where unsightly foliage is not in constant view. At any rate, it is probably best not to plant standard daffodils in a dooryard garden or in close and constant view of windows or near the garden living area. However, miniature daffodils (treated as a separate entry below) have less obtrusive foliage and are thus suitable for close-up viewing.

HOW TO PLANT: Select a site with good drainage in full sun or partial shade. Prepare the soil as described above (see p. 150). For standard-height daffodils (eighteen to twenty-four inches) excavate to a depth of about twelve inches, mix in one tablespoon of 9-9-6 fertilizer (Holland Bulb Booster) per square foot of planting area, fill the hole to within eight inches of the top, pat down the soil, set the bulbs in place about six inches apart, cover them with soil, tamp the surface, and water thoroughly. If you are naturalizing them in meadows or under deciduous trees, toss the bulbs gently on the ground and plant them where they land by digging a hole about eight inches deep for each, adding a half teaspoon of 9-6-6 fertilizer, setting the bulb in place, covering it with soil, tamping it down, and watering thoroughly.

MAINTENANCE: After bloom, remove all the spent flowers, and allow the foliage to wither before removing it. The following spring, when shoots emerge, work in one tablespoon of 9-9-6 fertilizer (Holland Bulb Booster) per square foot.

TIPS: After bloom, cover bare spots with annuals, or refer to chapter 4 for recommended permanent bulb overplanting varieties. Should bloom become sparse and foliage very thick as the years pass, overcrowding is probably the problem. Dig up the entire clump after bloom, separate the bulbs, and replant immediately as above. Or wait until the foliage has ripened and withered, dig up the bulbs, clean them, store them in mesh bags or old nylon stockings in a cool, dry, shady spot, and replant them in the fall.

In addition to the test-planting trial on Long Island, the Netherlands Bulb Industry conducted a series of four-year trials at North Carolina State University. Here again, some varieties of daffodils performed better than others. Below is a list of those that produced the best displays year after year:

- Barrett Browning
- Brighton
- Carbineer
- Estella de Mol
- February Gold
- Fortune
- Flower Record
- Gigantic Star

- Ice Follies
- Jumblie
- Salome
- Sugarbush
- Tahiti
- Thalia
- Tresamble
- Trevithian

Miniature Daffodils, Zones 4–10

Because they are so often overlooked by the novice gardener, I have opted to include miniature daffodils as a separate entry. There are so many ways you can use these charming spring flowers: in rock gardens, at a dooryard entrance, naturalized, in drifts among foundation plantings, or along walkways. Varieties range in height from three inches to fifteen inches and are available in a wide range of shapes and color combinations. Like the standard varieties, they are unproblematical, rodent free, and nearly pest free. When you plant, install at least twenty-five of the taller and fifty of the shorter varieties. If you use fewer, the display will appear insignificant, and disappointing.

HOW TO PLANT: Select a site with good drainage in full sun or partial shade. Prepare the soil as described above (see p. 150). Bulb size varies according to variety, but a good rule of thumb is to excavate to a depth of about three times the bulb's maximum diameter. The shoulder of the bulb (the area at the top that widens to the full circumference), rather than the tip, should be at this depth. Work in one tablespoon of 9-9-6 fertilizer (Holland Bulb Booster) per square foot of planting area, pat down the soil, set the bulbs in place (about two inches apart for those under one inch in diameter, four inches apart for those over one inch in diameter), cover them with soil, tamp the surface, and water thoroughly. If naturalizing, toss the bulbs gently on the ground and plant them where they land simply by digging a hole about three inches deep for small bulbs, six inches deep for larger bulbs, adding a half teaspoon of 9-9-6 fertilizer (Holland Bulb Booster), setting the bulbs in place, covering them with soil, tamping it down, and watering thoroughly.

MAINTENANCE: After bloom, remove all spent flowers, and allow the foliage to wither before removing it. In spring, when shoots emerge, work in one tablespoon of 9-9-6 fertilizer (Holland Bulb Booster) per square foot of planting area.

TIPS: After bloom, cover bare spots with annuals, or refer to chapter 4 for recommended permanent bulb overplanting varieties. Should bloom become sparse and foliage very thick as the years pass, overcrowding is

Some Available Miniature Daffodil Varieties

VARIETY	HEIGHT	DESCRIPTION
April Tears	7″	Deep yellow
Baby Moon	9″	Buttercup yellow
February Gold	10″	Lemon yellow
Gold Drops	8″	Yellow and white
Hoop Petticoat	6″	Bright yellow
Jack Snipe	8″	Creamy white
Kewpie Doll	9″	White with yellow cup
Liberty Bells	7″	Yellow
Lintie	3″	Yellow with orange rim
Little Witch	6″	Deep yellow
Peeping Tom	14″	Deep yellow
Rip van Winkle	7″	Clear yellow
Suzy	15″	Yellow with orange cup
Tête-à-tête	5″	Yellow with long cup
W. P. Milner	9″	Sulphur and white
Triandrus Albus	7″	Creamy white

probably the problem. Dig up the entire clump after bloom, separate the bulbs, and replant them immediately. Or wait until the foliage has ripened and withered, dig up the bulbs, clean them, store them in mesh bags or old nylon stockings in a cool, dry, shady spot, and replant them in the fall.

Hyacinth, Zones 4–10

Though gardeners everywhere cherish the heady scent of hyacinths, they can be somewhat problematic, for their very stiff, formal appearance often looks awkward in an informal scheme. The most familiar and readily available variety is *Hyacinthus orientalis*—the one you'll find for sale in pots at Easter time. Colors include blues, pinks, yellows, white, salmon, reds, and purples. Eight- to ten-inch-high spikes of clustered blossoms grow on twelve-inch stalks. For best results in an informal planting, plant in drifts, using perhaps two different colors plus white. Blooming around the end of April in most parts of the country, hyacinths are effective when planted in an area somewhat distant from the dooryard, where their flamboyant colors deliver a splash of welcome relief from the otherwise dreary early spring landscape. If a subtle display is what you have in mind, select from the pale blue, cream, white, and pink varieties rather than the more garish electric blue, red, and salmon ones.

Hyacinths' flowering spikes tend to loosen up a bit each year after planting, and for this reason I find them to be much more attractive and versatile in the garden scheme after several years. Instead of the tight, formal spikes, jammed with individual blossoms, fewer flowers placed irregularly up and down the stalk make them more attractive in informal borders as well as in foundation plantings. They work well at this stage in woodland gardens, resembling *Scilla hispanica*, but blooming from four to six weeks earlier. Use no fewer than twelve bulbs per drift.

HOW TO PLANT: Select a site with good drainage in full sun or partial shade. Prepare the soil as described above (see p. 150). Excavate to a depth of about ten inches, mix one tablespoon of 9-9-6 fertilizer (Holland Bulb Booster) into the bottom of the hole and fill to within six inches of the top. Pat down the soil, set the bulbs in place six inches apart, cover them with soil, tamp the surface, and water thoroughly.

MAINTENANCE: After bloom, cut off spent flower spikes, but allow the foliage to ripen and wither before removing it. Each spring, when shoots emerge, work in one tablespoon of 9-9-6 fertilizer (Holland Bulb Booster) per square foot of planting area.

Some Available Hyacinth Varieties

VARIETY	DESCRIPTION
Amethyst	Violet mauve
City of Haarlem	Bright yellow
Delft blue	Porcelain blue
Gypsy Queen	Soft orange
Jan Bos	Scarlet red
Lady Derby	Delicate soft pink
Pink Pearl	Rich rosy pink
Queen of the Blues	Sky blue
White Pearl	Pure white

TIPS: After bloom, cover bare spots with annuals or refer to chapter 4 for recommended permanent bulb overplanting varieties.

Tulips, Zones 3–7

In Holland, and indeed throughout Europe, most gardeners treat tulips as annuals; that is, they plant them in fall and then, after bloom, dig them up and throw them away. They do this because they know that most tulips produce less and less bloom with each passing year. Here in America, however, we tend to think in terms of permanent, perennial plantings, so we plant tulips and then, several years down the line, wonder why they are no longer producing spectacular bloom. The reason is that tulip bulbs divide into small bulbs each year, and if the planting is not fertilized and the soil structure and climate are not ideal, they deplete. Even under optimal conditions, the blooms usually become smaller and smaller, eventually disappearing.

Therefore, for landscape purposes, most tulips cannot be counted on to enhance your scheme after a year or two. Some varieties are more prone to "perennialize" than others—that is, to provide a continuing display year after year—but they must be fertilized properly to achieve this effect. Beyond this, conditions vary to such an extent from area to area, from garden to garden, and even within an individual garden, that you cannot count on true perennialization of tulips. However, tulips are so beautiful that it is certainly worth experimenting with those varieties that do tend to perennialize.

There are many types of tulips available. Species tulips, most of which are the earliest to bloom and the closest genetically to the original wild tulips, are classed as Kaufmania, Fosteriana or Emperor, and Gregii. All of these tend to perennialize and multiply, providing beautiful displays year in and year out. Another early-blooming variety, early-blooming double, does not. Of the other varieties, midseason Cottage and Triumph, later-blooming Rembrandt, Parrot, Lily-flowering, and Vridiflora, and the hundreds of varieties of Darwins are not prone to perennializing, usually producing less and less bloom each year.

The spectacular Darwin hybrids, a cross between the Fosteriana or Emperor tulip and the Darwin, does tend to perennialize if conditions are favorable. I have a planting of Darwin hybrid Golden Apeldoorn now in its fifth year, more beautiful and with more blooms than when it was planted.

In addition to the above, there is a class of wild or near-wild tulips that truly does perennialize. Small in stature and bloom, these tulips usually multiply freely and can be used in rock gardens, dooryard gardens, or anywhere where they can be viewed closely. Most are early bloomers and are available from most mail-order sources.

So then, if you are looking for tulips that perennialize, stick to the low-growing, early-blooming species Kaufmania and Gregii, the tall, early-blooming Fosteriana or Emperor tulips, the "wild" tulips, and for later display, to the Darwin hybrids. Of course, the lovely shapes and colors of Lily-flowering, Cottage, Darwins, and others may be more than you can resist. If so, by all means plant them, but be prepared for the fact that after a few years they will probably deplete and have to be replaced.

Some Available Kaufmania Tulip Varieties

VARIETY	HEIGHT	DESCRIPTION
Fritz Kreisler	6″	Salmon-pink
Gold Coin	6″–8″	Scarlet-edged yellow
Heart's Delight	10″–12″	Carmine red and rose
Kaufmania	6″	Cream with yellow center
Shakespeare	6″–8″	Blend of salmon, orange, and apricot
Show Winner	6″–8″	Scarlet red
Stresa	7″	Gold with orange border
Vivaldi	7″	Yellow and crimson
Waterlily	7″	Cream with carmine red markings

Some Available Fosteriana or Emperor Tulip Varieties

VARIETY	HEIGHT	DESCRIPTION
Golden Emperor	12″–18″	Gold-yellow
Orange Emperor	12″–18″	Bright orange
Pink Emperor	12″–18″	Pink
Red Emperor	12″–18″	Red
White Emperor	12″–18″	White

Some Available Gregii Tulip Varieties

VARIETY	HEIGHT	DESCRIPTION
Cape Cod	12″–14″	Orange-red, yellow inside
Engadin	12″	Yellow-edged deep red
Lovely Surprise	18″	Gold and red
Oriental Splendor	20″	Lemon-edged carmine red
Plaisir	12″	Cream-edged carmine red
Red Riding Hood	6″–8″	Brilliant scarlet
Royal Splendour	20″	Scarlet
Scheherazade	12″	Scarlet
Sweet Lady	8″	Soft pink and ivory

Some Available "Wild" Tulip Varieties

VARIETY	HEIGHT	DESCRIPTION
Biflora	8″	Yellow and white
Chrysantha	8″	Bright yellow and red
Clusiana (Clusius)	8″	Rose and white with violet base; fragrant
Dasystemon (Kuenlun)	3″–6″	Yellow and white
Hageri (Hager)	6″	Deep red
Patens (Persian)	6″–9″	Yellow and white; fragrant
Praestans (Leatherbulb)	12″–18″	Light red
Pulchella (Dwarf Taurus)	4″–6″	Pale purple
Turkestanica	8″	White with yellow center

Beyond the general recommendations above, the Netherlands Bulb Industry has run trial plantings of specific varieties of tulips for four years, in conjunction with North Carolina State University. The varieties that performed best are listed below. Some are readily available from suppliers; others are not so easy to locate. I suggest you refer to the bulb source list on page 248, send for a dozen or so catalogues, go through them, and select from the recommended list.

There are other ways to prolong tulip bloom, though the results are never assured. Some suggest planting bulbs at a depth of twelve to eighteen inches. This tends to slow down the process of bulb division, thus prolonging bloom. Frederic Doerflinger of the Northern Horticultural Society of Great Britain experimented with tulips at Harrowgate, Yorkshire, in England, by planting them at the recommended six-inch depth, but set-

Midseason-Blooming Tulip Varieties Recommended for Perennialization

VARIETY	DESCRIPTION
Candela	Yellow
Diplomat	Red
Frankfurt	Red
Golden Apeldoorn	Yellow
Golden Oxford	Yellow
Golden Parade	Yellow
Gudoshnik	Yellow-fringed orange
Hoango	Yellow
Ile de France	Red
Jewel of Spring	Yellow-edged red
Los Angeles	Red-edged yellow
Merry Widow	Red-edged white
Monte Carlo	Yellow
Negrita	Purple
Orange Emperor	Orange
Oscar	Red
Oxford	Red
Princess Victoria	Red-edged white
Spring Song	Red-edged white
Striped Apeldoorn	Yellow-striped red
Yellow Dover	Yellow
Yokohama	Yellow-edged red

Late-Blooming Tulip Varieties
Recommended for Perennialization

VARIETY	DESCRIPTION
Ad Rem	Red-edged yellow
Burgundy Lace	Red
Delmonte	White-fringed purple
Don Quichotte	Red-orange
Duke of Wellington	White
Dyanito	Red
Gordon Cooper	Red-orange-edged red
Jimmy	Red-orange
Karel Diorman	Red-edged yellow
Kees Nelis	Red-edged orange
Makeup	White-edged red
Orange Bouquet	Orange
Parade	Red-edged yellow
Smiling Queen	Red-orange-edged pink
Sorbet	Red-orange

ting each bulb on its side instead of on its base. He claims this method prolongs bloom by several years.

The trials run by North Carolina State University were planted in zones 7, 8, and 9—among the milder climatic regions of the country. This does not necessarily mean that these tulips will not do as well in cooler zones. However, be advised that in any case, similar results in your own garden, no matter where it is, are most assuredly not guaranteed. And, although some Darwins, Triumph, Parrot, and double early tulips received high ratings for perennialization, the majority of those with high ratings were the Darwin hybrids.

When you plan your scheme, be sure to keep the following basic design principles in mind: do not plant tulips in a single straight line, or in a circle, as they look unnatural; and do not plant rainbow mixtures, as they fail to make a color statement. Rather, plant in drifts or clumps of at least twelve bulbs of one variety. There are hundreds of colors available, in every conceivable gradation and combination except true blue. Keep in mind that many are very flamboyant: brilliant oranges, reds, sulphur yellows, bright purples, oranges lined with yellow or red, and so forth. Unless you select your varieties carefully, the end result may be an unpleasing clash of dominant colors. However, there are pale cream colors, pale lilac, pinks, and white to choose from as well. On the other hand, you may decide that a vivid display is exactly what you want. If so, by all means go ahead with your planting. But keep in mind that you can divide the colors in a flamboyant scheme with white tulips. This will help tone down the scheme considerably and will also help avoid color clashes.

HOW TO PLANT: Select a site with good drainage in full sun or partial shade. Prepare soil as described above (see p. 150). For Darwin hybrids, Lily-flowering, Fosteriana or Emperor, Triumph, Cottage, and other larger bulbs, excavate to a depth of about one foot and mix in one tablespoon of 9-9-6 fertilizer (Holland Bulb Booster) per square foot of planting area. Fill in the hole to within six inches of soil surface and set bulbs six inches apart. Cover them with soil, tamp down the soil surface, and water thoroughly. Plant varieties with smaller bulbs about four inches deep.

MAINTENANCE: After bloom, remove spent blossoms and allow the foliage to ripen and wither before removing it. The following spring, when shoots emerge, scratch in one tablespoon of 9-9-6 fertilizer (Holland Bulb Booster) per square foot of planting area.

TIPS: After bloom, cover bare spots with annuals or refer to chapter 4 for permanent bulb overplanting varieties.

Scilla hispanica or Spanish Bluebells, Zones 4–10

Spanish bluebells bloom later than most spring-flowering bulbs—usually in mid-May—and sport a series of bell-shaped blooms similar to individual hyacinth blossoms, on stalks from eight to twelve inches high. Colors are white, medium blue, and pink. The pink variety is not a true pink but has colorations of lavender that I feel have a washed-out look. But the blue and white varieties are quite beautiful and produce a dramatic display when in bloom. As with most bulbs, drift planting is most effective. Spanish bluebells prefer light shade and even flourish under the low-light conditions of more dense shade—one of the few bulb varieties that does. They are ideally suited to woodland gardens, meadows, or beneath deciduous trees and are effective when viewed from a distance. To my mind, they are too tall to plant in a dooryard bulb garden, and since they bloom later than most bulbs, they are ineffectual when used to create color patterns with other bulbs. Use them in combination with perennials or by themselves in woodland settings or borders. Once planted they multiply readily and can be left undistrubed for years. Unfortunately, many mail-order houses offer mixtures of the three colors. Avoid these and order either blue or white, or both.

HOW TO PLANT: Select a site with good drainage in partial shade. Prepare the soil as described above (see p. 150). Excavate to a depth of about eight inches and work in one tablespoon of 9-9-6 fertilizer (Holland Bulb Booster) per square foot of planting area. Fill the hole to within three to four inches from soil surface, pat the soil, set the bulbs from six to eight inches apart, cover them with soil, tamp the soil surface, and water thoroughly.

MAINTENANCE: Spanish bluebells multiply readily and also throw seeds. If you do not wish them to spread rampantly, remove the blossom stalks when spent. Allow the foliage to ripen and wither before removing it. It is not necessary to fertilize after initial planting.

TIPS: Since they are late bloomers, use Spanish bluebells in conjunction with May-blooming perennials. See chapter 4 for appropriate varieties.

Chapter Four

♦

THE FOURTH YEAR

The Permanent Colors of Spring, Summer,
and Fall: Perennials

The Big and Beautiful Five

The Perennial Encyclopedia

Fences and Hedges

Well, here it is the fourth year of your landscape project. By now you should be quite experienced in growing annuals and vegetables. This spring you should be harvesting your asparagus and enjoying the bulb plantings you installed last fall. Continue to care for the trees you planted during the second year of your project and evaluate them carefully in terms of selection and location. If you decide that you have made a mistake, now is the time to remove trees or replant new ones elsewhere. Do the same with your shrub borders and foundation plantings. Take extensive notes on your bulb plantings, recording dates of bloom, colors, and other features. Now is the time to begin to correct any mistakes you might have made in installing bulbs. Do not dig them up and move them until after all foliage has withered and turned brown. Be sure you identify each variety with a label, as once the leaves wither, it will be nearly impossible to distinguish one variety from another. Continue to install annuals around your property for color. And, after all danger of frost, install annuals over bulb plantings to cover the withering foliage and bare spots that will be evident after your bulbs go into summer dormancy.

This year, in addition to maintaining the projects of the previous three years, it is time to install fences and/or hedges and to plant your perennials—perhaps the most aesthetically rewarding of all your landscape projects.

The Permanent Colors of Spring, Summer, and Fall: Perennials

Perennial flowering plants provide the backbone of color in a garden. They are permanent and winter hardy; that is, they die down each fall when they have finished blooming but grow again the following spring. You do not have to plant them each spring as you do annuals. For this reason it is wise to plan carefully before you install perennial flowering plants.

Perennials are more expensive than annuals, but when you consider that they are a one-time investment, the cost amortized over the years is very reasonable. With literally thousands of varieties available, there is a perennial suitable for every possible location and growing condition. I have included only those perennials that are relatively unproblematical, readily available, and to a great extent pest and disease free. Should you become interested in growing perennials on a larger scale, there are worlds beyond what is included here with which you may wish to familiarize yourself. There are many books available on the cultivation of perennials alone, including some that deal exclusively with one kind of perennial, such as peonies, irises, delphiniums, primroses, and so forth. However, the information included here will give you a healthy start in landscaping your property with these workhorses of the garden world.

Where can I buy perennials? With a few exceptions, most perennials are difficult to grow from seed. Because very special conditions must often be provided, this is a task best left to experienced gardeners or professionals if you are just starting out with your landscaping. This means that you must buy established plants in order to install your planting.

In spring, most nurseries and garden centers offer perennial plants, usually in containers. However, unless the nursery specializes to a certain extent in these plants, the selection will probably be very limited. This can be frustrating for a homeowner who wishes to install a perennial bed or border in his or her landscape scheme. Friends or neighbors who like to garden often know of nurseries that may not be in the immediate area but that offer a wide selection of perennial plants. Once you've decided which plants you want, a visit to a nursery with a wider selection is certainly worth the effort.

Beyond the nurseries and garden centers in your area, you should tap the vast resources of the mail-order garden supply houses, for the range of available varieties is almost unlimited. The best way to begin is to send away for some of the catalogues that mail-order suppliers offer. Many advertise in newspapers or in national magazines and provide coupons that you clip out and mail in. On receipt of these coupons, they send a catalogue, usually free of charge. Before long, you will find that unsolicited catalogues will begin to arrive, as many of these companies share their mailing lists. Advertisements will begin to appear in the media around December or January. It is best to act quickly and send for catalogues early. This will allow you to see what each company offers, make your selection, and not risk the disappointment of having them run out of desired items. For a list of mail-order sources, see page 248.

As with anything else you buy, it is a good idea to comparison shop, as you will find that prices vary from one source to another. Usually, the newer varieties of any cultivar are the most expensive, but this does not necessarily mean that they are right for your garden scheme or that they will provide more satisfaction in terms of bloom or vigor.

In addition to the above-mentioned outlets, friends, family, and neighbors can be excellent sources for stock, since most experienced gardeners know that to maintain vigor, perennials must be divided regularly and replanted. Ask them if they have any planting material to offer you. Most gardeners are only too glad to share extra material. In fact, they undoubtedly received some of their stock in the same way. One word of caution, however: try to find out the name of each plant you are given and the color of the bloom. This will help ensure a harmonious planting of perennial flowers. A mixed bag of irises, for example, if planted in a border together, will result in a hodgepodge of color that you will probably decide to do away with. At first, you will probably take anything offered, but the sooner you learn that it is best to be discriminating in accepting giveaways, the more successful you will be in creating a landscape of harmony and beauty.

An alternative to turning down unfamiliar giveaways, or even unfamiliar plants that you purchase yourself, is to plant them in your nursery area. You can then wait several years to see what their mature size is and what color the flowers are, and move them into a permanent position if they please you.

Often, well-meaning friends or family will either purchase plants at nurseries or order them from mail-order sources and give them to you as gifts. If at all possible (and as tactfully as possible, of course), ask them to send gift certificates instead so that you can select according to your needs and taste.

Where can I plant perennials? Like spring-blooming bulbs, perennials can be planted anywhere you want spring, summer, or fall color. However, they are perhaps best used to create herbaceous borders or island beds. That is, use them for spectacular displays to brighten the landscape after spring-blooming bulbs have finished. They are also quite useful for adding dashes of color to monotonous foundation plantings, along driveways and walks, on hard-to-maintain slopes or in rock gardens, around birdbaths, garden furniture, and mailboxes, in boggy areas, and in woodland areas. There are perennials suitable for almost every conceivable growing condition.

Here are a few planting tips:

• With the possible exception of peonies, a single plant of which is substantial enough to make a statement, always plant at least three of each variety. If you plant only one, the effect will be hodgepodge and spotty.

• Perennials are best used in an informal rather than a formal manner. Most perennial plants are loose in structure, grow to varying heights, and look best when planted in groups next to other varieties, creating varying textures, leaf colors, flower colors, blooming times, and heights. Stiff, geometrically planned beds simply do not work aesthetically in most contemporary landscapes.

• Remember that many varieties of perennials bloom very early in the spring. Use these interplanted with spring-blooming bulbs and, as with bulbs, consider the planting not only from the outdoor point of view but from indoors through windows, as you will probably be spending most of your time indoors at this time of year. Late spring, summer, and fall plantings can be planned strictly from an outside point of view if you wish, since chances are that at these times of the year you will be spending a considerable amount of time outside in your garden.

• Perennials can be used for splashes of color in distant parts of the garden. Plant large groups of each variety for the best visual results. Do not plant symmetrically; rather, try to emulate nature and plant informally. When planning a distant planting keep in mind that the hot colors—red, yellow, and orange—will make the planting seem closer to the eye, while the cool colors—blue, purple, and green—will recede and appear to be more distant.

Where in the country can I plant perennials? Consult the zone designations included in each entry of the perennial encyclopedia (see pp. 205–18) to determine which varieties of perennials are appropriate for your particular location. You will find that there are varieties suitable for every area of the United States and Canada, regardless of how cold or warm the temperature may be.

How do I select a site for a perennial planting? The most important consideration is light. Some varieties prefer full sun, some like partial sun, and others thrive even in deep shade. Consult the encylopedia to determine which varieties are suitable for each light condition. Then consider drainage. Obviously, a well-drained area is desirable for most varieties you might wish to grow. However, some perennials will thrive in (and indeed prefer) wet and even boggy conditions. Thus, you have a wide range of sites from which to select. Once again, to test a site for drainage, dig a hole to a depth of about one foot and fill the hole with water. Allow the water to soak in. Repeat this two more times. If water remains after that, drainage is not sufficient for growing some varieties of perennials. Consult the encyclopedia and select only those that are tolerant of wet conditions. If the water does drain, the site is suitable for almost all varieties of perennials.

How do I plan my perennial planting? As always, it is best to work out your plan on graph paper. Using a scale of one block on the graph paper to two inches of garden space, sketch out the area you wish to plant. Then, keeping the following in mind, give your creative impulses free reign:

● There are advocates of herbaceous or perennial *borders* and those of herbaceous or perennial island *beds*. Borders are the traditional way of installing perennials. They date back to the English gardens of the nineteenth century, when vast (fifty-foot-long) plantings of perennials provided a spectacle all during the growing season. The only problem with borders is that to be effective, they must be at least six feet, and preferably eight feet, deep. They should also have a backdrop of a wall or a tall green hedge. This makes maintenance very difficult, as access is limited to one side—the front. In the days of inexpensive labor, gardeners took care of maintenance, but these days, most homeowners maintain their properties themselves. For this reason, island beds are preferred today. These can be of any shape—square, rectangular, circular, oval, or freeform. However, square or rectangular beds, set in the middle of a lawn, look particularly ugly during the winter when the garden is bare of bloom and foliage. For most landscape purposes, it is best to design an informal, freeform island bed, perhaps six to ten or twelve feet across at its widest point. For the most pleasing visual effect, the bed should be perhaps three times as long as it is wide and placed off center in a lawn area. That is, don't set it squarely in the middle of a lawn area. In this way, even though the bed will be bare in winter, it will not be situated so that it is the focal point in the yard. An island bed is also recommended for easy maintenance, as it is accessible from all sides.

● If you plan an herbaceous or perennial border, tall plants should be placed in the rear, medium-height plants in the middle, and low-growing plants in the front. If you plan an herbaceous or perennial island bed, taller plants belong in the middle, low-growing plants on the border, and medium-height plants in between.

• The tendency of most novice gardeners is to go through plant catalogues, selecting this or that plant because the flower is very beautiful, and totally ignoring the overall effect they wish to create. You want to strive for a harmonious bed, with colors that blend rather than clash. So don't be tempted by a particular plant just because its flower is a magnificent bright red, shocking pink, or brilliant orange. Start with an overall plan and stick to it.

• Some mail-order supply houses offer perennial garden packages, already planned for color combinations, gradation of height, and growing conditions. These are usually a good investment for the gardener who has neither the time nor the imagination to plan his or her own.

• Plant perennials in groups of at least three of each variety, preferably five or seven (except for peonies, which are substantial enough in size and bloom to stand alone). Avoid planting two, four, or six of each variety, as an even number of plants tends to appear as a block of foliage and color in the garden, which you should avoid if you want to achieve an informal look.

• Never plant in straight rows. Instead, stagger your planting to secure the informal effect appropriate for perennials.

• White-flowering plants are essential to break up color patterns. At least one-fourth of your planting should be white.

• Have a color scheme in mind. Blue, purple, and pink interspersed with white and an occasional red is one suggestion. Blue, white, and yellow with an occasional purple, or red, yellow, and white with an occasional blue are other possibilities. Experiment with colors by using a paint box to see which combinations please you. As a rule, orange is an extremely difficult color to use in a perennial border, as it is too bright and will dominate the scheme. Most experienced gardeners avoid using orange in flower beds.

• Consult the perennial encyclopedia (pp. 205–18) to see what time of year various plants bloom. Remember that a plant without flowers in May provides green, silvery, gray, or blue foliage, and thus provides color even though not in bloom. Try to plan your scheme so that there is something in bloom throughout the season.

• Always think about the color, texture, and shape of the foliage when you select perennials. If a certain cultivar sports a beautiful flower, but its foliage is problematical or ugly, avoid that variety. Remember that most plants bear flowers for only a short period during the growing season while foliage, with a few exceptions, is present all during the season. Some varieties are evergreen and add interest to your border or bed during the winter months.

● When you are ready to install your perennial garden, take your chart to the garden with you along with a ruler to measure spacing and depth of plantings.

● As a rule, tall-growing plants should be planted two feet apart, medium-height plants eighteen inches apart, low-growing plants twelve inches apart, and tiny, miniature plants about six inches apart.

How do I prepare the soil? Most perennials prefer a moderately fertile soil, enriched with some organic matter. Some prefer sandy soil, some will thrive in moisture-laden soil, and some do best in poor soil. As a rule, however, if you enrich the soil moderately, almost all varieties you may wish to grow will thrive and bloom. Stake out your perennial bed and dig to a depth of one foot. Then mix the excavated soil with about half as much organic material, such as sphagnum peat moss (available in garden centers or nurseries) and/or compost. Then replace the mixture into the excavated bed. If the soil has a high clay content, a considerable amount of sand may be added to lighten it. Once finished, water thoroughly. Do this a week or two in advance of planting your bed.

When do I plant perennials? Spring is the best time for most varieties, although many will thrive if planted in early fall. If you do install a fall planting (after the first heavy frost), cover the entire planting with a six-inch layer of salt hay mulch. This will prevent plants from heaving as a result of alternating freezing and thawing of the soil during the winter.

How do I plant perennials? Once you have designed your garden, purchased your plants, and fortified your soil, it is time to install your garden. Bring your chart and a ruler to the garden with you. Place the plants exactly where they are to be installed. Dig holes and one by one, plant the perennials at the depth that they were grown in the nursery. If your plants were ordered by mail and arrive dry root, inspect them closely and you will find that you can usually see the soil line between the roots and the stems. Firm the soil around each plant and water thoroughly. Check the encyclopedia (pp. 205–18) and fertilize only if instructed to do so.

Should I mulch my perennial planting to protect from winter cold? It is a good idea to mulch a new planting during the first winter. After the first killing frost, place a six-inch layer of salt hay over the entire planting as a mulch. This is not done to protect the roots from the cold—they are quite hardy—but, as mentioned above, to prevent the heaving of plants due to freezing and thawing of the ground during the winter. Should your plants heave anyway—that is, should they end up above the soil level at which you planted them—don't worry. On a warm day, when the soil is workable, simply push them back into the soil and firm the soil around them.

How do I maintain my perennial garden after the first season's bloom? Different varieties have different needs. Some must be fertilized each year, some should never be fertilized. Some must be divided periodically to maintain vigor, others can be left undisturbed. Check the encyclopedia (pp. 205–18) for information pertaining to each individual variety.

What about mulching during the summer? This is always a good idea, as mulch helps keep weeds down and maintains moisture, cutting down on dreary maintenance work. A three- to six-inch mulch of shredded pine bark compost is perhaps most effective. There are many mulches available, but not all of them are recommended. Peat moss should not be used as a mulch as it forms a crust and prevents moisture from entering the soil. Cocoa bean shells emit a strong chocolate odor, which most people find inappropriate for the garden. Shredded newspaper is ugly. Grass clippings are acceptable, but they tend to leach nitrogen from the soil, requiring yearly fertilization to compensate for this loss.

What about watering my perennial garden? Although not all perennials need regular watering, in order to afford yourself the widest selection, it is a good idea to plan on watering thoroughly to a depth of one foot during summer drought periods. You can install an expensive sprinkler system, but it's not really necessary. Even with an ordinary hose system, you can water effectively with a minimum of effort. Rather than dragging a hose around the garden all summer, buy a hose with holes punctured in it. These hoses are readily available and reasonably priced. They can be laid down in the garden under the foliage and will be virtually invisible. To water your garden, simply attach this hose to the hose attached to your outdoor water supply and let it run for several hours.

Can I plant perennials in a rock garden? By all means; they are ideally suited for rockeries. Select the low-growing varieties—those that endure drought if the garden is in the sun—and combine them with a planting of spring bulbs. Fill in with annuals after the bulbs have bloomed, or over-plant bulbs with perennials from the list on page 218 and you will enjoy the glorious display of a rock garden.

Are there any varieties of perennials I can plant in the woods or in a shady spot? Yes indeed, there are many. Check the encyclopedia (pp. 205–18) for varieties recommended for shady woodland conditions.

Are there any varieties of perennials I can plant in an area with poor drainage or where water stands for a long time after rain? Yes. Again, check the encyclopedia for recommended varieties. Japanese iris, a plant with a spectacular bloom, is particularly suited for this condition.

Are there any varieties of perennials I can count on if I don't have time to water regularly during the summer? Yes. Check the encyclopedia for recommended drought-resistant varieties.

After several years, some of my perennials no longer bloom so profusely. What should I do? This almost always means that it is time to divide the plant. In the spring, dig up the plant, cut it into pieces with a sharp knife, or pull the shoots apart with your fingers, and replant according to the instructions above.

What about pests and diseases? Most of the perennials included in the encyclopedia are relatively pest and disease free. However, just in case problems arise, listed below are the cures for the most common ailments. Chemical cures are available at most nurseries and garden centers. Always mix them according to manufacturer's instructions. Complete guidelines appear on labels. Read them carefully to protect your health.

Red spider. One of many varieties of mites that might strike perennials. Plants become yellow and weak. Undersides of leaves are dirty-looking when examined. This is the result of soil sticking to the fine webs that mites weave. These webs first appear near the ribs or margins of leaves and then over the entire surface. Larger mites can be seen with the naked eye. Use tedion if trouble is just beginning or kelthane for more advanced problems. This mite usually does not appear until the heat of summer.

Powdery mildew. Leaves become disfigured by a white fuzz. This disease is usually caused by lack of air movement, by very humid night conditions, or by evening dew, which begins around the end of July. Use captan or benomyl from midsummer until early September.

Aphids and chewing insects. Small, green insects that suck juices from buds, then leaves, then stems. Malathion is good for a quick kill; Sevin is useful for longer protection.

Borers. About the only perennial that may suffer from this pest is iris. See page 196 for detailed instructions on combatting borers.

The Big and Beautiful Five

Because they are so readily available, so spectacular, so easy to grow, and so versatile in the landscape, daylilies (*Hemerocallis*), plantain lilies (*Hasta*), iris, lilies (*Lilium*), and peonies are treated separately here, with detailed growing instructions.

Hemerocallis or Daylily, Zones 3–10

Daylilies have all the qualities the busy gardener could ask for. They are completely pest and disease free, are resistant to drought, adapt to all kinds of soil and light conditions, and grow so thickly that once established they choke out weeds and bloom flamboyantly all summer long. They have been grown in gardens for centuries and actually are not true lilies (i.e., members of the genus *Lilium*) at all but belong to the genus *Hemerocallis*, which derives from the Greek words for "day" and "beauty" and means "beautiful for a day." The name is appropriate because each blossom lasts no more than one day. But each stem sports a score or more of buds, and each day a new one unfolds, then fades, with the next opening the following day. Some varieties produce such an abundance of buds that the total bloom time may last from thirty to forty days.

During the past few decades, hybridizers have created hundreds of new varieties, many of which are a far cry from the lemon lilies of grandmother's day and their relatives, the tiger lilies, commonly seen along roadsides during the summer. Lovely pastel shades of melon, peach, ivory, yellow, pink, and lavender, intense gold, orange, red, and purple, and combinations thereof are all readily available. Some varieties sport blossoms that are eight inches across, while some miniatures are a mere three inches across. Heights range from one foot to three feet or more, so there are varieties available for every conceivable landscape use. By planting early, midseason, and late-blooming varieties, your garden can be a glittering showcase all summer long. There are also varieties available that open in the evening, should you care to create a twilight garden to enhance outdoor entertaining. Add to this the fact that many daylilies now exude a subtle gardenia fragrance, and you have what may be the perfect flowering plant. Plant them anywhere you want a spectacle of color during the late spring, summer, or early fall. If you have a difficult slope or an area of your property that presents maintenance and mowing problems, plant daylilies. They can serve as accents in borders and island beds, or they can be used to break up monotonous foundation plantings, to line driveways, and even as ground cover.

HOW TO PLANT: Daylilies can be planted anytime during the growing season, even while plants are in bloom, but early spring and fall are the ideal times in most parts of the country. For best results, select a site that is in partial shade—preferably one that receives about four hours of sun a day—for the relentless hot, full sun of summer tends to fade daylilies' blooms. You can expect reasonable results even if you do plant in full sun. Deep shade is not suitable, however, although you can expect some bloom even under this adverse condition. Though not particularly fussy about soil, daylilies will probably not survive in waterlogged soil of a claylike consistency. Since they grow vigorously and form a dense mat in a few years, space plants at least two feet apart. Miniature varieties can be spaced one foot apart. Although they adapt to a wide range of soil types, for best results, fortify the soil as instructed on page 183.

MAINTENANCE: Although your plants will probably survive the first winter without mulch, it is wise to place about six inches of salt hay on top of the planting to prevent heaving. Remove this mulch in spring when the first signs of growth appear. If you find in early spring that your plants have heaved—that is, that they have been raised from soil level—simply firm them back to ground level. Daylilies thrive in moist soil, so during the hot, dry, summer months, water them thoroughly to a depth of about one foot at least once a week. To help retain moisture, it is a good idea to apply a two- to three-inch mulch of sphagnum peat moss, wood chips, or compost. This mulch will also help keep weeds down until the planting is established.

When new growth emerges in spring, and again after bloom, scratch one tablespoon of 5-10-5 fertilizer into the soil around the plant. To maintain an attractive planting, remove spent blossoms as they fade, and in fall, after foliage has withered, remove and dispose of it.

TIPS: After four or five years, your daylily planting may show signs of being overgrown. Bloom may become sparse because the roots have used up most of the nutrients in the soil. This is the time to dig and divide—a little work, but the reward will be a renewed bed, full of bloom, plus many additional plants to use in your landscape. Daylily roots are tough, and division requires some effort. The best way to divide them is to drive two spading forks into the clump, back to back, and then pull the clump apart. Once it is divided in half, you can use either a sharp knife or an ax to divide the plant further, or pull the divisions apart with your hands. Each division should be about the size of a head of cauliflower and have at least three stems with all of the roots attached. Cut the foliage back to five or six inches and replant. When you replant, either fortify the existing bed as you did when planting initially or plant in fortified soil in a new site. In either case, fresh soil is important. You can divide daylilies in spring or fall, though fall, after bloom time, is preferable. The following year bloom and growth may be sparse, but after that your daylilies will once again grow vigorously and bloom will be profuse. You will have to repeat this process every four or five years.

Daylilies lend themselves to cut-flower arrangements, and if you have a planting of them, you can enjoy bouquet after bouquet indoors. In the evening, cut stems with several well-developed buds and submerge them in cold water up to the buds. Leave them there overnight. The next day, place them in a vase, and each day thereafter, cut off the spent blooms. A location that is cool and not in direct sunlight will help the blossoms last. If you would like a bouquet of daylilies for an evening party, simply place the stems in water in the refrigerator during the day, and they will open at night when you take them out. Because of the short span of each bloom, daylilies are best used in bouquets rather than arrangements.

And last, but far from least, daylily buds are edible! The lily buds used in Chinese cooking are one and the same. To process lily buds for cooking, pick them before they have opened, dry them thoroughly in the sun, place them in air-tight containers in a cool, dark place, and use them to create delectable Chinese dishes for your guests.

Some Available Hemerocallis or Daylily Varieties

Below is a list of some of the more readily available varieties of daylilies. Here is a key to the symbols used:

E - Early blooming. In most parts of the country, June.
M - Midseason blooming. In most parts of the country, July and early August.
L - Late blooming. In most parts of the country, late August and early September.
OE - Opens in the evening rather than in the daytime.
Repeat - This indicates that the variety may sport a second bloom later in the season.

Red and Purple Shades

VARIETY	HEIGHT	DESCRIPTION
Gala Greetings	34″	M, OE, 5″ blooms; bright cherry red with gold throat
Jug of Wine	34″	E, M, Repeat, OE, 6″ blooms; velvety fuchsia red with a gold heart
Plush	36″	E, M, 4″ blooms; ruffled raspberry red with velvety finish
Saucy Sue	32″	E, M, Repeat, 5″ blooms; velvety garnet red
Sleigh Ride	20″	M, Repeat, OE, 5″ blooms; very ruffled strawberry red
Swiss Strawberry	34″	M, Repeat, 5″ blooms; light strawberry red with darker veins

Pastel Pink and Rose Shades

VARIETY	HEIGHT	DESCRIPTION
Abstract Art	32″	M, Repeat, 6″ blooms; coral amber petals with honey buff sepals

VARIETY	HEIGHT	DESCRIPTION
Away We Go	28"	E, M, 5" blooms; intense cantaloupe with much pink, ruffled and crimped
Bee Haven	25"	M, 7"–8" blooms; smooth melon with orchid overtones
Beyond Call	20"	M, Repeat, 5" blooms; pale amber peach with pink ribs
Broadway Melody	26"	M, Repeat, 5" blooms; creamy, pale pink
Chatter of Color	22"	M, L, Repeat, 5" blooms; green heart opens to melon pink with orchid ruffles
Coral Princess	40"	M, Repeat, 7" blooms; orange apricot with coral ruffles
Cup Race	36"	M, Repeat, 4" blooms; salmon pink
Glistening Beauty	36"	M, 5"–6" blooms; ruffled orchid pink with green heart
Little Girl	28"–30"	M, 4" blooms; light orchid pink, ruffled
Little Wart	24"	M, Repeat, Fragrant, 3" blooms; deep lavender with green heart
Lovely Dancer	22"	M, Repeat, OE, 6" blooms; opens pale amber peach and changes during the day to deep rose pink
Nob Hill	36"–38"	E-M, Repeat, OE, 6"–7" blooms; pale lavender pink and green bitone
Paradise Kitten	22"	M, L, Repeat, 4"–5" blooms; round, frilled, orchid pink
Pink Garland	30"–36"	M, Repeat, OE, 5"–6" blooms; salmon pink shading to creamy pink
Silver Pink	32"	M, OE, 5" blooms; true pink with green throat
Snow Valley	18"	M, L, 6" blooms; ruffled, star-shaped, snow pink
That's Different	20"	M, OE, 5"–6" blooms; tangerine heart blending to deep rose-pink frills

Gold and Orange Shades

VARIETY	HEIGHT	DESCRIPTION
Etched in Gold	27″	E, M, OE, 6″ blooms; gold ruffles with melon-edged petals and primrose heart
Golden Candles	35″	M, Repeat, OE, 8″ blooms; huge, triangular shaped, gold
Golden Gift	32″	M, Repeat, OE, 5″ blooms; ruffled and quilted, pure gold
June Prom	20″–24″	M, Repeat, 6″ blooms; sparkling pale-orange sherbet
Little Love	25″	M, Repeat, 5″ blooms; multiple small, melon-gold flowers
Rembrandt	28″	M, Repeat, 7″ blooms; huge, orange with a hint of pink ribs
Sea Gold	22″–24″	E, M, Repeat, OE, 4″ blooms; amber gold shading to pale peach
Toyland	20″–24″	M, OE, 2″ blooms; bell-shaped flowers of tangerine and orange-pink
Wild Welcome	34″	M, L, Repeat, OE, 4″–5″ blooms; gold apricot shading to apricot pink

Cream, Lemon, and Yellow Shades

VARIETY	HEIGHT	DESCRIPTION
Alice in Wonderland	32″	M, 5″ blooms; frilly, ruffled, lemon yellow
Arrowmaker	27″	E, M, OE, 6″–7″ blooms; large, lemon yellow with a touch of rose
Close Up	26″–32″	E, M, 6″ blooms; clear lemon with a touch of rose, ruffled
Dream Baby	28″	E, M, 3″ blooms; small, ruffled, pale yellow
Empire	30″–32″	M, 6″–7″ blooms; chrome yellow, ruffled

VARIETY	HEIGHT	DESCRIPTION
Hotel de Ville	32″	M, OE, 6″–7″ blooms; ruffled, yellow with hint of pink
Mary Todd	34″	M, L, 6″ blooms; golden yellow
Miniature King	22″–24″	E, M, 3″–4″ blooms; butter yellow
Winnie the Pooh	36″	M, 2″–3″ blooms; round, ruffled, and curved; yellow with golden throat
Young Countess	26″	M, Repeat, 4″–5″ blooms; pale yellow blending into pale orchid pink

Hosta or Plantain Lily, Zones 3–10

Among the easiest plants of all to grow, this old-fashioned cultivar is enjoying an unprecedented renaissance, due to its adaptability to a wide range of growing conditions, its near indestructibility, its suitability as a ground cover in low-maintenance landscapes, and, perhaps most important, because of the fact that it grows beautifully under shady conditions. Although *Hosta* sports delicate blossom spikes in white, lilac, and lavender from June to September, depending on the variety, it is grown primarily for its lush foliage, which is often variegated and always tidy. Its leaves range in size from less than one inch to more than one foot across, in colors ranging from yellow to light green, dark green, gray, and near steel blue, often edged or speckled with white, cream, or yellow. Leaf texture varies; some varieties have smooth leaves, others ribbed, others delicately twisted. The mature plants range in diameter from around one to three or four feet. They range in height (without bloom) from several inches to almost four feet. Flower stalks range from just above foliage height to five feet.

Use *Hosta* to edge foundation plantings, shrub borders, or herbaceous perennial borders. Larger-growing varieties can be used as specimen plants; that is, they can be planted singly within a border or to complement a foundation planting or shrub border. Although they won't grow to full size in areas of deep shade under such trees as maples and beeches (primarily because the roots of these trees absorb most of the moisture and nutrients from the underlying soil), older varieties will survive and often thrive under such conditions, providing a reliable ground cover in areas where almost nothing else will grow. Ideal growing conditions are semishade, rich soil, and adequate moisture, but *Hosta* will thrive even in full sun. Once established, clumps can be left undisturbed for years. Or, should you decide that you want more plants, and you undoubtedly will, propagation by division is a simple task. Simply dig the clump in early spring when shoots begin to emerge, or in fall after bloom, cut it with a knife, allowing perhaps three shoots per division, and replant. *Hosta* is perhaps one of the best "friends" a gardener or homeowner can have.

HOW TO PLANT: Although spring planting is preferred, *Hosta* can be installed in fall or even transplanted in summer. Select a site in deep shade, partial shade, or full sun. Prepare the soil as described on page 183. Space small-leaved *Hosta* eighteen to twenty-four inches apart and large-leaved varieties twenty-four to thirty inches apart. Excavate to a depth of about one foot and work in sphagnum peat moss or compost in a ratio of one part soil to one part additive. Mix in two tablespoons of 5-10-5 fertilizer. Replace the soil, then dig a hole large enough to accommodate the plant or division, set the plant in the hole, firm the soil around the plant, and water thoroughly.

MAINTENANCE: Each spring, when shoots emerge, scratch in about one tablespoon of 5-10-5 fertilizer around each plant. After bloom, remove spent flower stalks. In fall (after frost), remove dead foliage once it has browned, or do so in early spring. During periods of extreme summer drought, deep watering once a week is recommended for best results, although *Hosta* is drought resistant and will survive even if neglected.

TIPS: You will probably find, as I have, that you can't have enough *Hosta* in your landscape. A good way to increase your stock without paying a fortune for new plants is to ask friends, relatives, or neighbors who have established plantings for divisions. Then plant them in areas that are ideally suited for raising *Hosta*—that is, partial shade, with rich, moist soil. I have found that they grow rapidly, and although the divisions are small, I can divide each spring. In the course of a few years, I have increased my stock from one of each of eight varieties to a dozen of each. Since *Hosta* is not in full leaf until late May or early June, it makes an excellent overplanting for spring-blooming bulbs. If you decide to do this, it is probably best to plant the *Hosta* in the fall, after you have installed the bulbs.

PESTS AND DISEASES: *Hosta* is almost totally pest and disease free, with one occasional exception: snails or slugs. Antislug sprays are available at garden centers or nurseries should this unlikely situation arise. Apply according to the manufacturer's specific instructions. It is interesting and heartening to know that as plants get older, they become more resistant to slug damage.

Some Available Hosta Varieties

VARIETY	DESCRIPTION
Frances Williams	Blue-green foliage with white and golden yellow borders that intensify during the season; plant forms large clumps; white flowers; a variety of *Hosta sieboldiana*
August Moon	Large, yellow, rounded leaves that stay attractive all during the summer; white flowers with a touch of pale lavender
Brigham Blue	Heart-shaped, rich blue leaves; lavender flowers
Halcyon	Light blue leaves with smooth, elegantly pointed tips
Krossa Regal	Frosty blue foliage with upright leaves that grow to 3′ tall; lavender flowers on 5′-high stalks
Ginko Craig	A good, small plant to use for edging; lance-shaped leaves are edged in white
Golden Tiara	Low-growing to about 10″ high and 1′ in diameter, with 2″ long, medium green leaves, edged in chartreuse, turning bright gold in summer

Iris, Zones 3–10

The magnificent tall, bearded, or German iris is the flower that most people associate with this genus, and there is a vast selection of varieties available in every color except pure red. However, there are many other varieties of iris that are far more suitable for landscape purposes. Oh indeed, the tall, stately, bearded variety is a sight to behold when in bloom, and by all means grow it if you wish. But if you are creating a border or a bed, bear in mind that bearded irises are not well suited to this purpose for several reasons: they are very formal and rigid, they grow to a height of three to four feet and thus often need staking to protect them from wind and heavy rains, and their very flamboyant coloring tends to overwhelm other culti-vars. If you decide that you simply must have them in your garden, install them in a separate, formal bed, where other less spectacular cultivars will not have to compete with them during bloom time. Most varieties of iris bloom in late spring, but a few bloom in early spring and early summer, and during the past decade or so, varieties have been developed that repeat bloom—that is, they bloom once in spring and then again in late summer. There are dwarf, medium-height, and tall-growing varieties as well. All have the characteristic spearlike foliage, although some varieties have less rigid leaves than others. Most irises require the same kinds of growing conditions, though there are exceptions.

Use irises in perennial beds and borders, in foundation plantings, in shrub borders, or in separate beds—wherever you want a reasonably maintenance-free planting. Use Japanese irises in swampy areas with poor drainage, for they thrive under these conditions. Some varieties are effective in bouquets, but the tall, bearded varieties are perhaps too flamboyant for this use, except in combination with other flowers.

Although irises are available at garden centers and nurseries, for the best selection and prices, I suggest that you order through mail-order houses specializing in irises.

After the initial preparation of the soil and planting, irises are virtually maintenance, pest, and disease free, with one exception: iris borers and accompanying bacterial soft rot, both of which are easily controlled if recognized in time.

HOW TO PLANT: If you order irises by mail, they will probably arrive bare root, with the foliage trimmed in the shape of a fan. Plant as soon as possible after arrival. If you purchase container-grown irises from a nursery or if friends give you divisions, it is best to plant them after bloom. Most mail-order houses deliver after bloom—that is, from late July through September. Select a sunny, well-drained location and prepare the soil as described on page 183. Irises require shallow planting, with the rhizome, or gnarled root, planted at the soil surface. Dig a hole just deep enough to accommodate the root system. Fill in the hole with fortified soil after planting, tamp down, and water thoroughly. Do not mulch bearded varieties, although Japanese and Louisiana irises should be mulched to preserve the moisture they so crave. Plant at least three of each variety if you are creating a border or bed, and arrange them in a triangle with the fan-shaped foliage facing toward the outside of the arrangement. In this way, as they grow, they appear to be one large clump rather than three small ones. Larger varieties should be spaced about ten inches apart, with dwarf and intermediate varieties spaced about eight inches apart.

MAINTENANCE: Irises need to be fertilized only once in a season. The best time to fertilize is in the spring, when they begin to grow. Scratch in about one tablespoon of all-purpose 5-10-5 fertilizer per plant. After bloom, cut the stalks from the plants and in fall, to avoid pest and disease problems, carefully remove all withered foliage. After a number of years, bloom will become sparse and plantings overcrowded. This means it is time to dig and divide your iris bed. After bloom, dig up iris clumps and separate them. Dispose of any diseased rhizomes and break off young plants from the main rhizomes. Dispose of main overgrown rhizomes. These overgrown rhizomes are knobby and produce few, if any, bloom stalks. Remove most of the foliage by trimming it to a fan shape, and replant as above.

PESTS AND DISEASES: Iris borer and bacterial soft rot are the only pests you will have to be concerned with, and these primarily if you grow bearded irises. But if you maintain a tidy bed by removing spent foliage in the fall, borer and accompanying rot should not strike. Bacterial soft rot enters the iris through wounds made by the borer. It multiplies rapidly and is detectable by its very offensive odor. It appears as a soft, water-soaked spot on the leaf. The infection often follows the borer down the leaf to the rhizome, rendering it a vile-smelling mush. If detected early, borers can be removed from the leaves with minimal damage to the plant. If not detected soon enough, it may be necessary to remove an entire leaf from the plant. Should the infection become very severe, there are chemicals that are effective. Malathion, available at garden centers and nurseries, applied according to manufacturer's directions, can solve the borer problem. To protect bearded irises against borers, never use mulch, as the drier the tops of the rhizomes, the more impervious they are to borer attack.

TIPS: Since irises multiply rapidly, if you plan ahead you can purchase single plants, put them in a nursery area, and, after three years or so, divide them and have enough for a substantial border or bed planting.

Some Available Iris Varieties

BEARDED IRIS: There are six different divisions of this cultivar: miniature dwarf, standard dwarf, intermediate, miniature tall, border bearded, and tall bearded. The tall bearded are the most universally planted and are available in more than a thousand different colorations. These bloom in late spring. Although staggeringly beautiful, they do not adapt well to border planting. The intermediate bearded, miniature tall bearded, and border bearded are more adaptable to border and bed treatment and also bloom in late spring. The dwarfs flower early in spring, around April, and are useful in rock gardens.

JAPANESE IRIS (*Iris kaempferi*): Japanese irises are hardy only to zone 5. They grow to around four feet tall and thrive in moist soil, even in bogs or pools. The blossoms are flat, often up to one foot in diameter, and are available in white, yellow, purple, and light blue. This is the only iris that thrives under swampy conditions. Plant rhizomes so that the tops are at soil level.

SIBERIAN IRIS *(Iris sibirica)*: These are highly recommended for perennial beds and borders, for the blossoms are less rigid than those of the bearded varieties, and the foliage is more graceful. They grow to a height of two to four feet and are available in shades of blue, purple, wine red, and white. They are quite pest and disease resistant and do not become overcrowded, although you can divide them a few years after planting if you want more stock.

LOUISIANA IRIS: Only recently available to northern gardeners, hybrids of this wild variety are already taking their place in garden schemes around the country. They thrive in full sun and do not need moist soil, although they prefer it. For this reason it is a good idea to apply several inches of mulch over the planting. They grow from three to four feet tall and are available in yellow, copper, blue, and a true red, the first iris known of that color.

DUTCH IRIS AND RETICULATA IRIS: These are bulbs and must be planted in the fall. They are not included here because although they can be used in beds and borders, they are problematical in some of the colder zones.

Lilium or Lilies, Zones 3–10

Although lilies are technically summer-flowering, hardy bulbs, they are included here as perennials, because they serve the same purposes in your landscape scheme. And, unlike dahlias and gladiolas, the bulbs are winter hardy and do not have to be dug in fall and stored indoors over the winter. A wealth of varieties is available, so you must be careful to select those that will best suit your purpose(s). You can use lilies in perennial borders and island beds, for masses of color among shrub borders, or incorporated within foundation plantings to add zest to their usual monotony. They are ideal for bouquets and cut-flower arrangements. Lilies are available in just about every color except blue and range from two-foot-high dwarfs to towering seven-foot-high specimens. There are early, midseason, and late-blooming varieties. The latter, which bloom in August, are particularly useful because little else blooms at this time of year. Their foliage is dark green and remains attractive all during the growing season. After the initial preparation of the soil and planting, they are practically maintenance free.

Of particular note is their fragrance, which ranges from light to very heavy, depending on the variety. A stand of some of the heavily scented varieties will perfume your entire garden and will also attract hummingbirds.

Lily bulbs are sometimes available in garden centers and nurseries, but for a wider selection it is best to order from mail-order houses that specialize in bulbs (see p. 248). In order to make an effective "statement" with lilies, plant at least three bulbs of each variety in a given location rather than one variety only or one each of several different varieties.

HOW TO PLANT: Although you can plant lilies in the fall, or even move them during the summer, spring is the best planting time. Select a site with very good drainage, for lily bulbs will rot if planted in boggy soil. Plant in full sun or partial shade. Prepare and fortify the soil as described on page 183. Then dig a hole one foot across and one foot deep and mix a handful of all-purpose 5-10-5 fertilizer in the bottom of the hole. It is a good idea to mix about one tablespoon of an acid-type fertilizer such as Miracid into the hole as well. A good rule of thumb is to plant all lily bulbs about six inches deep. However, fist-sized bulbs should be set about eight inches deep. Tamp down the soil and water thoroughly. After planting, mulch heavily, as lilies thrive in cool, moist soil. Space bulbs from six to eighteen inches apart, depending on the variety. See the section on varieties of lilies below for specific spacing information.

MAINTENANCE: As the flower stalks grow, taller-growing varieties will have to be staked. To do this drive a one-inch-by-two-inch wooden stake about six feet long into the soil next to the lily. Take care not to drive the stake too close to the stalk, as you might injure the bulb. Then tie the stalk to the stake with twine, preferably green in color. Shorter varieties usually do not need staking, so if you don't think you will have time to install stakes, plant only the shorter-growing varieties. After bloom, remove spent blossoms. In fall, after killing frost, remove withered stalks. If you cut lilies for bouquets, do not cut long stems, as food for next year's bloom is contained in the stems and leaves. Renew the mulch each year to ensure cool growing conditions for the roots. Each spring, scratch in a handful of acid-type fertilizer around the base of each plant. If the plants become crowded, dig them up after bloom, separate the bulbs, and replant as described above.

PESTS AND DISEASES: Lilies are almost totally pest and disease free, though aphids might occasionally attack. The best thing to do in this case is to spray the stalks with water from a hose. If the problem persists, dust with rotenone, available at garden centers and nurseries, or spray with any indoor or outdoor house and garden spray.

TIPS: When cutting lilies for bouquets or to give as gifts, it is best to remove the stamens from the bloom, for the pollen can stain fabric. Simply cut the stamens with scissors or pinch them out with your fingers. Try to be careful not to let any pollen fall on the flower petals, as it detracts from the beauty of the bloom. If you do decide to pick an entire bouquet of lilies to place in the house, the scent may be too overwhelming, indeed funereal. It is probably better to mix one or two stalks of lilies with other flowers.

Some Available Lily Varieties

The array of lilies available can be overwhelming when you sit down to make a selection for your garden. It took me many years to figure out which varieties were best suited to my purposes, and I made a number of mistakes in the process. For example, because I had a location ideally suited to the growing of lilies, those I selected—the Aurelian hybrids— which were supposed to grow to about four feet, reached a towering seven feet and looked absurd in their surroundings. The following breakdown should help you make intelligent selections.

AURELIAN HYBRIDS: These are the towering trumpet lilies that can grow to seven feet. They look magnificent as a backdrop for a very wide border, but for most landscape purposes they are simply too tall. If conditions are less than ideal—that is, if they are planted in full sun and left without mulch—they will dwarf. However, this is best left to more experienced gardeners who have the time and are willing to make the effort to experiment with different locations for lily plantings. They bloom from the end

VARIETY	HEIGHT	DESCRIPTION
Pink Perfection	5'	Huge, 2½' flower heads of rich pink
Golden Splendor	4'–5'	8–20 flowers of rich gold
Regale Lilies	4'	Large blooms of white with a gold throat
Green Magic	4'–6'	8–20 flowers of white with pale green overtones
African Queen	4'–6'	Huge, deep gold-orange flowers

of June to the end of July in most areas of the country. This variety always needs staking.

HYBRID LILIES: These are much more manageable and sensible for the average home landscape than the Aurelian hybrids, as they grow to between two and four feet, depending on the variety. The flowering spike is compact with many blooms, some in solid colors, others speckled. They bloom from mid-June to mid-July in most parts of the country and rarely need staking. Be very careful when selecting colors, as some can be quite startling, even garish.

VARIETY	HEIGHT	DESCRIPTION
Bravo	2'–3'	Mellow red to orange-red, unspotted
Fireball	2'–3'	Rich red, unspotted
Freckles	2'	Bright yellow with magenta spots
French Vanilla	2'–3'	Soft creamy yellow
Heritage	2'–3'	Warm mellow red with small spots
Matchless	2'–3'	Rich orange-red, unspotted
Melon Time	3'–4'	Melon orange, unspotted
Mont Blanc	2'–3'	Pure white
Rosefire	3'–4'	Orange-red bicolor
Utopia	2'–3'	Bright buttercup yellow
Venture	2'–3'	Intense burgundy red
Zephyr	3'–4'	Clear rose-pink, spotted

HYBRID ASIATIC LILIES: Although these lilies grow taller than the above hybrids, the stems are quite strong and support the abundance of blooms. Thus, they usually do not require staking. They are early bloomers, from mid-June to July. The petals are turned back, and many varieties are speck-

VARIETY	HEIGHT	DESCRIPTION
Enchantment	3'	10–16 nasturtium red blooms per plant
Connecticut King	4'	Large yellow with gold overtones
Prominence	2½'–3'	Glowing cherry red
Connecticut Yankee	4'	Apricot orange with secondary buds that extend bloom
Sterling Star	4'–5'	Ivory, star-shaped flowers with wine-colored spots
Gypsy	4'	Candy pink, star-shaped flowers with carmine spots and yellow throat

led. Enchantment, which is a brilliant red-orange, is difficult to blend with other perennials. Again (and as always, this is a highly subjective matter), select colors carefully to blend in with other plantings, as some are overwhelming.

SPECIOSUM LILIES: Many consider these the most beautiful of all the lilies. Certainly the *Speciosum rubrum* is one of the most popular of all the lilies and is even available now in florist shops. Although they can grow to four or even five feet, they rarely need staking. There are many varieties available, with more being introduced each year. Order them early from mail-order bulb suppliers, as these are the first of the lilies they run out of, since they are very popular with gardeners. They are rarely available at garden centers and nurseries. They bloom from late July through August.

VARIETY	HEIGHT	DESCRIPTION
Stargazer	18″	A new variety; deep pink flowers with dark red spots and bright white petal edges of taller and older varieties
Album	3′–4′	Pure white; new and expensive, but a show stopper
Auratum Lily (*Lilium* Goldbanded)	3′–4′	Large flowers of pure white with golden yellow bands and allover dark red spots; petal edges are attractively ruffled; very fragrant
Bi-Centennial	3′–4′	Large flowers of glowing rose with white edges
Uchida (*Speciosum rubrum*)	4′–5′	The best known of this category, graceful large flowers of rich pink shading to brilliant crimson at the center of the petal, with dark red spots all over

TIGER LILIES (*Tigrinum splendens*): Most of these varieties are spotted, with the petals turned back. They bloom from late July to September, filling a gap in garden color. Each produces from twelve to twenty flowers per stem. They reach a height of three to four feet. Here again, be careful in your color selection, as some varieties tend to be garish.

VARIETY	DESCRIPTION
White Tiger	Pure white flowers with maroon dots and stamens
Yellow Star	Bright buttery yellow, with black dots
Tigrinum Rose	Lovely rich pink flowers with black dots
Red Fox	Intense red, with black dots and satin sheen
Torino	Delicate cream white with a hint of yellow and wine red dots
Tigrinum Fortuneii	Large flowers of gleaming salmon orange with black dots
Sunny Twinkle	Bright, shining, yellow-gold flowers with black dots

Paeonia or Peony, Zones 2–8

There are two kinds of peonies: *tree peonies*, also called *shrub peonies*, and *herbaceous peonies*, also called *Chinese* or *garden peonies*. Tree peonies are not really trees but small shrubs, growing to about four feet in height. They lose their leaves in winter, but the woody framework does not die down. Because their foliage and bloom are more lush than tree peonies, herbaceous peonies are better for landscaping purposes (and are therefore the focus of this section). They die down to the ground in winter, only to emerge again in spring. Although most varieties bloom during a two- to three-week period from late May to early June, by selecting from early, midseason, and late-blooming varieties, the bloom season can be extended to around six weeks. Peony blooms are spectacular, often measuring up to eight inches across, and are available in a wide range of pink, red, white, and pale yellow colorations, single, semi-double, and double, set above two- to four-foot-high foliage that remains strikingly handsome after the bloom period. Peonies are virtually indestructible, are pest and disease free, and are so beautiful that they deserve a place in any landscape. If you plant them in a spot well suited to their needs, they can live one hundred years or more.

Use them in borders, as specimen shrubs, in foundation plantings, as a hedge, for masses of color, and for cutting. Although it is generally advisable, when installing a perennial border or island bed, to plant three or more plants of each cultivar together, one peony in each spot will usually suffice, unless you are planning a large border. You can repeat this single plant throughout your border or bed if you wish. Remember that peonies are very flamboyant, so be cautious about the colors you select. If you want to achieve a subtle effect, select from the whites, pinks, and pale yellows. If a more dramatic display is desired, use the red or red and white varieties.

HOW TO PLANT: Late summer or early fall is the time to install peonies. Although they are often available at garden centers or nurseries during spring, all experts agree it is not advisable to plant at that time of year. This is because the plant is dormant in late summer or fall. In spring the plant is sending forth new growth that is best left undisturbed. Select a site with good drainage in full sun. It is a good idea to be very selective about the site, since peonies take several years to establish themselves and loathe being moved. Fortify the soil as described on page 183, but instead of fortifying to a depth of one foot, dig to a depth and diameter of one and a half feet. While adding sphagnum peat moss, well-rotted manure, or compost, add several substantial handfuls of 5-10-5 fertilizer to the soil. Then fill the hole with soil so that the buds or "eyes" on the fleshy roots are exactly between one and one and a half inches below the soil surface. These "eyes" are easy to spot, as they are creamy white with a touch of pink. If you are installing a peony that was grown in a container, plant it so that the soil surface in the container is even with the surrounding soil surface. Take a ruler with you when planting to ensure proper depth of planting. If you plant peonies too deep, there will be little or no bloom. Tamp the soil down firmly, water thoroughly, and apply a two-inch mulch around the plant. If you are planting more than one peony, space them about four feet apart.

MAINTENANCE: After the first hard frost, cover the entire plant with about SIX inches of salt hay or other mulching material to prevent heaving. In early spring, when shoots begin to emerge from the ground, remove the mulch. After the first year, it is not necessary to mulch peonies during the winter. Overfertilizing is probably the best way to kill a peony, so refrain from feeding until around the third year after installation. Then scratch in a handful of 5-10-5 fertilizer in early spring as the shoots emerge. Wait another three years or so before feeding again. Dead-head or remove all spent blossoms after bloom. After several years, when the plants reach maturity, you may find it necessary to stake the flower heads when they are in bloom. (See p. 198 for information on staking.) After the first killing frost, cut withered foliage to one and a half inches above the soil line.

PESTS AND DISEASES: It is unlikely that disease will strike your peonies, with one exception: botrytis blight. The signs of this blight are wilting foliage

Some Available Peony Varieties*

VARIETY	HEIGHT	DESCRIPTION
Belle Center	30"	E; semi-double, deep mahogany red bloom; entire flower is attractively cup-shaped
Early Scout	18"	E; single, very dark red blooms with finely cut foliage; blooms before all other hybrids
Fernleaf Double Red	15"	E; an old favorite, double red blooms on short bush with compact growth; these peonies were carried in covered wagons by garden-loving pioneers to their new homes on the great midwestern prairies
Ann Cousins	32"	M; large, double white blooms with a rose fragrance
Becky	32"	L; large, double pink flowers
Butterball	36"	M; pink-blossomed with a yellow butterball center
Cincinnati	32"	M; double crab apple-blossom pink, with petals edged in silver; dense, dark green foliage
Dixie	34"	L; double, very dark red; strong stems
Doreen	32"	M; single bloom of flashy pink with silvery yellow center; light-colored foliage; fragrant
Elsa Sass	30"	L; double bloomer resembling a pure white camellia
Hermione	36"	L; large apple-blossom pink, double blooms, with occasional red speckles
La Lorraine	36"	M; tall-growing double white with pink center, opening to pure cream
Lotus Queen	34"	M; single, pure white with glowing sulphur yellow center; slight fragrance
Minnie Shaylor	36"	M; semi-double, pure white blooms with red and yellow center
Mischief	36"	L; apple blossom shades of pink
Mrs. F. D. Roosevelt	34"	M; double blooms of seashell pink
Sarah Bernhardt	36"	L; double flowers of soft seashell pink with red flecking
White Wings	36"	M; single white, very large flowers up to eight inches in diameter

*See page 189 for key to symbols used in descriptions.

that eventually turns black and dies, or a dust resembling mildew that appears on buds. Should either or both of these occur, remove all diseased foliage and stalks, and dispose of them in the garbage. Then spray with a fungicide such as captan or benomyl, available at nurseries and garden centers, according to manufacturer's instructions. Tidy gardening will help prevent this and other diseases that may strike your plants. In the fall, remove all spent foliage and dispose of it in the garbage. You may notice black ants crawling on buds in spring. Do not worry: they are harmless and are merely attracted by the sweet secretions on the plant.

TIPS: Should you decide you want larger blooms on your plants, pinch off all side buds on each stalk as they emerge. You can propagate peonies by digging clumps in early fall, dividing them into four or five sections by cutting them with a sharp knife, and replanting. Each division should have from three to five eyes and at least one strong root.

The Perennial Encyclopedia

Cultivars marked with asterisks are easily grown, while others can sometimes be problematical for one reason or another. Spring is the best time to install most perennials.

Achillea or Yarrow, Zones 3–10

Light: Full sun.
Soil: Moderately fertile, but tolerates sandy soil.
Moisture: Drought resistant once established.
Bloom time: July to September.
Color range: Yellow, white, and pink.
Height: 3–48 inches, depending on variety.
Tips: Dwarf variety, *Achillea tomentosa*, suitable for rock gardens. Coronation Gold and Gold Plate may be too intensely yellow for overall effect. Moonshine is a pale, primrose yellow variety that blends nicely with other colors in a border.

Aconitum or Monkshood, Zones 3–8

Light: Full sun or partial shade.
Soil: Rich, well-drained soil.
Moisture: Moderately moist.
Bloom time: July to September.
Color range: Blue, violet, white, yellow, and dark red.
Height: 24–48 inches.
Tips: To keep plant vigorous, divide every three years. Roots are poison-
ous if eaten. Care should be taken when handling this cultivar, espe-
cially if you have cuts or abrasions on your hands, as painful swelling
can occur if plant juices come into contact with healing sores.

**Althaea or Hollyhock,* Zones 3–10

Light: Full sun.
Soil: Moderately fertile.
Moisture: Tolerates drought.
Bloom time: July to August.
Color range: Yellow, white, red, and pink.
Height: 60 inches.
Tips: Use for screens or as tall accents at the rear of borders. Tall varieties
may require staking. Unless sprayed regularly, foliage becomes dis-
eased and ugly during summer.

**Alyssum saxatile or Basket-of-Gold,* Zones 3–10

Light: Full sun.
Soil: Moderately fertile, but tolerates sandy soil.
Moisture: Drought resistant once established.
Bloom time: April to May.
Color range: Yellow.
Height: 12 inches.
Tips: Spreading plant used for borders and rock gardens. Most available
varieties are a very intense, often overpowering, yellow. Citrina is a
pale lemon color and Dudley Neville a buff or pale apricot. Both are
subtle and preferable to other varieties for an overall effect.

Anemone (Japanese), Zones 5–9

Light: Partial shade.
Soil: Moderately fertile.
Moisture: Moderately moist.
Bloom time: August to September.
Color range: Pink, white.
Height: 24–48 inches.
Tips: Because it is late-blooming, *Anemone* provides color when little else does. Good for cutting.

*Anthemis or Golden Marguerite, Zones 3–9

Light: Full sun.
Soil: Not fussy.
Moisture: Drought resistant.
Bloom time: July to killing frost.
Color range: Yellow.
Height: 30 inches.
Tips: Nearly indestructible. Divide each spring, discarding the woody center growth and planting the new side shoots. Dead-head throughout the summer to keep plant tidy. May need staking.

Aquilegia or Columbine, Zones 3–9

Light: Full sun or partial shade.
Soil: Moderately fertile and cool.
Moisture: Moderately moist.
Bloom time: June to July.
Color range: A wide range of colors and bicolors including yellow, red, pink, peach, coral, salmon, violet, purple, cream, white, and blue.
Height: 18–30 inches.
Tips: Use in borders, woodland plantings, rock gardens, and for cutting.

*Arabis or Rock Cress, Zones 3–9

Light: Full sun.
Soil: Moderately fertile.
Moisture: Moderately moist.
Bloom time: May.
Color range: White.
Height: 12 inches.
Tips: Ideal for rock gardens; also suitable for edging borders and beds.

*Armeria or Thrift, Zones 3–9

Light: Full sun.
Soil: Not fussy.
Moisture: Drought resistant.
Bloom time: May to June.
Color range: Pink, white.
Height: 12 inches.
Tips: Useful in rock gardens or for edging borders and beds.

*Artemisia or Mugwort, Zones 4–9

Light: Full sun.
Soil: Not fussy.
Moisture: Drought resistant.
Bloom time: No bloom; grown for its silver foliage.
Color range: Silver foliage.
Height: 12 inches.
Tips: Useful in beds and borders for foliage contrast.

Aster or Michaelmas Daisy, Zones 5–10

Light: Full sun.
Soil: Moderately fertile.
Moisture: Moderately moist.
Bloom time: May to July.
Color range: Pink, red, blue, violet, and white.

Height: 8–24 inches.
Tips: A perennial that is not used enough in this country. Useful in borders and rock gardens. Taller varieties must be staked and sometimes appear rangy, but shorter and medium-height varieties adapt well to border and bed treatment.

Astilbe, Zones 5–9

Light: Full sun or partial shade.
Soil: Moderately fertile.
Moisture: Moderately moist.
Bloom time: June to July.
Color range: White, pink, and red.
Height: 12–24 inches.
Tips: Feathery blooms on delicate foliage. Useful in borders, beds, and interspersed in foundation plantings. Adapts well to shady locations, combining well with *Hosta*. Adequate moisture must be provided, so it is best not to install under maple and beech trees, whose surface roots draw a great deal of moisture and nutrients from the soil.

*Bergenia, Zones 2–7

Light: Full sun or partial shade.
Soil: Not fussy.
Moisture: Drought resistant.
Bloom time: April to May.
Color range: Pink, red, and white.
Height: 12 inches.
Tips: Evergreen, useful at the front of a border or as edging. Should be divided every spring.

*Brunnera or Forget-Me-Not, Zones 3–9

Light: Partial shade.
Soil: Moderately fertile.
Moisture: Tolerates dry shade.
Bloom time: April to May.

Color range: Sky blue.
Height: 12–18 inches.
Tips: One of the few perennials that tolerates dry, shady conditions such as those found under maple and beech trees.

*Campanula, Zones 5–9

Light: Full sun or partial shade.
Soil: Moderately fertile.
Moisture: Moderately moist.
Bloom time: May to August, depending on variety.
Color range: Blue, purple, lavender, and white.
Height: 6–36 inches, depending on variety.
Tips: There are many varieties available, ranging from dwarfs—useful in rock gardens and as edging for borders or beds—to tall-growing varieties—useful in the middle of borders or beds.

*Chrysanthemum, Zones 5–9

Light: Full sun.
Soil: Moderately fertile.
Moisture: Drought resistant.
Bloom time: July through frost.
Color range: A wide range of colors including yellow, white, rust orange, red, purple, and lavender.
Height: 8–36 inches.
Tips: Use in borders, beds, containers, or for cutting.

*Coreopsis, Zones 4–10

Light: Full sun.
Soil: Tolerates poor soil.
Moisture: Drought resistant.
Bloom time: May to killing frost.
Color range: Yellow.
Height: 24 inches.
Tips: Use for borders and cutting. Very easy to grow.

The Fourth Year

Daisy, Gloriosa, Zones 3–10

Light: Full sun.
Soil: Tolerates poor soil.
Moisture: Drought resistant.
Bloom time: July to August.
Color range: Yellow to mahogany.
Height: 18–36 inches.
Tips: Use for borders and cutting. Easy to grow.

Daisy, Painted, Zones 4–10

Light: Full sun or partial shade.
Soil: Moderately fertile.
Moisture: Moderately moist.
Bloom time: May to June.
Color range: White, pink, and red.
Height: 24 inches.
Tips: Use for borders and cutting.

*Daisy, Shasta, Zones 4–10

Light: Full sun or partial shade.
Soil: Moderately fertile
Moisture: Moderately moist.
Bloom time: June to August.
Color range: White.
Height: 12–42 inches.
Tips: Use for borders and cutting. Remains evergreen down to 5°F.

Delphinium, Zones 3–10

Light: Full sun or partial shade.
Soil: Requires very rich soil.
Moisture: Moderately moist.
Bloom time: June to July.
Color range: White, blue, purple, and pink.

Height: 26–60 inches.

Tips: Useful as a background in borders or cutting. Stems must be staked. Cut flower heads off after bloom and plant may bloom again in the fall. Can be difficult unless conditions are ideal, but because of their spectacular beauty they are worth the effort.

*Dianthus or Pink, Zones 4–10

Light: Full sun or partial shade.
Soil: Prefers sandy loam.
Moisture: Drought resistant.
Bloom time: May to June.
Color range: White, pink, and red.
Height: 8–18 inches.
Tips: Useful in rock gardens, for edging, and in borders. Beautiful clove fragrance.

*Dicentra or Bleeding Heart, Zones 3–9

Light: Partial shade.
Soil: Moderately fertile.
Moisture: Moderately moist.
Bloom time: May.
Color range: Pink, white.
Height: 12–36 inches.
Tips: An old-time favorite, easy to grow, useful in shady areas.

*Gaillardia or Blanket Flower, Zones 3–10

Light: Full sun.
Soil: Not fussy.
Moisture: Tolerates drought and heat.
Bloom time: June to September.
Color range: Yellow, red, and bicolors.
Height: 12–30 inches.
Tips: Use in borders and for cutting.

Geranium or Cranesbill,
Zones 3–10

Light: Full sun or partial shade.
Soil: Moderately fertile.
Moisture: Moderately moist.
Bloom time: Throughout season, depending on variety.
Color range: Blue, purple, and pink.
Height: 6–24 inches, depending on variety.
Tips: This is the perennial form of geranium, not the startling red flowers, which are annuals. Most are wild in origin and are quite easy to grow. Perhaps the reason they are so often overlooked is that many gardeners don't know that they are different from the annual geranium.

Geum, Zones 5–10

Light: Full sun.
Soil: Moderately fertile.
Moisture: Moderately moist.
Bloom time: June to September.
Color range: Red, yellow, and orange.
Height: 20 inches.
Tips: Use for borders and cutting. Often short-lived.

Gypsophila or Baby's Breath,
Zones 4–9

Light: Full sun.
Soil: Well-drained and fertile.
Moisture: Moderately moist.
Bloom time: June to July.
Color range: White, pink.
Height: 18–36 inches.
Tips: Use in borders. Sprays of these tiny flowers are ideal for arrangements or bouquets.

*Heliopsis or Sunflower, Zones 3–9

Light: Full sun.
Soil: Tolerates poor soil.
Moisture: Tolerates drought and heat.
Bloom time: August to September.
Color range: Yellow.
Height: 24–36 inches.
Tips: This is not the common sunflower, which is of the same genus, but because its blooms are smaller in size and plant height is from 2 to 3 feet rather than 6 to 8 feet, it is a variety more adaptable to the landscape.

*Heuchera or Coralbells, Zones 4–9

Light: Full sun or partial shade.
Soil: Moderately fertile.
Moisture: Drought resistant.
Bloom time: June to September.
Color range: Red, pink.
Height: 12–18 inches.
Tips: Use for borders, edging, and cutting.

*Iberis or Candytuft, Zones 3–10

Light: Full sun.
Soil: Moderately fertile.
Moisture: Drought resistant.
Bloom time: May to June.
Color range: White.
Height: 10–12 inches.
Tips: An evergreen, useful as a ground cover in rock gardens, beds, or borders.

Lavender, or Lavandula Officinalis, Zones 5–10

Light: Full sun.
Soil: Moderately fertile.
Moisture: Drought resistant.
Bloom time: July to August.
Color range: Lavender-blue flowers, gray-green foliage.
Height: 12–24 inches.
Tips: Use for borders and edging. Flowers and foliage have a haunting fragrance.

Liatris or Gayfeather, Zones 3–10

Light: Full sun or partial shade.
Soil: Not fussy about soil.
Moisture: Moderately moist.
Bloom time: July to August.
Color range: Purple, lavender, and white.
Height: 15–18 inches.
Tips: Maintenance free. Never needs dividing.

Monarda or Bee Balm, Bergamot, Oswego Tea, Zones 4–9

Light: Full sun or partial shade.
Soil: Not fussy about soil.
Moisture: Prefers moisture, but will survive drought.
Bloom time: June to September.
Color range: Red, white, purple, and pink.
Height: 24–48 inches.
Tips: Red varieties can be overpowering in a border, but Croftway Pink is subtle and blends nicely with other perennials. The leaves can be dried and used as an herbal tea. Mildew can strike during the summer, making the plant unattractive. Spray regularly with captan or benomyl, available at garden centers and nurseries, according to manufacturer's instructions. If you spray, do not use the leaves for tea.

*Nepeta or Catmint, Zones 4-9

Light: Full sun, partial shade, or deep shade.
Soil: Not fussy.
Moisture: Drought resistant.
Bloom time: May to September.
Color range: Lavender-blue.
Height: 12 inches.
Tips: Spreading, bushy plants useful in borders and beds. Foliage is scented.

*Oenothera or Evening Primrose, Zones 4-9

Light: Full sun or partial shade.
Soil: Not fussy.
Moisture: Drought resistant.
Bloom time: May to July.
Color range: Yellow.
Height: 6-18 inches.
Tips: Some varieties are night bloomers. Very easy to grow.

*Papaver or Oriental Poppy, Zones 3-9

Light: Full sun.
Soil: Moderately fertile.
Moisture: Drought resistant.
Bloom time: May to June.
Color range: White, pink, and red.
Height: 36 inches.
Tips: Reds may be too startling for an overall effect. Poppies resent being moved, so locate them in a permanent position. Their foliage dies down in summer, leaving bare spots that must be filled in with annuals.

Phlox, Zones 3-9

Light: Full sun.
Soil: Moderately fertile.
Moisture: Moderately moist.

Bloom time: June to September.
Color range: White, pinks, purple, red, lavender, and orange.
Height: 48 inches.
Tips: Must be sprayed throughout the summer for mildew or plant will look messy. Use captan or benomyl, available at nurseries and garden centers, according to manufacturer's instructions. Divide every three years to maintain vigorous bloom.

*Potentilla or Cinquefoil, Zones 5–9

Light: Full sun or partial shade.
Soil: Moderately fertile.
Moisture: Moderately moist.
Bloom time: May to July.
Color range: Pink, rose, white, yellow, orange, and copper.
Height: 6–18 inches, depending on variety.
Tips: Resents heavy, wet soil. Divide every three years to maintain vigorous bloom.

Primula or Primrose, Zones 5–9

Light: Partial to deep shade.
Soil: Moderately fertile.
Moisture: Moderately moist.
Bloom time: April to May.
Color range: Many colors and bicolors, including yellow, white, blue, red, purple, pink, gold, and salmon.
Height: 6–8 inches.
Tips: Primula vulgaris is the most reliable variety. Pacific hybrids, most readily available in garden centers and nurseries, tend to be short-lived.

Viola, Zones 3–10

Light: Partial shade.
Soil: Moderately fertile.
Moisture: Moderately moist.
Bloom time: June to killing frost.

Color range: Purple, lavender, yellow, white, and apricot.
Height: 6–12 inches.
Tips: Requires cool, moist conditions and rich soil. Dead-head as blooms fade or plant will become rangy. The familiar Johnny-jump-up is the most reliable variety.

Perennials Useful as Overplantings for Spring Bulbs

Ajuga†
Arabis
Artemesia
Aubrieta*
Geranium, perennial varieties
Helianthemum*
Iberis
Nepeta
Oenothera
Potentilla
Sedum*
Thymus*
Viola

Fences and Hedges

Unless your need for privacy has been so pressing that you have already installed fences or hedges earlier in your landscape project, now is the time to do so.

What are fences and hedges used for? Fences and hedges can be used to secure privacy, to screen out ugly views, to break up your property into a series of smaller areas, to enclose patios, vegetable gardens, or specialty gardens attractively, or to dress up driveways, paths, and steps.

†See the "Ground Cover Encyclopedia," page 132.
*See "Rock Gardens," pages 231, 232, 234, and 235.

The Fourth Year

I have decided that I want to install living fences, or hedges. What should I do? First, decide what kind of hedge you want to install. Do you want an evergreen hedge? Do you want a flowering deciduous shrub hedge? Do you want a low-growing or high-growing hedge? Do you want a hedge of trees? Check the tree and shrub encyclopedias in chapter 2 for further information. Although most communities do not have ordinances concerning living fences, it is a good idea to check with the local building department before you install a hedge, just to be sure. Once you have decided what kind of plant you wish to use for your hedge, order the planting material through a mail-order nursery or purchase stock at a local garden center or nursery.

What time of year should I install a living fence? Although spring is the best time to install most plant material, some varieties of shrubs or trees can also be planted in the fall. Check with the mail-order nursery or other source of your planting material for recommendations.

How do I install a living fence? Reread the shrub and tree sections in chapter 2 for information on installation.

How do I ensure a thickly growing hedge? Regular trimming of hedges forces thick growth. When you purchase stock for a hedge, inquire at the point of purchase about maintenance and trimming.

I have decided to install a fence. Before I do so is there anything I should check out? Yes. Many communities have ordinances about fence height and distance from adjoining properties, and some require building permits to install a fence. If you install a fence without the required permit, you may have to dismantle it if it is not in keeping with local ordinances.

Can I install a fence myself? That depends on the size, height, and type of fence you plan on installing. Low fences—picket, stockade, or basket weave—are easy to install. Taller fences are somewhat more complicated and often require considerable expertise. My advice to you is to have taller fences installed professionally.

What materials do I need if I wish to install a low fence myself? In addition to energy and time, you will need a posthole digger. You can usually rent one from a garden center or nursery for a minimal fee. Inquire at the point of rental about how to use this tool. You will also need something with which to tamp down and secure the soil. Tamping tools can also be rented, but you can use anything with a flat base that can be hammered with an ax or sledge hammer, as long as it tamps and firms the soil. A two-by-four hammered into the surrounding soil will do the trick.

What kind of wood should I use for my fence posts? You can treat ordinary lumber with preservatives, but pretreated lumber and fence posts are available at all lumber yards. I suggest you use this pretreated material rather than treating the wood yourself—a messy and complicated business.

What kind of fences should I install? There are many different kinds of fences available. I suggest that you go to a local fencing company and discuss your needs with them. They can recommend the proper type of fence for your property and needs. Most also install fences and offer some kind of guarantee on their work. Some will replace any posts that rot out after a few years, but most guarantee only materials; if a replacement should be necessary, you will have to pay the labor costs. Try to select a fence that is stylistically in keeping with the architecture of your house. Picket fences, for example, are appropriate for traditional American Colonial architecture, but generally do not work with contemporary architecture. Split-rail fencing is quite versatile and works with most styles of architecture. Consult a fence company about other styles.

What else should I do before installing a fence or hedge? Either buy a book on fences or go to the library and borrow one. There are so many options that it is impossible to outline them all here.

What about fence maintenance? A painted fence can look very attractive, but it must be repainted every few years to keep it looking that way. Many types of wood weather to a lovely gray color. These require an initial coat of wood preservative, but beyond that, no painting. To reduce maintenance, I recommend you go the natural route, using only wood preservative on bare wood.

I have installed my fence. How do I dress it up? You can install shrub or perennial plantings in front of it, or you can plant certain kinds of vines or climbing plants on it. You can also install planters or pots on the fence itself.

What kinds of vines or climbing plants can I install on a fence, on trellises attached to the house, on other buildings on my property, or on arbors? There are many kinds of climbing plants and vines, both annual and perennial, which are suitable for these purposes. You must select very carefully, however, because some grow so rampantly that they require heavy annual pruning in order to keep them in bounds.

Unfortunately, most perennial climbing plants are very fast growing and are thus not suited to the average property. Wisteria, with its lovely scented purple, pink, or white flowers, requires heavy pruning once established or it will take over the fence or building. The trunks ultimately become as thick as those of trees, and the weight of the plant, if allowed to run rampant, can topple a fence or even a house. Trumpet vine and honeysuckle are other perennial vines that are *not* recommended for the average property. However, there is one climbing perennial that is perfectly suited for your purposes. That is clematis, and I strongly recommend restricting yourself to this cultivar. Available in scores of varieties and a range of colors—pink, white, purple, and blue—clematis requires cool roots and full sun. For this reason, overplant the area where the roots will grow with ground cover, low-growing shrubs, or perennials. Each year in spring, work about one tablespoon of lime into the soil around the plant, as clematis thrives when grown in alkaline soil. Clematis cannot be easily grown from seed. Purchase plants from mail-order nurseries or from local garden centers or nurseries.

There are many annual climbing vine plants that are appropriate for fences, trellises, and arbors. These include morning glory, moonflower, *Thunbergia* or black-eyed Susan vine, canary creeper, *Tropaeolum* or nasturtium, and cardinal climber. These can all be planted from seed after all danger of frost.

How do I secure climbing plants to fences? You will have to provide some sort of support—something for the tendrils of these plants, which wind around support surfaces, to hold on to. You can locate trellises along the fence wherever you want to install a climbing plant, though this can be costly. I have found that a nearly invisible trellis, made of heavy-duty fish line tied to and wrapped around galvanized nails that have been hammered into the fence at intervals, is an inexpensive and aesthetically pleasing way to provide support.

Chapter Five

◆

THE FIFTH YEAR

The Finishing Touches: Specialty Gardens

Rock Gardens

Rose Gardens

Garden Structures and Decorations

It has been four years since you began your landscape project. By now, the trees you planted during the second year should be approaching semimaturity. No longer simple little sticks in the ground, each year they send new growth up to the sky, becoming more and more grand in stature. Your foundation plantings have filled out and have begun to assume their mature, graceful proportions. If you've installed perennial or shrub borders, they too have grown to near maturity. Your yearly annual planting has become far more complex in design and the use of color. Your bulb plantings are multiplying, and where you once had a display of several dozen daffodils, there are now hundreds. Screens or fences have been erected for privacy, and your outdoor living area has offered scores of evenings of pleasant dining and relaxation. Most of the drone work has been accomplished, and now you are ready for the finishing touches.

The Finishing Touches: Specialty Gardens

By this time, if your thumb has grown greener (and it undoubtedly has), you will probably have begun to think about planting some sort of small, specialized garden—it is inevitable if you have become addicted to gardening. Here is a list of specialty gardens you might consider. Some are small and intimate, others quite grand; some are utilitarian, others purely decorative:

- A dwarf conifer garden
- Herb gardens according to interest: herbal teas, aromatic herbs, kitchen herbs, medicinal herbs, all mint, all thyme, herb garden for sachets and potpourris
- An azalea and rhododendron garden

- A delphinium garden
- An iris garden
- A peony garden
- A *Hosta* garden
- A blue garden, featuring all blue-flowering plants
- A white garden, featuring all white-flowering plants, particularly effective in the evening and at night
- A red garden, featuring all red-flowering plants, particularly popular in Britain
- A Shakespearean garden, featuring plants mentioned in the bard's plays and sonnets. (There are more than 100.)
- An English cottage garden
- A wildflower garden
- A shade garden, featuring plants adapted to shady conditions
- A naturalized woodland garden
- A naturalized meadow garden
- A summer bulb garden, featuring tender bulbs that bloom in summer and must be dug in winter
- A chrysanthemum garden
- A summer lily garden, easily maintained
- A daylily garden
- A primrose garden
- A garden of everlasting flowers grown for dried arrangements
- A lilac grove
- A container garden for the patio
- A garden to attract birds
- A cut-flower calendar garden that provides cutting material all year long
- A Chinese vegetable garden
- A gourmet French vegetable garden
- A berry patch
- A fruit-tree orchard
- A salad garden
- A Japanese garden
- A medieval knot garden, featuring trimmed boxwood and other cultivars planted in the form of a knot
- A water garden with a small pool and fountain and aquatic plants
- A fragrance garden with heavily scented plants
- A garden with only traditional, old-fashioned varieties planted

Quite a list indeed, and something for everyone's taste or interest. There are scores of other specialty gardens in addition to those listed above. All it takes is the desire to specialize in any particular kind of plant and you have a specialty garden.

However, there are two specialty gardens that are unquestionably the most popular of all: the alpine garden or rockery, commonly called a rock garden, and the rose garden. For this reason, detailed instructions on how to install both are included in this chapter. An alpine garden, once installed, requires very little maintenance. A rose garden does require some attention, although not nearly as much as is generally thought.

Rock Gardens

The rock garden, or, more precisely the alpine garden, has long been prized by gardeners for its charm and beauty. And these days alpine gardens are enjoying renewed popularity, for once installed, they are virtually maintenance free. Problematic slopes, always difficult to landscape and maintain, can be turned into enchanting gardens, reversing the uphill battle of mowing and weeding. Even a monotonous flat landscape can accommodate a corner of mountain greenery, a small part of the Jungfrau, if you will, providing a pleasing change of grade as well as a major focal point.

When do I install an alpine garden? You can do this anytime during the growing season. The best time to install an alpine garden, however, is in late summer or early fall, as you will want to plant not only perennial blooming plants and probably a few dwarf conifers, but spring-blooming bulbs as well. And just think about the anticipation and excitement come spring, when your efforts will be rewarded with a spectacular progression of the intensely colorful blooms of alpine plants and miniature bulbs. And then, year in and year out, with a minimum of time and effort, your alpine garden will grow ever more beautiful.

How do I install the superstructure of an alpine garden? If you wish to install an alpine garden on a flat area of your yard, you will have to define and contain it. Six-by-six-inch railroad ties, available at lumber yards, sunken two inches into the ground, can be used for this purpose. The standard length of these ties is eight feet, so a total of eight ties will contain a sixteen-square-foot garden. You will also need soil to provide sufficient elevation for your minialpine landscape. Either move earth from another part of your property or have a landscape contractor provide it for you. For a sixteen-square-foot garden you will need three cubic yards of fill or subsoil, ideally composed of about half sand and half clay, and one cubic yard of topsoil. Once the subsoil is in place within the framework, dig in the topsoil to a depth of a garden spade, along with the contents of a three-cubic-foot bale of sphagnum peat moss. This will provide nutrients for the plants as well as drainage. If you already have a natural slope on your property, the above will not be necessary, for you can use that slope to shape your garden.

How do I shape my mini-landscape? Once you've defined your area and secured fill for elevation (or, if you have a natural slope, have added fill where necessary), you will be ready to shape your landscape. In nature, mountain areas contain outcroppings of boulders and rocks; this is the effect you wish to achieve. It might be a good idea to drive to a nearby hilly area to look closely at how rocks outcrop in nature. Note that some are at angles, and almost all are partially buried in the earth.

Start by moving the earth around to create "shelves"—steplike layers at various levels. If you are working with an established slope, excavate to create these "shelves." You will want to install at least three large boulders, each about two cubic feet in volume, in any alpine garden, perhaps more, depending on the size of the project. You will also want to install from fifty to one hundred smaller rocks, depending, again, on the size of the garden.

Using a thick-walled pipe or a two-by-four with a wedge, move the boulders into place. Use the wedge as a fulcrum placed near the rock; then insert the pipe or lumber beneath the rock and slowly ease it into place. Then "plant" the rocks to approximate a natural outcropping effect. One-third of the volume of the boulders should be buried beneath the soil level. Do not simply place boulders and smaller rocks on the surface of the soil —this will look ridiculous. Rock material that is native to your area is almost always the most aesthetically pleasing, and usually the least expensive. Artificial rocks are sometimes available in garden centers, but they never look natural. Once the largest boulders are in place to your satisfaction, "plant" the smaller rocks, being sure to create nooks and crannies to contain alpine plants and to leave flat areas free of rock material to accommodate mass plantings of bulbs and annuals.

You might want to install a birdbath in your garden. Do this after you've installed the rocks. Sink the saucer part of the birdbath into a level area. You can mask the circumference of the saucer with rocks if you wish.

What do I plant first in my alpine garden? Once you've completed your superstructure, plant specimen dwarf conifers or evergreens, which are slow-growing, tough, and very attractive plants. Although there is a wide range to choose from, you will need only a few to provide focal points. Consult the dwarf conifer encyclopedia (pp. 122–26) to determine which are best suited to your landscape. When you make your selection, be sure to vary your specimens to provide contrasts in shape, texture, and foliage color. Depending on the size of your garden, select two or three vertical, pyramidal, columnar, or conical-shaped specimens, several horizontal, low-growing, spreading varieties, and one nonconiferous plant, such as a golden, swordleaf yucca.

Vertical conifers should be planted on the upper levels of your garden, with the low-growing horizontal plants on the descending levels. This will help lead the eye from level to level.

Once you've made your selection but before you plant, set the specimens where you think you might want them. Then step back from the garden to see if the effect you have chosen pleases you. If not, move the plants around, step back again, and continue this process until you are sure the specimens are where you want them. Then set them in the ground permanently.

Although you should consult the dwarf conifer encyclopedia in chapter 2 for more extensive information, here is a list of dwarf conifers especially suited for alpine gardens:

- *Arborvitae:* Low-growing, green- to yellow-foliaged plants of many varieties.
- *Chamaecyparis* or false cypress: Low-growing and spreading with blue, green, or yellow foliage, depending on variety.
- *Cryptomeria japonica:* Low-growing and spreading with bright green foliage.
- *Picea* or spruce: Alberta is upright and conical, with medium green, dense foliage. Birdsnest is low-growing and moundlike, with medium green, dense foliage.
- *Pinus* or pine: Mugho is low-growing and moundlike, with medium green foliage. Aristata is upright and conical, with medium green foliage.

What is the next step in planting my alpine garden? The next step is to install alpine perennials. A vast variety is available, but keep in mind height, foliage texture and color, and flower shape, size, and color when you make your selection. Some alpine perennials are busy minishrubs, some evergreen, some deciduous, some spreading and matlike, some globular, and so forth. Most bloom from early to late spring and sport intensely colorful blooms. Look at your garden and try to calculate how much planting material you will need. As you do this, keep the following in mind:

- Alpines grow vigorously, and most spread somewhat as they do, so be sure to leave space for future growth.
- Plant at least three of the same variety together. A large splash of color at bloom time is more effective than a hodgepodge of different colors.
- Some plants, such as the sedums, thymes, and sempervirens, or "hens and chicks," are best planted in crevices of the rock structure, which usually accommodate one plant only.
- Try to keep a color scheme in mind and select perennials accordingly. Designing your scheme on graph paper before you purchase plants will help you decide which cultivars suit your purposes.
- Leave open spaces for planting spring-blooming bulbs.

Whether you've ordered your perennials from a mail-order nursery or purchased them at your local nursery or garden center, they will probably be in containers. As with the specimen evergreens, place the plants on your superstructure and step back to see if the effect pleases you. If not, move the plants around, step back again, and continue this process until you are sure the plants are where you want them. Then dig a hole, remove the plants from their containers, and install them. Water thoroughly after planting and continue to do so all during the fall.

The following perennial plants are well suited to an alpine garden. They all adapt to either full sun or partial shade and are, for the most part, drought resistant and very hardy. For more information on these and other perennials, consult the perennial encyclopedia (see pp. 205–18).

Achillea or yarrow
Alyssum saxatile or basket-of-gold
Arabis or rock cress
Armeria or thrift

Campanula carpatica or bellflower
Dianthus or pinks
Geranium calmaticum or cranesbill
Heuchera or coralbells
Iberis snowflake or candytuft
Potentilla fragiformis or cinquefoil

In addition to the perennials included in the encyclopedia, there are probably thousands suitable for alpine gardens. Here is a short list of other perennials that are unproblematical; that is, they will thrive in most parts of the country, resist drought, and require no special soil conditions.

Aethionema or Warley Rose, Zones 6–9

Light: Full sun.
Soil: Light, well-drained.
Moisture: Water regularly during summer drought.
Bloom time: May to July.
Color range: Rose to pink.
Height: 12 inches.
Tips: Cut back after bloom and plant will remain a compact bush for years. Part of the top may be winterkilled. If so, in early spring, cut back to green wood and scratch one tablespoon of lime around the plant.

Aubrieta or Purple Rock Cress, Zones 4–9

Light: Full sun.
Soil: Light, well-drained.
Moisture: Water regularly during summer drought.
Bloom time: April to June.
Color range: Blue, purple, and violet.
Height: 8 inches on low-growing mats of silver-gray foliage.
Tips: A very versatile plant that complements spring bulb plantings of daffodils and *Muscari*. After bloom, shear back heavily to encourage new growth. In early spring, scratch one tablespoon of lime around plant.

Catananche or Cupid's Dart, Zones 3–9

Light: Full sun.
Soil: Sandy, well-drained.
Moisture: Drought resistant.
Bloom time: All summer.
Color range: Lavender-blue with darker eyes.
Height: 12 inches.
Tips: To propagate, divide in early spring. Flowers may be dried for winter use in arrangements.

Chrysogonum virginianum or Golden Star, Zones 3–8

Light: Full sun to shade.
Soil: Ordinary.
Moisture: Water regularly during summer drought.
Bloom time: All summer.
Color range: Yellow, daisylike.
Height: 6–9-inch stems on 3-inch-high rosettes of coarse, toothed foliage.
Tips: A native American plant that adapts well to most conditions.

Draba sibirica, Zones 3–8

Light: Full sun to partial shade.
Soil: Well-drained.
Moisture: Water regularly during summer drought.
Bloom time: Early spring and midfall.
Color range: Yellow.
Height: 2 inches.
Tips: Divide after bloom. A charming plant that is among the earliest of all alpines to bloom.

Helianthemum or Wisley Primrose, Zones 6–9

Light: Full sun.
Soil: Well-drained.
Moisture: Water regularly during summer drought.

Bloom time: May to June.
Color range: Pink or yellow.
Height: 8–10 inches.
Tips: Little known, but one of the loveliest of all perennial flowering plants. Suitable for borders as well as alpine gardens. Easy to grow and highly recommended.

Leontopodium alpinum or Edelweiss, Zones 4–7

Light: Full sun.
Soil: Gritty, well-drained.
Moisture: Drought resistant.
Bloom time: June to August.
Color range: White on silver foliage.
Height: 8-inch stems over 2-inch, matlike foliage.
Tips: Though you may think that no alpine garden would be complete without edelweiss, you might actually find that it is rather disappointing—the flowers are not particularly attractive. There are other white-flowering alpines such as *Arabis* and *Iberis* that are far more interesting in the rockery.

Myosotis alpestris marina or Forget-Me-Not, Zones 3–8

Light: Full sun.
Soil: Ordinary, well-drained.
Moisture: Water regularly during summer drought.
Bloom time: May, June.
Color range: Sky blue.
Height: 10-inch stems over 2 to 3-inch mats of short-leaved foliage.
Tips: Grows easily from seed.

Opuntia or Prickly Pear, Zones 4–9

Light: Full sun.
Soil: Ordinary, well-drained.
Moisture: Drought resistant.
Bloom time: May, June.

Color range: Yellow or orange.

Height: 5–6 inches.

Tips: The only cactus that will thrive in northern zones, prickly pear is an oddity, and an interesting one. However, the plant self-seeds rampantly, and because of thorns, weeding between plants is downright dangerous. Despite its interesting aspects, I'd advise you not to install this cultivar.

Sedum, Zones 3–9

Light: Full sun to partial shade.

Soil: Ordinary, well-drained.

Moisture: Drought resistant.

Bloom time: Spring to fall, depending on variety.

Color range: Red, yellow, rose, and white, depending on variety.

Height: 2–18 inches, depending on variety.

Tips: Select from low-growing varieties. Sedums are ideal for alpine gardens, as they are succulent: that is, they retain moisture in their leaves. Foliage is green, red, or yellow, depending on variety.

Sempervivum or Hen and Chickens, Zones 5–10

Light: Full sun to partial shade.

Soil: Ordinary, well-drained.

Moisture: Drought resistant.

Bloom time: Summer.

Color range: Yellow, pink, or red, depending on variety.

Height: Foliage mats are from 2 to 4 inches high, with blooms sometimes 1-foot high.

Tips: Another ideal alpine succulent that retains moisture in its leaves. Grown primarily for its colorful and interesting foliage. There are hundreds of varieties to select from.

Spiraea japonica alpina or Japanese Spiraea, Zones 5–9

Light: Full sun.

Soil: Well-drained and sandy.

Moisture: Drought resistant.

Bloom time: June to July.
Color range: Pink.
Height: 12–14-inch stems on low, globe-shaped, medium green foliage plants.
Tips: Easy to grow. Divide in early spring for more plants.

Thymus or Thyme, Zones 5–9

Light: Full sun.
Soil: Light and well-drained.
Moisture: Drought resistant.
Bloom time: Throughout the season, depending on variety.
Color range: Pink, crimson, lavender, and purple, depending on the variety.
Height: 2–4 inches.
Tips: Easily grown. Divide in spring or summer for more plants.

Veronica minuet or Speedwell, Zones 4–9

Light: Full sun.
Soil: Ordinary, well-drained.
Moisture: Water regularly during summer drought.
Bloom time: May.
Color range: Pink.
Height: 12-inch stems over mats of dusty green foliage.
Tips: Surefire. Easily grown from seed, or by division in spring.

The final phase in installing your alpine garden is to plant spring-flowering bulbs. Here too, there is a wide selection from which to choose. When you make your selection of spring-flowering bulbs, keep the following in mind:

- The miniature, so-called minor bulbs and low-growing minidaffodils and species tulips are ideal for rock gardens because they are low growing, dwarf in stature, and because they are native to areas with similar physical characteristics.
- Avoid standard daffodils and tall-growing Emperor, Darwin, lily, and Darwin hybrid tulips, as they are too tall for rock gardens.
- Dutch hyacinths are out of place in rockeries. They are too rigid and formal for the natural looking landscape you want to create.

- Purchase bulbs in quantity, at least twenty-five of each variety. The small bulbs—crocus, snowdrop, glory-of-the-snow, *Iris reticulata* and *danfordiae, Puschkinia,* minidaffodils, and the smaller species tulips (Kaufmania)—should be planted in groups of fifty to ensure a dramatic display.

If you order bulbs by mail, they will arrive in bags of each variety. If you buy them in garden centers or nurseries, bags are usually provided for you. When you get ready to plant your bulbs, place the bags where you think you might want to plant the bulbs, step back and view your scheme, and readjust accordingly.

Excavate the area for planting bulbs to the proper depth and plant as recommended in chapter 4 (see p. 183). Disregard the spacing information provided in the instructions that accompany your bulbs. Plant them *half* the recommended distance apart to ensure a dramatic display in the spring.

Here are some bulbs you might wish to include:

- *Anemone blanda:* pink giant, white splendor.
- *Chionodoxa* or glory-of-the-snow.
- Crocus, Dutch: Early Perfection, Golden Goblet, Joan d'Arc, Little Dorrit, Peter Pan, Pickwick.
- Crocus, species: Blue Giant, Blue Pearl, Cream Beauty, Golden Bunch, Lady Killer, Miss Vain, Moonlight, Princess Beatrix, Sieberi, and Snow Bunting.
- Daffodil, miniature: April Tears, Baby Moon, February Gold, Jack Snipe, Little Witch, Rip van Winkle, Tête-à-Tête, and Thalia.
- *Galanthus* or snowdrop.
- *Iris danfordiae* or *reticulata.*
- *Leucojum* or snowflake.
- *Muscari:* Blue Spike, Early Giant (blue), Early Giant (white).
- *Puschkinia libanotica*
- *Scilla* or squill.
- *Scilla campanulata* or wood hyacinth.
- Tulip: Bathalinii Bright Gem, Chrysantha, Kolpakowskiana Linifolia, Plaisir, Purissima, Red Riding Hood, Saxatilis, Shakespeare, Show Winner, Stresa, Tarda, Turkestanica

How do I protect my alpine garden during the first winter? Now that you've completed the planting, wait until a deep winter frost and then cover the entire garden with a three-inch-deep layer of salt hay. This mulch is placed on the garden during the first winter *only*, to protect the newly planted perennial alpines from heaving.

What do I do in the spring to maintain my garden? Before spring growth commences, remove the straw hay and scratch a handful of Holland Bulb Booster around each planting of bulbs. Then place a two-inch layer of pine or cedar bark chips, available at garden centers and nurseries, on the entire garden to conserve moisture and cut down on weed growth. By March, the early crocuses and snowflakes will bloom. Then, week by week, the glorious parade of bulbs and alpine perennial bloom will continue.

As explained in chapter 4, once bulbs have bloomed, do not remove foliage, but permit it to dry naturally, as food for next year's bloom is contained in the leaves.

What do I do to my alpine garden to provide color interest throughout the summer and fall? Fill in the spent bulb areas with low-growing annuals such as *Lobelia*, dwarf marigold, *Dianthus*, *Portulaca*, miniature snapdragon, sweet alyssum, and verbena. Since most cultivars suitable for alpine gardens and bulbs bloom in spring, the annuals will provide color during the summer. In the fall you might wish to plant here and there some low-growing cushion chrysanthemums, which bloom profusely, for color.

What about watering my alpine garden? Although most cultivars suitable for alpine gardens are very tough and drought resistant, during the dry summer months, it is a good idea to water thoroughly once a week. Leave the sprinkler on for about two hours.

Where can I get more information about rock gardens? If you have a keen interest in alpine gardens, you might want to consider joining the American Rock Garden Society. Membership is open to all and costs around fifteen dollars a year. Information is available from the secretary, Norman Singer, Norfolk Road, South Sandisfield, Massachusetts 01255. Members have access to the society's seed list, which includes over forty-five hundred rare varieties from every corner of the world.

Rose Gardens

Certainly one of the most popular of all specialty gardens is the rose garden—and with good reason, for throughout the ages, the rose has been considered the most beautiful of all flowers. Mention has been made of it in writings from the beginning of recorded history, and it has been reproduced by artists and sculptors countless times. The Greek poet Sappho wrote of her beloved roses, and Cleopatra is said to have had rose petals waist high in the room where she first received Mark Antony. From Shakespeare to Gertrude Stein, roses have been lauded by the world's most renowned poets, playwrights, and authors. Small wonder, for what could be more devastatingly lovely than a rose—in a bouquet, in a garden, or all alone in a bud vase.

Modern roses, bred from the wild through the centuries, fall into several categories, and can serve any landscape purpose you can imagine. And now, with the hybridization of disease resistant miniature roses, they are easily grown in the rock garden as well. Here's a brief rundown on the different types available:

- Hybrid teas: these are perhaps the best known, ranging in height from two and a half feet to seven feet. Most are from three to five feet tall and produce a single flower on a long stem.
- Grandifloras: somewhat larger than the hybrid teas, the result of a cross between hybrid teas and floribundas, these produce up to a half-dozen blooms on each stem. They are vigorous and most are fragrant.
- Floribundas: small plants, from two to four feet high, extremely vigorous, hardy, and disease resistant. They are usually covered with blossoms, smaller than hybrid teas or grandiflora blooms.
- Climbers: plants do not attach themselves to surfaces but must be tied to trellises, fences, and other supports. Many grow to from ten to twelve feet.
- Tree roses: these are hybrid teas and grandifloras grafted onto root stock and trained into tree form with a trunk by careful pruning methods. They need substantial protection in winter in cooler areas. In the Deep South and the Southwest, they are very popular and need no winter protection.
- Shrub roses: tough and very floriferous, growing to six to ten feet. They serve as fences and barriers to keep intruders out.

● Miniatures: rarely growing above one foot, these are tiny replicas of all other forms. They are used for edging, borders, and as houseplants in containers.

Regardless of what you may have heard, roses are quite easy to grow and require only a moderate amount of care and maintenance. And the rewards are great—armfuls of magnificent roses all summer long. If you decide you wish to create a specialty garden of roses, here's how you do it.

How do I buy rose bushes? You can order rose bushes by mail. There are many reputable suppliers in the United States, and you can almost always count on receiving healthy, vigorous plants. Do not order roses from any house that does not offer a replacement guarantee if your plant dies. If you buy from a nursery or garden center, here's what to look for. First, check for grade number. Roses are rated #1, #1½, and #2, with #1 being the highest rating (and hence the most expensive). Ratings are determined by size and number of canes, or stems. Sometimes a #2 grade rosebush will produce excellent roses, although usually it takes a few more years and more care and feeding than a #1 or #1½. At this point, you would do well to buy only #1 grade roses to ensure that you have the best possible stock to start out with. Second, check to see if the bushes have pale or thick canes. If they do, avoid them, as they have been neglected in the nursery. Finally, if there are swellings, strange dark colors, or growths on the canes and roots, disease is probably present, so avoid these.

When do I plant roses? Roses shipped from mail-order nurseries are almost always sent at the proper planting time for your area. Bushes available at nurseries and garden centers are usually also sold and stocked at the appropriate planting time too.

Where can I plant roses? Roses are not fussy about planting sites, but they do require between four and six hours of sunlight a day, depending on variety. They prefer morning light, so an eastern exposure—that is, the side of your house that faces east—is ideal. A dappled southern exposure, and northern or western exposures in full sun are also satisfactory. Good drainage is important, so be sure to test your site for drainage. It is best also to select a site with adequate air circulation in order to prevent disease.

How do I plant a rose bush? To plant all varieties except miniatures, dig a hole about two feet across by one and a half feet deep. For miniatures, a hole one foot deep and one foot across is sufficient. Although roses are not fussy about soil, it is a good idea, regardless of your soil type, to mix compost, sphagnum peat moss, or other organic matter in with the soil removed from the hole in a ratio of about two parts soil to one part additive. If there is a drainage problem on tne site, fill the bottom of the hole with rocks or broken flowerpot shards.

Then fashion a cone about six to eight inches high in the bottom of the hole with some of the soil mixture. If the plants are bare root, remove any damaged, dried out, or overly long roots with pruning shears. Position the plant in the hole so that the roots fall over the cone and the graft (the knobby growth just above the roots) is even with or just below soil level in zones 4 and 5 or above soil level in zones 6 through 9. Then fill in the soil several inches at a time and tamp it firmly, until the soil level around the rose bush is even with the surrounding area. Then water thoroughly to remove air pockets in the soil.

Some rose bushes are sold in ready-to-plant boxes or containers. Follow the instructions above for digging and amending the soil. There are two schools of thought on planting these roses. The mail-order nurseries' instructions always indicate that it is not necessary to remove the paper cartons in which these roses are planted—the paper will simply rot. Others feel (and I agree) that it is perhaps better to remove the cartons and spread the roots out somewhat before planting. Observe the graft level as above and water thoroughly.

How far apart should I plant rose bushes? Hybrid teas, grandifloras, and floribundas should be spaced about two feet apart from center of bush. Miniatures should be spaced about one and a half feet apart; climbers should be spaced six to eight feet apart along fences and about four feet apart on trellises. Shrub roses should be planted about three feet apart.

How do I water roses? As a rule, water thoroughly once a week in the morning so that the soil is soaked to a depth of one to one and a half feet. If you place an empty coffee can next to the rose bushes while watering, when one inch of water is in the bottom of the can, surrounding soil will be soaked to a depth of from one to one and a half feet. Of course there are many variables including humidity, rainfall, and the use of mulch that may affect this schedule. Use common sense. If there has been substantial rainfall, don't water. If there is a summer drought, water thoroughly. Overhead watering can be employed if you spray your roses regularly with a fungicide. If you do not regularly spray with fungicide, water on leaves can cause fungus problems. However, it is perhaps best to invest in a hose that seeps water into the ground. (These are available at garden centers and nurseries and are quite inexpensive.) This will discourage the growth of fungus diseases. If you do water with a regular hose, try to avoid wetting the leaves.

How do I fertilize roses? There are many fertilizers on the market, but those specifically labeled "rose fertilizer" are your best bet. Ortho sells a product that is a combination fertilizer–systemic pest killer–weed killer. It is available at most garden centers and nurseries and is called Ortho 3-way Rose and Flower Care. You can save yourself a substantial amount of maintenance if you use this product. Apply it three times during the season according to the instructions on the package.

What about pests and diseases? Roses are subject to some pests and diseases, but these are easily controlled. As a preventative, spray with a dormant oil spray, available at garden centers and nurseries, according to manufacturer's instructions. Do this in early spring, before leaf growth starts, to smother any insects and fungi that may have survived the winter. Three diseases may attack your roses. They are:

- Rust: small, powdery orange spots that first appear on leaf undersides and spread, ultimately causing the leaves to die. Severe infestation can cause the plant to die.
- Powdery mildew: a white, powdery substance that appears on stems and buds. If allowed to spread, it can also cause the plant to die.
- Black spot: small, black circles that appear first on leaf undersides and then spread to the entire leaf, weakening the plant and ultimately causing it to die.

At the first sign of any of the above problems, spray with Funginex, an Ortho product recommended by the American Rose Society, according to the instructions on the bottle. As a preventative, it is a good idea to apply this spray while the plants are dormant and then once a week during the growing season, particularly after heavy rains. As a further preventative measure, water roses only in the morning so that moisture will evaporate during the day and not leave foliage wet, which leads to disease.

Insects such as aphids, spider mites, and thrips are easily controlled with rose dust or a systemic insect killer. Systemics, which are absorbed into the plant and kill insects on contact, are preferred to rose dust because they do not leave unsightly residues and water does not wash the poison away. Ortho's 3-Way Rose and Flower Care, containing weed killer, and systemic poison, applied three times during the season, is an easy way to control most insect problems. Japanese beetles are best controlled by hand-picking. If you have an infestation of this insect, a Japanese beetle trap, available at most garden centers or nurseries, is recommended.

Should I mulch roses? Yes, it is a good idea. A mulch helps to retain moisture and reduce weed growth. Although there are many different kinds of mulches available, homemade compost or shredded pine or cedar bark is recommended.

How do I prune my roses? In the fall, when roses stop blooming and go into dormancy, prune only the tallest branches to about three feet high. This will prevent winter winds from damaging the plants. Spring is the time for annual pruning, but different kinds of roses require different pruning techniques. However, if you follow these general rules, you should have success:

- Wait until new growth begins, when buds begin to emerge from the canes. Then prune out dead cane to the *crown* or base of the plant. The crown will be brown or black and dried out. Use sharp pruning shears, loppers, or a small saw to do this.
- Prune out frost-damaged canes to healthy wood, which is white or light green all the way through the cane.
- Make all pruning cuts at a 45° angle about one-third of an inch above a bud that faces away from the center of the bush.
- Open the center of the bush; that is, prune out thin twigs and stems near the middle. This is particularly important with floribunda varieties.
- Prune out suckers emerging from below the graft, the knobby growth at the base of the plant. These grow from root stock and will not produce blooms true to the variety you have planted.
- Thin out all but four to seven canes. The remaining canes should be at least as thick as a pencil. If large "specimen" flowers are desired, prune to about one foot. If more extravagant displays but somewhat smaller flowers are desired, prune lightly to about two feet.
- When finished, apply Elmer's glue or shellac to all exposed cuts to prevent moisture evaporation and insect infestation.

How do I cut roses? During summer, when you cut roses for bouquets or remove spent blossoms, always cut to just above a five-point leaf, as opposed to a three-point leaf. New flowering branches will generally not grow from above three-point leaves.

How do I prune climbers? Climbers require a few special techniques. Most form flowering *laterals*, or side shoots, from the main branches. In spring, cut these back to from three to six inches with three or four buds each. During summer, remove faded flowers to force new blooms. So-called ramblers, which bloom only in June, should have all two-year-old canes cut to their source after flowering.

How do I provide winter protection for my roses in colder climates? In colder areas of the country, where temperatures regularly fall below zero, winter protection of rose bushes is necessary. Wait until after a killing frost (15–20°F), bring in some soil, and mound it up around the trunk of the bush to a height of six or seven inches. In spring, wait until the weather has warmed up and new growth has commenced before removing the earth mound.

What about old-fashioned roses? While most of us are content with the lovely modern roses that are readily available, a look back at some of the old-fashioned varieties can be very rewarding. And more and more rose enthusiasts are doing just that. Fairy polyantha, for example, offers clusters of enchanting, seashell pink blooms all summer long. The rugosa shrub rose, tough as nails, will survive the most difficult growing conditions. Damask and cabbage roses have a heavy scent that one rarely finds in modern offerings. Such varieties as the lovely pinkish-white Comtesse de Murianais, the Baronne Prevost, the Austrian Copper, and the hybrid China roses such as Old Blush, Slater's Crimson, Hermosa, and Viridiflora are all worth investigating.

What about the aesthetics of rose gardening? At first, you will probably want one of each of many varieties. However, as you gain more experience with rose gardening, you may find that some of the cultivars are too garish for your taste. Consider this at the start, for some colors clash badly with others. You might want to plan a color-coordinated rose garden. In this case, use white roses to break up color patterns and select three of each variety to plant in a block rather than three separate varieties in each block.

This, of course, is all a matter of personal taste, but do give it some thought before investing money in rose bushes.

Which rose varieties are right for my climate? Although your local garden center or nursery can advise you as to which roses are best for your area, here are some guidelines for hybrid tea roses, set forth by different rose societies throughout the country, to help you make your selection.

- Hybrid tea roses for hot, dry climates, recommended by the Tucson, Arizona, Rose Society: Charlotte Armstrong, Chrysler Imperial, Double Delight, First Prize, Granada, Miss All-American Beauty, Mister Lincoln, Oldtimer, Peace, Royal Highness, Sutter's Gold, and Tropicana.
- Hybrid tea roses for hot, humid climates, recommended by the Gulf Coast Rose Society: Bewitched, Chrysler Imperial, Double Delight, Fragrant Cloud, Garden Party, Honor, Lady X, Mister Lincoln, Paradise, Pascali, Peace, Perfume Delight, Red Masterpiece, Royal Highness, Tiffany, Toro, and Tropicana.
- Hybrid tea roses for cool climates (all have won the city of Portland, Oregon, gold medal): Double Delight, Fragrant Cloud, Pascali, Peace, Princess Margaret, Prominent, and Red Devil.
- Hybrid tea roses for cold climates, recommended by the Northern Chicagoland Rose Society: Big Ben, Double Delight, First Prize, Fragrant Cloud, Garden Party, Granada, Mister Lincoln, Paradise, Pascali, Peace, Pristine, Sunblest, Swarthmore, and Tropicana.

Which roses are the most fragrant? Since many gardeners complain that most modern roses have little scent, here is a list of the most fragrant:

NAME	SCENT	COLOR
Chrysler Imperial	Heavy clove	Red
Confidence	Spicy true rose	Light pink to yellow
Double Delight	Apple, spice, damask	Cream and red
Fragrant Cloud	True rose	Bright coral
John F. Kennedy	Lemon, damask	White
Medallion	Fruity, apple	Apricot buff
Mister Lincoln	Apple, damask	Red
Paradise	Sweet, lemon	Silver lavender
Perfume Delight	Rose, clove	Pink
Peace	True rose, lemon	Pale yellow, white, pink

NAME	SCENT	COLOR
Presence	True rose	Coral pink
Seashell	Sweet, lemon	Peach-apricot
Sweet Surrender	True rose, spicy	Lavender-pink
Tiffany	True rose	Pink rose
Tribute	True rose, hint of apple, lemon, strawberry	Cerise
Tropicana	Fruity apple, strawberry	Orange

Garden Structures and Decorations

By now, your landscape scheme is probably well on the way to being reasonably mature. At this time, you can start adding all the little touches that make a garden personal and charming. Birdbaths and sundials can be installed to add focal points to borders and beds.

Container-grown plants can now be placed in areas of deep shade to provide color in these otherwise dreary spots. Grow them in the sun and place them in the shade when you are entertaining or enjoying that part of your landscape. Then place them back in the sun for several days.

You may find that you wish to install garden benches here and there around your property, so that you can sit and peacefully enjoy particular parts of your garden. You can do this easily yourself.

More elaborate projects, such as adding a gazebo or a pergola, must be thought out carefully. If you are experienced with carpentry, you can probably purchase a set of plans for these garden structures and do it yourself. Either buy a book on garden structures or borrow one from the library for more information. Beyond that, at the back of many of the women's and family magazines, various companies advertise sets of plans for garden structures, with some offering complete do-it-yourself kits. You should be able to put these together yourself. If custom work is in order and you are not an experienced carpenter, it is perhaps best to hire someone to do the job for you.

You may wish to install a permanent outdoor grill or barbecue pit near your patio. Read books on how to do these projects, most of which are reasonably easy to construct and which you can probably handle yourself.

Don't overlook some of the old-fashioned garden appointments such as gliders and arbors. They add great charm to a garden.

At the same time, and at the risk of dictating taste, here are some "don'ts," which you may or may not wish to abide by: Avoid littering the landscape with plastic pink flamingos, pinwheels, sunflowers and ducks, cement stags or elks, and mirrored balls on pedestals. Let your landscape, wrought from nature, make your statement rather than relying on some of the tacky garden paraphernalia available.

Although from here on in you will undoubtedly have to replace certain plants in your garden for one reason or another and will have to maintain your property, for the most part, your work is complete. Now is the time to let your imagination dictate what else you wish to do with your property. Beyond that, sit back and enjoy the landscape you have created. You've worked hard, invested time, thought, and money, and you deserve all the credit you can get. And do remember, all of that time and expense has added substantially to the value of your property.

Sources for Planting Material

There are thousands of sources for planting material, but the following list should get you headed in the right direction. You will find, after you have written for some of the catalogues listed below, that you will start to receive unsolicited catalogues as well, since many mail-order nurseries share their mailing lists. Drop postcards to all of the companies listed here and use their catalogues not only as sources of planting material but as sources of information, since most include a great deal of that.

Annual, Perennial, and Vegetable Seeds

George W. Park Seed Company, Inc., Highway 254 North, Box 31, Green-wood, South Carolina 29647. (803) 374-3741. In business since 1868, Park offers a large selection of annual and vegetable seeds, as well as perennial seeds and plants, shrubs, bulbs, and trees.

Le Jardin du Gourmet, Box 44, West Danville, Vermont 05873-0044. A broad selection of European vegetables, herbs, and shallot sets.

Thompson & Morgan, Box 1308, Jackson, New Jersey 08527. (201) 363-2225. Toll free outside New Jersey between 8:30 A.M. and 8:30 P.M. For information call 1-800-367-7333. This company has the most comprehensive offering of annual seeds of any I know. Most are imported from Great Britain. The catalogue contains a great deal of information about how to grow the varieties, along with many color photographs illustrating the offerings. Beyond the annual varieties included in the encyclopedia of this book, Thompson & Morgan offers many less-known cultivars, certainly worth experimenting with once you have established your landscape.

W. Atlee Burpee Company, 300 Park Avenue, Warminster, Pennsylvania 18974. (215) 674-4900. In business since 1876, this company offers a large selection of annual seeds.

Bulbs

Van Bourgondien Bros., Box A, 245 Farmingdale Road, Route 109, Babylon, New York 11702. (800) 645-5830, in New York (800) 832-5689. Probably the most comprehensive offering of Dutch bulbs, both spring-blooming and summer-blooming. Prices are reasonable.

Perennials

Bluestone Perennials, 7211 Middle Ridge Road, Madison, Ohio 44057. (216) 428-7535. One of the best sources for perennial plants at very reasonable prices. These are small plants, available in either three-packs or six-packs. They offer a package called a perennial starter garden, which contains fifty-one plants for around $40. This comes with a predesigned planting scheme. All plants are guaranteed to reach you in good condition and to grow. If they do not, the company will reship immediately or refund your money if you are not satisfied.

Wayside Gardens, Hodges, South Carolina 29695. (800) 845-1124. Offers a large selection of perennial plants as well as unusual shrubs and trees. Expensive, but plants are well established.

White Flower Farm, Route 63, Litchfield, Connecticut 06759-0050. (203) 567-0801, 567-4565. Offers a broad selection of perennial plants and shrubs. Expensive, but plants are well established. Catalogue costs $5 but contains a great deal of valuable information.

Roses

Jackson & Perkins Co., Box 1028, Medford, Oregon 97501. (503) 776-2400. The largest grower of rose bushes in the country. However, they do not offer old-fashioned roses.

Heritage Rose Gardens, 40350 Wilderness Road, Branscomb, California 95417.

(707) 984-6959. Offers an excellent selection of old-fashioned roses. Catalogue costs $1.

Trees and Shrubs

Girard Nurseries, P.O. Box 428, Geneva, Ohio 44041. (216) 466-2881. A wide selection of conifers, azaleas, rhododendrons, and deciduous trees. They also sell seedlings, which can be put in a nursery for a few years until of reasonable planting size.

Kelly Nurseries, Dansville, New York 14437. (800) 828-6977, in New York. (800) 462-6836. Primarily offers fruit trees, berry bushes, and nut trees, but has an interesting selection of shrubs and trees as well, including Golden Chain trees (*Laburnum*).

Musser Forests, P.O. Box 340-M, Indiana, Pennsylvania 15701-0340. (412) 465-5685, 465-5686, 465-5687. One of the largest growers of trees and shrubs. Prices are very reasonable and selection is extensive.

Beyond the brief list above, avail yourself of coupons in magazines and newspapers for nursery catalogues. Should you be interested in a comprehensive book on gardening by mail, I recommend *Gardening by Mail* by Barbara J. Barton, Tusker Press, 1986. This useful volume, now in its second edition, lists thousands of sources.

Index

◆

Index

Baby's breath, 213
Bachelor's button, 44
Backfill, 68
Baltic ivy, 134
Barbecue pit, 245
Basket-of-gold, 206
Bearberry, 133
Bearberry cotoneaster, 133
Bearded iris, 196
"Bedding plants," 27–29
Bee balm, 215
Begonia, 41–42
Berberis julianae, 114
Bergamot, 215
Bergenia, 209
Betula, 72–73
"Big and beautiful five" (perennials),
    186–92
    daylily, 186–92
    iris, 194–97
    lily, 197–202
    peony, 202–205
    plantain lily, 192–94
Birch trees, 72–73
Birdbaths, 56, 229, 245
Bird feeders, 55–56
Birdhouses, 56
Birds, 19, 55–57
    attracting, 55–57
    birdbaths, 56, 229, 245
    bird feeders, 55–56
    birdhouses, 56
    "junk" birds, 55
    learning about, 56–57
Black locust, 11
Black spot, 241
Blanket flower, 212
Bleeding heart, 212
Blood meal, 153
Bloom Sequence Chart (bulbs), 152
Borers, 186
Boxwood varieties, 114
Brachycome, 42
Broad-leaved evergreen encyclopedia,
    113–22
Broad-leaved evergreens (shrubs), 95, 103, 113–
    22
    encyclopedia of, 113–22
Brunnera, 209–10
Buddleia davidi, 105
Bulbs. *See* Bloom Sequence Chart (bulbs);
    Dutch bulbs; Early-blooming bulbs; Rock
    gardens
Burning bush, 107
Buttercup shrub, 110
Butterfly bush, 105
Buxus microphylla, 114
Buxus sempervirens, 114–15

Calendula, 42–43
California poppy, 43
Calliopsis, 43–44
Calluna vulgaris, 115
Camellia, 115–16

Camellia japonica, 115–16
Camellia sasanqua, 116
Campanula, 210
Candytuft, 135, 214
Carnations, 47
Carpet bugle, 132
Carrots, 22
Catalogues (mail-order nurseries), 5, 247–49
Catalpa tree, 11
Catananche, 232
Catmint, 216
Cauliflower, 21–22
Cedar tree, 79
Celery, 22
Celosia, 44
Centaurea, 44
Ceris canadensis, 86
Chaenomeles japonica, 105–106
Chamaecyparis, 79–80, 123–24
Children's play areas, 40
Chinaberry tree, 92
Chinese holly, 118
Chionanthus virginica, 87
Chionodoxa, 161–62
Chrysanthemum, 210
Chrysogonum virginianum, 232
Cinquefoil, 217
Cladrastis lutea, 87
Clarkia, 45
Clematis, 221
Cleome, 45
Climbing vine plants, 221
    securing to fences, 221
Cockscomb, 44
Coleus, 45–46
Columbine, 207
Common boxwood, 114–15
Common camellia, 115–16
Common winter creeper, 134
Compost heaps, 6–8
    defined, 6
    making of, 7–8
    manure for, 7
    moisture and, 7
    nitrogen and, 7–8
    organic materials for, 8
    phosphorus and, 7
    potassium and, 7–8
Conifers. *See* Dwarf conifers; Evergreen trees
Corabells, 214
Coreopsis, 43–44, 210
Corms, 156
Corn, 22
Cornflower, 44
Cornus, 87–88, 106
Cosmos, 46
Cotoneaster, 116
Cotoneaster conspicuus, 133
Cotoneaster dammeri, 133
Cotoneaster horizontalis, 134
County Cooperative Extension Service,
    4–5, 63, 97, 130, 131, 153
Crab apple tree, 91–92
Cranesbill, 213

252

Index

Index

Larkspur, 46–47
Lathyrus, 48
Lavandula officinalis, 215
Lavender, 215
Lawn(s), 127–37
  dethatching, 127
  "dream lawns," 127–28
  four alternatives to "dream lawns," 129
  installing new lawn, 129–30
  maintenance of, 131
  negative aspects of, 127–28
  renovating established lawn, 130
  replacing with ground cover, 128
  sod and, 129
Leatherleaf mahonia, 120
Leatherleaf viburnum, 122
Lebanon squill, 161
Leontopodium alpinum, 233
Lettuce, 23
Leucothoe fontanesiana, 119–20
Liatris, 215
Lilac, 111–12
Lilly, 197–202
  aurelian hybrids, 199–200
  hybrid Asiatic lilies, 200–201
  hybrid lilies, 200
  speciosum lilies, 201
  tiger lilies, 201–202
Liquidambar styraciflua, 76
Liriodendron tulipifera, 90
Little leaf boxwood, 114
Lobelia, 49
London plane tree, 76
Lonicera japonica, 136
Louisiana iris, 197

Magnolia grandiflora, 90–91
Magnolia soulangiana, 91
Magnolia stellata, 109
Mahonia acuifolium, 120
Mahonia bealei, 120
Maidenhair tree, 75
Malus, 91–92
Maple trees, 70–72
  varieties of, 71–72
Marigold, 52–53
Melia azedarach, 92
Michaelmas daisy, 208–209
Miniature daffodils, 164–66
  varieties of, 165–66
Mimosa tree, 10–11, 86
Miracid, 104
Mock orange, 109–10
Moles, 153
Monarda, 215
Monkshood, 206
Mountain laurel, 119
Mugwort, 208
Mulberry tree, 11
Muscari, 159–60
  varieties of, 160
Mulch, 6–7
  defined, 6
  purposes served by, 6–7

"Mules," 37
Myosotis alpestris marina, 233

Narcissus, 162–64
Nasturtium, 53–54
Necklace cotoneaster, 133
Nepeta, 216
Nicotiana, 49
Nitrogen, 7–8
Nursery area, 6

Oak, 77
Oenothera, 216
Opuntia, 233–34
Oregon holly grape, 120
Oriental poppy, 216
Ortho 3-Way Rose and Flower Care, 241, 242
Osage orange tree, 12
Oswego tea, 215
Outdoor grills, 245
Oxydendrum arboreum, 92–93

Pachysandra, 136
Painted tongue, 52
Papaver, 216
Patios, 15–16, 143–46
  aesthetics and, 145–46
  brick-in-sand, 144–45
  concrete surface and, 145
  drainage and, 144
  easiest flooring for, 144–45
  enhancing, 146
  in first year, 15–16
  furniture for, 146
  shade and, 146
  weeds growing in cracks of, 145
  wooden decking, 145
Paulonia tomentosa, 93
Peach tree, 93–94
Pelargonium, 50
Peony, 202–205
  two kinds defined, 202
  varieties of, 204
Perennial encyclopedia, 205–18
Perennials, 177–218
  "big and beautiful five," 186–205
  borders and beds, 181–82
  comparison shopping for, 179
  defined, 177–78
  dividing plant, 185
  drought-resistant varieties, 185
  encyclopedia of, 205–18
  expense of, 178
  gifts of, advice about, 179
  maintenance after first season bloom, 184
  as overplantings for spring bulbs (list), 218
  pests and diseases, 185–86
  planning planting of, 181–83
  planting procedures, 183–85
  poor drainage and, 185
  purchasing, 178–79
  rock gardens and, 184–85
  shady woodland conditions and, 185
  sites for, 180–81

255

Index

"junk" trees, 10–12
  maintaining trees, 13
  replacement trees, planting of, 13
  treeless properties, 13
  tree surgeons, 13
Tree surgeons, 13
Trellises, 220–21
True cypress, 80
Trumpet vine, 221
Tsuga, 85
Tsuga canadensis, 126
Tulips, 148, 167–72
  Darwin hybrids, 168
  Fosteriana or Emperor varieties, 169
  Gregii varieties, 169
  Kaufmania varieties, 168
  late-blooming varieties, 171
  midseason-blooming varieties, 170
  "wild" varieties, 169
Tulip tree, 90

Ulmus, 78

Vegetable garden (first year), 16–26
  fertilizer for, 19
  insects and birds in, 19
  pests and diseases, 25–26
  planting from seed, 21
  planting procedures, 22–23
  problematic vegetables, 21–22
  rabbits and other animals in, 18–19
  reassessing site after harvest, 26
  site for, 17, 26
  size and shape of, 17
  soil evaluation for, 18
  tender vegetables, 23–25
  times to plant, 20–21

Vegetable garden (permanent), 137–40
  site for, 137–38
  See also Asparagus
Velvet flower, 52
Verbena, 54
Verey, Rosemary, 28
Veronica minuet, 235
Viburnum carlesi, 112
Viburnum dentatum, 112–13
Viburnum rhytidophyllum, 122
Vinca, 137
Viola, 217–18
Voles, 153

Walks (paths), 16
Warley rose, 231
Wax begonia, 41–42
Weigela eva rathke, 113
Weeping willow, 12
Wilder, Louise Beebe, 156
Willow, 77–78
Window-box annuals, 35–36
Wintergreen barberry, 114
Winter creeper, 117, 134
Wishbone flower, 53
Wisley primrose, 232–33
Wisteria, 221
Workable ground, defined, 18

Yarrow, 205
Yellowwood, 87
Yew, 84, 126

Zinnia, 37, 54